D I A G N O S I N G
LEARNING DISORDERS

DIAGNOSING
LEARNING DISORDERS
A Neuropsychological Framework

Bruce F. Pennington, PhD
UNIVERSITY OF DENVER

Foreword by
Martha Bridge Denckla, MD
THE KENNEDY INSTITUTE

THE GUILFORD PRESS
New York   London

Printed in the United States of America

This book is printed on acid-free paper.

Last digit is print number: 9 8 7 6 5 4 3 2 1

Library of Congress Cataloging-in-Publication Data

Pennington, Bruce Franklin, 1946–
    Diagnosing learning disorders : a neuropsychological framework /
Bruce F. Pennington.
        p.   cm.
    Includes bibliographical references and index.
    ISBN 0-89862-563-7
    1. Learning disabilities.   2. Autism.   3. Attention deficit
disorders.   I. Title.
    [DNLM: 1. Attention Deficit Disorders with Hyperactivity—
diagnosis.   2. Autism, Infantile—diagnosis.   3. Learning
Disorders—diagnosis.   4. Memory Disorders—diagnosis.
5. Neuropsychology.   WS 110 P414d]
RJ496.L4P46   1991
618.92′85′889075—dc20
DNLM/DLC
for Library of Congress   91-9558
                                                                     CIP

To my wife, Linda, without whose unending support and encouragement this book could not have been written.

To my parents, Frances and Jim, who started it all.

To my mentors:
Lise Wallach and John Coie, who planted the seed.
Marshall Haith, Robert Heaton, and Arthur Robinson, who bent the twig.

To my students—carry it on.

Foreword

If, as the well-known saying goes, "actions speak louder than words," then the first and most important words for me to write about this book are those describing my actions: that is, I have already given out a manuscript copy of this book to a younger colleague seeking training in developmental behavioral neurology and I have made slides of several of the book's tables and figures for a presentation at Neurology Grand Rounds. Clearly, these early-1991 actions express how glad I am to be among the first to welcome this book by Bruce Pennington. Most of the book is precisely what I would have written myself, and it has provided me with that most comforting of professional experiences, consensual validation. Since Dr. Pennington and I work at nearly opposite ends of the country (two time zones away by telephone), come from different disciplines, and have different types of degrees as "doctors," this degree of consensual validation is all the more heart warming and mind satisfying. To find oneself saying "Yes, just so!" again and again in response to the words of a colleague who has arrived at such strikingly similar ways of thinking about research and practice is to be reassured that this field, call it what you will (Learning Disorders? Developmental Neurobehavior?), is making progress.

Dr. Norman Geschwind pointed out that in truth there are three types of neuropathology: acquired insult to mature brain, acquired insult to immature brain, and developmental. This book is mostly about that third pathology, the developmentally different brain. Dr. Pennington's book is organized along the dimensions or modules that serve to focus the reader on the best-known profiles constituting developmental differences. With the genetics of dyslexia as the prototype, Dr. Pennington's conceptual framework gives this book's readers the basis for reflection upon the biology of human neurological diversity.

Dr. Pennington is to be congratulated for the lucidity with which his model is laid out; he defines learning disorders in terms of dysfunctions of specific modules of brain function and makes overt comparison to Howard Gardner's well-known multiple-intelligences perspective. Dr. Pennington is also to be congratulated for the breadth of his knowledge of other related disciplines (developmental psychology, for one) and his generous appreciation of what these disciplines contribute to the neuropsychological model of modularity. Thus his brain–behavior orientation is never a narrowly deterministic one and his sensitivity to the multivariate nature of the relationships between underlying modular "risk factors" and real-life clinical outcomes is exemplary. Dr. Pennington's exposition of the diagnostic process is a courageously complex one, leaving no uncertainty as to how much he abhors oversimplification.

Having emphasized these outstanding features of the book and having declared myself to feel thoroughly "at home and at ease" with most of its contents (from the overarching conceptual framework down to most of the fine-grained descriptive details), I will claim the right of a "kindred spirit" to quibble with Dr. Pennington about a few items. After that, I will return to applauding certain statements that I wholeheartedly endorse. But the highest praise is, surely, that one finds a colleague worthy of some disagreement, for it is in such debate that much clarification is born.

The scope of Dr. Pennington's book does not extend to the motor domain, nor does he refer to it in connection with associated or concomitant aspects of several disorders. Perhaps it is not surprising that it is with respect to the motor domain that Dr. Pennington should be less impressed than is a neurologist, since a neurologist's training so heavily emphasizes reliance upon motor dysfunction per se as well as motor "markers" as co-localizers. Also, a behavioral neurologist is probably somewhat more likely than a neuropsychologist to be consulted about children whose motor function is a major, if not central, concern. This "referral artifact" may skew the population seen and evaluated by the behavioral neurologist even when the very same chief complaints (reading, calculating, etc.) are equally in the presenting clinical picture. To put it another way, the very decision-making process that leads to neurological referral of a learning-disordered (LD) child may be heavily biased by motor dysfunctions and may place those motor dysfunctions "front and center" in the chief complaint to the behavioral neurologist. There have been *direct* and *indirect* implications of motor dysfunction for (1) dyslexia and (2) executive dysfunction (under its many names over the years). The direct implications in both disorders converge upon recommendations for "treatment" of handwriting, a school skill the lack of which can become a "bottleneck" for many LD students. Thus, it is my experience that documentation of age-referenced slowness, dysrhythmia, or postural instability relevant to handwriting is important in support of a treatment program that detours around this common "bottleneck." Although motor proficiency is an associated or concomitant domain to reading disability's phonological processing or ADHD's executive dysfunction, the direct implication for academic program accommodations (these days, extensive use of wordprocessor) seems to me worthy of note.

Indirect relevance of motor findings to underlying brain–behavior relationships is also helpful to the researcher and the clinician. My past research, and that of several others, has established that age-referenced *motor* inhibitory capacity, as indexed by the orderly developmental disappearance of associated (also called extraneous or overflow) movements elicited by neuromotor examination, is an observable "tip of the iceberg" where the "iceberg" is *mental* inhibitory capacity—an important facet of executive function. Similarly, choreiform movements, irregular small deflections off course, or tremulousness bespeaking postural instability of fingers or tongue may index *attentional instability*. And for the dyslexic, slow-for-age tongue wiggles and finger sequencing (persistent even in adults) testify to the subtle left-hemisphere-mediated inefficiencies that often spill over somewhat from the prototype phonological-processing territory as "neighborhood markers."

Dr. Pennington's relative emphases in the dyslexia and executive function chapters (4 and 5) on oral language and attentional processes mean that other issues are not discussed in full. In Chapter 4, he superbly handles the prototype phonological deficit in its pre-reading form, although he does not stress the longevity of the effects of this and other subtle language deficits upon higher academic, vocational, and even social achievements or adjustments. The reader needs to hear from us as clinicians that subtle language deficits affect much wider-ranging skills than reading, that reading skill is but the most easily measured of the subtle language deficits and may paradoxically be the "salvation" (the *relative* strength) in higher education of the poor phonological processor/producer who cannot follow lectures or "shine" on oral examinations. I would like the reader to know how subtle language deficits weave in and out of centrality in the life of patients over the long term (I believe the medical reader would recognize "protean" manifestations, but even such a term falls short of the complexity with which compensation, cognitively speaking, enters into the clinical picture of dyslexia over the lifespan).

In Dr. Pennington's discussion of executive function and attention deficit hyperactivity disorder (Chapter 5) the reader should be aware of the overlap of these categories, one (EF) assessment-derived and dimensional, the other (ADHD) historically derived and categorical. I avoid making hierarchical relations between the terms because in neurological analysis executive function, identified by Dr. Pennington (in traditional fashion) as prefrontal in localization, stands at the top of a distributed network for attentional and intentional control processes; hence ADHD may represent a label for a heterogeneous group of dysfunctions related to each of the several identifiable "nodes" along the distributed attentional/intentional network (anywhere from posterior fossa—e.g., cerebellum—up to and including prefrontal cortex). So, although I agree profoundly with Dr. Pennington that the EF/prefrontal top end of the system is probably the most common and intrinsically most important piece of the internally heterogeneous ADHD category with respect to learning disorder, it is not the only piece that is encountered clinically. Dr. Pennington's beautiful first chapter itself reminds us how much subcortical brain tissue must remain under our consideration when we analyze learning disorders: The ADHD category, to my way of thinking, exemplifies the need to broaden our differential localization beyond prefrontal cortex to include neural substrates of activation, orientation, motivation, and vigilance as these connect with and influence executive function. In simple words: Don't neglect "bottom up" in favor of "top down" in approaching the phenomenology of mental control.

Dr. Pennington is to be commended for his courage in placing the autistic spectrum (even the much-disputed Asperger's) in juxtaposition with the other learning disorders; for cleaving the "nonverbal, right hemisphere" category along the social cognition/spatial relations boundary line; for the honest exposition of what clues we clinicians discern yet what gaps in our knowledge leave these clues tantalizingly fragmentary; for the thoughtful discussion of the different levels and types of functions subsumed under "spatial relations" and, again, under "social cognition"; and most importantly for writing a book that is "state of the art" yet honest enough about the limitations of that art, such that I predict it will become something of a late-20th-century classic, a book that will not become embarrassingly dated because it points the way to future research needs, eschewing premature closure.

—**Martha Bridge Denckla, M.D.**
The Kennedy Institute
Baltimore, Md.

Preface

The main goals of this book are to (1) propose a nosology of learning disorders in children, (2) review the research evidence supporting such a nosology, and (3) provide a usable, practical guide for practitioners in various disciplines faced with the clinical problem of diagnosing and treating learning disorders in children. Every effort has been made to base the recommendations for clinical practice on the best available research. Gaps in our current scientific knowledge of learning disorders are highlighted and core issues discussed. This book is intended for both researchers and clinicians; this relatively new and rapidly evolving area of child clinical practice requires a close connection between research and practice.

Despite the limitations in our current scientific knowledge, provisional answers are needed for clinical practice. Clinicians evaluate very large numbers of children with learning problems every year, but very little information exists in the way of uniform standards or approaches, either within or across disciplines. For instance, virtually every school district in the country has an interdisciplinary team that evaluates children and compiles extensive test data and recommendations. These teams often lack a theoretical framework that permits them to integrate the information from different disciplines into a succinct and comprehensive diagnostic formulation. Likewise, child health care practitioners outside of schools commonly encounter children with school problems, but very often lack specialized training in how to diagnose or treat learning disorders. This book is for all such practitioners who encounter children with learning problems. Although the book uses neuropsychological theory as an organizing framework, it is not specifically a book for neuropsychologists.

I have intentionally focused this book on learning disorders rather than learning disabilities, which I see as a subset of learning disorders. The term learning disorders includes both mental retardation and learning problems due to acquired etiologies. Historically, mental retardation was the first learning disorder to be described and studied. The domains of function discussed here are important for understanding the strengths and weaknesses of retarded individuals, who rarely have evenly depressed cognitive profiles, but mental retardation is a topic for another book.

By definition, a learning disorder involves dysfunction in one or more. neuropsychological systems that affect school performance. A child can have poor school performance without having a learning disorder, when the poor school performance is due entirely to emotional, motivational, or cultural factors.

In the category of learning disorders, I also include autism spectrum disorder and acquired learning disorders, which are not included in the category of learning disabilities. Likewise, attention deficit hyperactivity disorder without an accompanying learning disability is not currently included in the category of learning disabilities, yet all of these non-learning disabled children have problems with learning and need educational services. The task for the diagnostician faced with a child with school problems is broader than deciding whether the child has a learning disability. He or she needs to determine why the child is having learning problems and devise and implement an appropriate treatment plan. The traditional category of learning disabilities is unduly restrictive given the nature of the clinical problem.

This book is organized into two broad sections. Part I covers background issues that are important for understanding the chapters on specific learning disorders. Part II consists of chapters on specific disorders. The last chapter considers implications for research and practice.

The first chapter in Part I provides a neuropsychological framework for the classification system (nosology) that will be used. Because a nosology is a set of syndromes, issues in syndrome validation are crucial for considering the overall validity of the diagnostic approach proposed here. Chapter 2 considers those issues. This chapter also provides a format for reviewing what is known about each of the disorders; the research review for each disorder in subsequent chapters follows this common format.

The third chapter reflects on the clinical processes of making diagnostic decisions and providing feedback. The essential task of the diagnostician is to map data from a variety of domains (symptoms, history, behavioral observations, and test data) onto a diagnostic scheme or nosology and evaluate "goodness of fit," so that some diagnoses are ruled out and others are considered. Because diagnoses are "fuzzy sets" that satisfy multiple soft constraints, the inference processes involved are rarely formal or exact. Nonetheless, the cognitive processes of an expert diagnostician are reliable and teachable. This book attempts to make those diagnostic inference processes more accessible and explicit. Similarly, communication of a diagnosis to parents, child patients, and other professionals requires clinical skill, but of a different sort. The second part of Chapter 3 provides guidelines for conducting this crucial portion of an evaluation.

Part II of this volume consists of five chapters that deal with five specific disorders: dyslexia, attention deficit hyperactivity disorder, right hemisphere learning disorder, autism spectrum disorder, and acquired memory disorder. Each chapter on a specific disorder has two sections. The first section reviews the research on the disorder and the second deals with differential diagnosis and treatment. The research reviews follow the format discussed in Chapter 2. Following a brief discussion of the basic definition of the disorder, the review considers four levels of analysis: etiologies, brain mechanisms, neuropsychological (functional) phenotype, and symptoms. Issues about continuities and discontinuities in the disorder's developmental course are also discussed. The second section of each chapter in Part II follows the format discussed in Chapter 3. Following information about presenting symptoms is a discussion of history, behavioral observations, test results, and treatment. Finally, case examples illustrate the diagnostic process. The case reports presented have been altered so the specific children and families are not identifiable. The test scores and pertinent aspects of the history have not been changed. The last chapter of the book deals with implications for research and practice.

Some children clearly have learning problems purely on the basis of either motivational/emotional factors or cultural ones. These are certainly important clinical issues, but it is beyond the scope of this book to address them. However, the use of the diagnostic procedures described here can rule out a learning disorder, making these other causes of learning problems more likely explanations.

ACKNOWLEDGMENTS

The research reported in this book was supported by the following grants to the author: A NIMH RSDA (MH00419) and project grants from NIMH (MH38820), NICHD (HD19423), the March of Dimes (12-135), and the Orton Dyslexia Society.
Many people helped me in the writing of this book. I am very grateful to Bruce Bender, Richard Crager, Munro Cullum, Geraldine Dawson, John DeFries, Gordon Farley, Deborah Fein, Randi Hager-

man, Marshall Haith, Richard Mangen, Sally Ozonoff, Lynne Sturm, Tish Thompson, Guy Van Orden, and Lise Wallach for their careful reading of an earlier version.

Suzanne Miller, Deborah Porter, and Patti Russell all provided extensive help with the sometimes taxing process of typing the manuscript, preparing figures, and assembling the bibliography. My computer phobia has been something of a joke in my lab, but the experience of writing a book on yellow pads has convinced even me to convert to using a word processor.

Finally, I would like to thank Sharon Panulla, Anna Brackett, and the other staff at the Guilford Press for their encouragement and the speed with which the book was produced.

Contents

PART   I. BACKGROUND

Chapter 1. **Neuropsychological Model**   3
Domains of Brain Function   5
Summary   22

Chapter 2. **Issues in Syndrome Validation**   23
Internal and External Validity   23
Symptom Categories and Subtype Validity   26
Categories versus Continua   30

Chapter 3. **The Clinical Process: Differential Diagnosis**   32
and Providing Feedback
The Process of Making Diagnoses   32
The Process of Providing Feedback   38

PART II. SPECIFIC LEARNING DISORDERS

Chapter 4. **Dyslexia and Other Developmental**   45
Language Disorders
Research Review of Dyslexia   45
Other Developmental Speech and Language
   Disorders   64
Diagnosis and Treatment of Dyslexia   67
Case Presentation 1   77
Case Presentation 2   79

Chapter 5. **Attention Deficit Hyperactivity Disorder**   82
Research Review of Attention Deficit Hyperactivity
   Disorder   82
Diagnosis and Treatment of ADHD   98
Case Presentation 3   102
Case Presentation 4   106

Chapter 6. **Right Hemisphere Learning Disorders**   **111**
Research Review of Right Hemisphere Disorders   *113*
Diagnosis and Treatment of Right Hemisphere Learning
Disorders   *121*
Case Presentation 5   *125*
Case Presentation 6   *128*

Chapter 7. **Autism Spectrum Disorder**   **135**
Research Review of Autism Spectrum Disorder   *135*
Diagnosis and Treatment of Autism Spectrum
Disorders   *149*
Case Presentation 7   *153*
Case Presentation 8   *159*

Chapter 8. **Acquired Memory Disorders**   **166**
Research Review of Acquired Memory Disorders   *166*
Diagnosis and Treatment of Memory Disorders   *169*
Case Presentation 9   *172*
Case Presentation 10   *176*

PART III. **CONCLUSION**

Chapter 9. **Implications for Research and Practice**   **183**
Implications for Research   *184*
Implications for Practice   *190*

References   **193**

Index   **219**

PART I

Background

CHAPTER 1

Neuropsychological Model

This chapter provides a theoretical framework for understanding the specific disorders discussed in subsequent chapters. This theoretical framework is explicitly neuropsychological—it is assumed that all of the disorders discussed here represent examples of specific brain dysfunction caused by genetic and environmental factors that disrupt brain development. A second implicit assumption is that a reciprocal relationship exists between progress in understanding the domains and mechanisms of normal brain development and progress in understanding developmental pathologies. The better articulated our understanding of normal developmental neuropsychology, the clearer our understanding of developmental disorders. Conversely, careful study of developmental disorders may provide insights into which domains of brain function are dissociable from each other and which are most vulnerable to genetic and environmental perturbation.

Two other assumptions are important to this approach: that brain functions are modular and that these modules are differentially vulnerable. Modularity means that there are brain systems specialized for processing rather specific kinds of information, and that these modules are autonomous to an important degree in both function and neural representation (Fodor, 1983). This notion of modularity is widely used by neuropsychologists (e.g., Shallice, 1988) without necessarily implying all Fodor means by the concept. For instance, Fodor's definition of modularity includes two assumptions: that control systems are not modular and that they do not have access to the workings of modules, neither of which is assumed here. As will be seen, one important component of control systems—executive functions—is characterized here as a dissociable module. Moreover, the integrity of executive systems can definitely affect how well modules function, partly because the executive system controls attention and changes in attention can modify even low level processes (Allport, 1989).

Differential vulnerability means that, because of their localization in the brain and their evolutionary and developmental histories, different modules have different susceptibilities to disruption by genetic and environmental factors. If all brain systems were equally vulnerable, we should find equal numbers of developmental disorders for each brain system. Instead, available data points to a very different conclusion: There are a small number of functional brain systems that are most vulnerable to developmental insult or variation. Among these, I would list the prefrontal cortices, which are involved in executive functions (e.g., planning, set maintenance, selective attention, inhibition, and initiation of both cognitive and social behaviors), and the left hemisphere language system, particularly the part of this system concerned with phonological processing. So I am proposing that two functional domains, executive functions and phonological processing, are the systems most vulnerable to developmental insult and therefore the substrates for the most common developmental disorders.

This proposal has an evolutionary justification: namely, brain systems that have evolved more recently are more likely to be subject to genetic and environmental variation, whereas older brain systems are more highly conserved and exhibit less variation, both within and across species. This theory is discussed in more detail by Lieberman (1984) with regard to the language system, which is clearly a part of the human brain that has a recent evolution. Similarly, we know that the prefrontal cortices have increased dramatically in relative and absolute size in recent evolution.

As pointed out in the Preface, *learning disorders* is a broader term than *learning disabilities* (which are a subset of learning disorders), because the term *learning disorders* does not exclude mental retardation or acquired etiologies. Historically, mental retardation was the first learning disorder to be described and studied. The domains of function discussed here are important for understanding the strengths and weaknesses of retarded individuals, who rarely have evenly depressed cognitive profiles. Similarly, the same dimensions of brain function are important for understanding the strengths and weaknesses of children who suffer acquired insults, such as those caused by a closed head injury or anoxia; these kinds of learning disorders will be discussed in Chapter 8.

DOMAINS OF BRAIN FUNCTION

In what follows, I provide a simplified model of domains of brain function, emphasizing those functions that are most relevant for understanding learning disorders in children (see Table 1.1). This model focuses on five functional domains: phonological processing, executive functions, spatial reasoning, social cognition, and long-term memory. Obviously, the human brain has many other functions, from perception to motor control. These five particular domains were chosen because they can account for all or nearly all the learning disorders encountered by most clinicians.

Some readers may feel there should be a category devoted to motor learning disabilities. Although motor problems are correlated symptoms in many learning disorders, the only learning disorders in which they appear to be primary are some cases of handwriting disorder, many other cases of which have a spatial reasoning component. Other readers may feel there should be a more differentiated set of language disorders that affect learning. But research on subtypes of language disorders and their relation to learning disorders apart from reading disorders is still in an early state of development. However, other speech and language disorders besides dyslexia are considered in Chapter 4.

A somewhat similar neuropsychological theory has been developed by Gardner (1983), called the theory of multiple intelligences. His list of intelligences includes linguistic, spatial, logical-mathematical, musical, bodily kinesthetic, and two personal intelligences. As in the current approach, he places a strong emphasis on neuropsychological data to validate these different intelligences as "natural kinds." Gardner also reviews evidence from prodigies, idiot savants, and other cultures to support his "parsing" of cognition into these seven fairly independent domains. Our two lists of domains agree on three categories: linguistic, spatial, and personal (which I call social cognition).

TABLE 1.1 Modular Brain Functions and Learning Disorders

Function	Localization	Disorder
Phonological processing	Left perisylvian	Dyslexia
Executive functions	Prefrontal	Attention deficit disorder
Spatial cognition	Posterior right hemisphere	Specific math/handwriting
Social cognition	Limbic, orbital, right hemisphere	Autism spectrum disorder
Long-term memory	Hippocampus, amygdala	Amnesia

Furthermore, two more of his domains, musical and bodily kinesthetic, certainly appear autonomous and modular, but are not relevant for a taxonomy of learning disorders in our culture, because children are rarely brought to clinical attention because of specific problems in these two areas. If our culture expected universal musical or athletic attainment, then it is likely many children would have learning disorders in these fields.

The real disagreement between the two lists is the inclusion of executive functions and long-term memory on my list and the inclusion of logical-mathematical thinking on his. Because both executive functions or long-term memory are horizontal rather than vertical faculties (i.e., they are not restricted to one content domain), they do not meet one of Gardner's criteria for an intelligence. However, because children can be specifically impaired in either executive functions and long-term memory, they do meet my criteria for learning disorders. Finally, his category of logical-mathematical thinking overlaps with my categories of spatial reasoning and executive functions.

Despite these differences, the spirit of the two approaches is very similar. Before Gardner's book, neuropsychological theories of intelligence were hard to come by, and previous research on intelligence neglected the important constraints provided by various exceptional populations.

Each of the five functional systems discussed here are subserved by different portions of the cortex (see Figure 1.1). In this figure, the top brain shows the lateral surface of the left hemisphere on which the perisylvian region is outlined, which is important in phonological processes (PP). The left prefrontal areas are also indicated, which are important in executive functions (EF). The middle brain shows the medial (middle) surface of the right hemisphere. The two small circled areas of the medial temporal lobe are the hippocampus and the amygdala, important for long-term memory (LTM). The C-shaped structure around the corpus callosum is the cingulate gyrus, which may be important for social cognition (SC), among other things. The other SC line points to the orbital frontal area, also implicated in social cognition. Finally the bottom brain depicts the lateral surface of the right hemisphere. Different portions of the posterior right hemisphere appear to be implicated in spatial reasoning (SR) and social cognition. The right frontal lobes are also indicated and, like their counterparts on the left, are important in executive functions.

Each function has a protracted developmental course, beginning in infancy and exhibiting developmental increases at least into adolescence. We will briefly discuss the localization and developmental course of each functional system in turn.

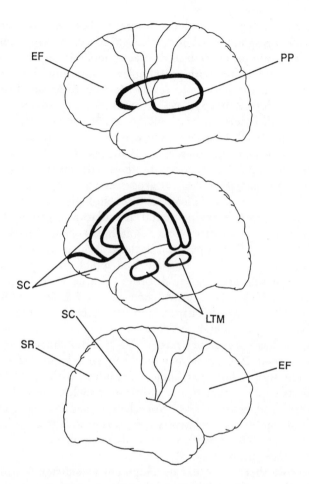

FIGURE 1.1. Localization of modular brain functions. EF, executive functions; PP, phonological processes; SC, social cognition; SR, social cognition; LTM, long-term memory.

Phonological Processing

Phonological processing in the majority of normal adults is subserved by the perisylvian areas of the left hemisphere, including Wernicke's area in the posterior left temporal lobe and Broca's area in the premotor portion of the left frontal lobe. Lateralization of speech processes to the left hemisphere is evident quite early in development (Witelson, 1987). Some discrimination of speech sounds may be present in neonates and is clearly present in infants by a few months of age (Eimas, 1974).

Although the ability to produce different phonemes is commonly viewed as emerging in the babbling phase of speech development, both the perception and production of discrete phonemic segments appears to be a protracted affair, with preschoolers processing words more at the syllabic than the phonemic level (Menyuk & Menn, 1979; Nittrouer & Studdert-Kennedy, 1987). Similarly, articulatory competence for the full repertoire of phonemes is not completed until about age 8 (Templin, 1957). Moreover, there are steady increases in articulatory speed at least into adolescence (Baddeley, 1986; Case, Kurland, & Goldberg, 1982): Consonant with their late evolution and protracted development, phonological processes are subject to considerable individual variation, and disorders of phonological processes have a high prevalence rate. Developmental articulation disorders have an approximate prevalence rate of 5% (Beitchman, Nair, Clegg, Ferguson, & Patel, 1986). Developmental dyslexia, which we will discuss as a developmental phonology disorder, and which overlaps somewhat with developmental articulation disorders (Catts, 1989; Lewis, Ekelman, & Aram, 1989), has a prevalence rate of 5%–10%. Stuttering, which also affects speech output, appears to be a disorder distinct from either developmental dyslexia or developmental articulation disorders, and has a prevalence rate of 1%–3%. Beitchman et al. (1986) found that about 20% of 5-year-olds had speech and/or language disorder; this figure, however, includes children with voice disorder, stuttering, as well as other primary disorders such as mental retardation, autism, and hearing loss. Nonetheless, because each of these confounding conditions is relatively rare, it is probably fair to estimate a prevalence of 10%–15% of 5-year-olds with an idiopathic speech and/or language disorder.

Obviously there are other developmental language disorders besides these three, just as there are other levels of language processing besides phonology. Developmental language disorders that affect only nonphonological language processes such as syntax, semantics, and/or pragmatics are rarer. Some of these rarer developmental language disorders overlap with autistic spectrum disorder, which is discussed in Chapter 7.

Spatial Cognition

Stiles-Davis, Kritchevsky, and Bellugi (1988) have edited an excellent recent book on the neuropsychology and development (both normal and abnormal) of spatial cognition; much of this brief overview is drawn from that book. Sometimes referred to vaguely with the exclusive term "nonverbal abilities," the domain of spatial cognition is increasingly studied in its own right and not just in contrast to language. Although the visual and spatial systems are closely linked in our thinking (hence the common term "visuospatial skills"), it is important to emphasize that spatial cognition, like language, is modality-independent (Kritchevsky, 1988). There are certainly spatial tasks with no visual input such as the Tactual Performance Test (which is performed by a blindfolded subject), just as there are visual tasks with at most minimal spatial requirements (such as skilled reading). This modality independence is dramatically demonstrated by the development of spatial cognition in congenitally blind children (Landau, 1988), an interesting counterpart to the development of manual language in the congenitally deaf. Like other neuropsychological domains considered here, this domain consists of a number of heterogeneous functions that are subserved by multiple brain systems, some of which operate in parallel.

A list of functions in this domain includes object localization and identification, short- and long-term visual or spatial memory, deployment of attention to extrapersonal space, mental rotations and displacements, spatial imagery, and spatial construction (e.g., drawing or building). These functions overlap with other functional domains discussed here, such as long-term memory (LTM) and attention; attention is discussed here in the domain of executive functions.

Given the heterogeneity of functions included in this list, it is not surprising that there is no one portion of the brain that attends to all of them. For instance, while the right hemisphere is clearly specialized for many spatial functions, Farah (1988) develops a convincing empirical case for the hypothesis that the generation of visual imagery has a left posterior localization. Moreover, the mediation of the transfer of visuospatial information into LTM depends on limbic memory structures, especially those in the right hemisphere. Attention to extrapersonal space depends on multiple, parallel, bilateral attention systems, both cortical and subcortical, though the posterior right hemisphere (parietal) system plays a special role. Spatial construction tasks are necessarily complex and draw on attentional executive, motor, and sometimes language systems, as well as spatial cognition. In the absence of a stimulus, such tasks also depend on memory and imagery systems. Finally, disorders of object recognition are dissociable from disorders of spatial reasoning per se. Animal models have demonstrated two cortical visual processing systems: an occipital–temporal system concerned with object recognition and an occipital–parietal system concerned with the analysis of extrapersonal space (Morrow &

Ratcliff, 1988). In humans, the right parietal lobe appears to be particularly specialized for the analysis of extrapersonal space; it appears to operate on an analog representation of external space that can be mentally rotated. This form of representation and transformation calls for specialized neural processes; hence the localization of function. In contrast, object recognition depends on different visual processes.

The purest example of a spatial cognitive task is the three-dimensional mental rotation task explored by Shepard & Metzler (1971); they found that time to completion is a direct linear function of the number of degrees one figure has to be rotated to be in the same orientation as another. This result implies there is a processor in the brain that actually performs a mental rotation. Normal performance on mental rotation tasks depends on the integrity of the right parietal lobe (Kritchevsky, 1988). Shepard (1988) argues that the long evolutionary experience organisms have had with changing perspectives in a three-dimensional world has led to neural processing structures that represent space in terms of possible transformations, such as rotations and displacements. This evolutionary argument implies that the neural mechanisms for spatial reasoning are much older, more highly conserved, and perhaps less subject to genetic variation than neural mechanisms that have evolved for much more recent representational tasks, such as those involved in phonological processing.

As is true for language processes, the relative specialization of the right hemisphere for spatial reasoning appears to emerge early in development (Stiles-Davis, 1988; Witelson & Swallow, 1988). However, spatial reasoning does not emerge as early in development as phonological processing. To a certain extent, the early development of spatial cognition may depend on motor experience, especially early locomotor experience (Acredolo, 1988; Benson, 1990). For instance, normal precrawlers when compared with crawlers of the same age perform worse on various measures of spatial cognition (Benson & Uzgiris, 1985; Campos & Bertenthal, 1989; Kermoian & Campos, 1988). It makes sense that the neural networks involved in processing spatial information would need to be tuned by experience with spatial transformations, such as the transformations encountered when navigating in space. Moreover, such experiential tuning is much more effective in the case of active versus passive movement (Held & Hein, 1963). Interestingly, the developmental course of spatial reasoning throughout the life span also appears to be different from that of verbal knowledge. Whereas verbal knowledge shows continuing increases into the later decades of life, spatial reasoning reaches a peak in adolescence and slowly declines thereafter (Horn, 1985). This differential life-span course likewise implies that different neural mechanisms underlie spatial versus language processing. Gardner (1983) points out that the decline of spatial cognition with age is not found in practicing painters or sculptors, so either continued practice or talent (or both) may protect spatial reasoning from the effects of age.

Although everyday experience suggests wide individual differences in spatial reasoning, we don't know whether the variation is as great as is observed in phonological processes. We also do not know what the true prevalence rate is for spatial cognitive learning disabilities. Clinical experience (and relative amounts of research literature) suggest that spatial cognitive learning disabilities (LDs) are considerably rarer than language-based LDs, but we don't know this in a rigorous way. If they are indeed rarer, two possible explanations suggest themselves. One is that the range of individual differences in spatial reasoning is actually smaller than for language skills, because, as argued above, spatial reasoning has a longer evolutionary history and should be less variable within a species. Gardner reviews evidence in favor of this explanation. Another explanation is that the range of individual differences for each skill is equal, but that what differs is the culturally based threshold of concern for problems in each skill. Illiteracy is of more concern in our society than innumeracy, and we even lack a term for ineptitude in the visual arts. These two possible explanations are not mutually exclusive, and both could be operating to produce what seems to be a much lower rate of spatial cognitive LDs.

Interestingly, the traditional (Orton, 1937), and still common lay theory of dyslexia is that it represents some kind of visual or spatial processing problem. However, recent research has shown very convincingly that the vast majority of dyslexics have impaired language processing skills, especially in phonological processes (Bryant & Bradley, 1985; Raynor, 1986; Vellutino, 1979).

Social Cognition

Recently, there has been increasing interest in social learning disabilities (Denckla, 1983; Rourke & Strang, 1978; Weintraub & Mesulam, 1983), which some investigators term "right hemisphere learning disability." This is a somewhat misleading designation, because social, cognitive, and pragmatic processes are not exclusively localized to the right hemisphere. In normals, in patients with acquired right hemisphere lesions, and in developmental learning disorders, spatial reasoning and social cognition are dissociable.

Prosody, pragmatics, and emotion perception do appear to be lateralized to the right hemisphere, based on both adult lesion and normal data (Bryden & Ley, 1983; Etcoff, 1984), but emotional and social cognition also appear to be subserved by the limbic system and by portions of the frontal lobe (Fein, Pennington, & Waterhouse, 1987) and possibly by the left hemisphere as well.

In the developmental literature the last 10 years has seen a revolution in our understanding of the social competencies of infants (Bruner, 1975; Stern, 1985; Trevarthen, 1977), and the earlier psychoanalytic notion of an asocial infant who very slowly develops social contacts has been abandoned.

Some social cognitive abilities emerge in the first year of life, including social interest, joint attention, differential emotional expression, and possibly differential emotional recognition (cf. Nelson, 1987). Imitation is likewise a fundamental social skill, which emerges very early in development and may be present in neonates (Meltzoff, 1987). The developmental course of social cognitive development is obviously quite protracted, and continues well into adulthood as new roles (spouse, parent, grandparent) require new social cognitive abilities.

Because of their enormous adaptive significance, we would expect social skills to emerge early in development and to be relatively immune to perturbation. Extreme deficits in social cognition (i.e., autism) are considerably rarer (0.02%–0.05%) than extreme deficits in general cognition (i.e., mental retardation, about 3%). The prevalence rate of milder forms of social cognitive deficit is unknown, although one form, Asperger's syndrome, may be less rare, 0.1%–0.26% (Gillberg & Gillberg, 1989). Short of actual deficits in basic social cognitive processes, there is obviously much greater variation in more complex social skills, such as those involved in making and maintaining friendships, marriages, and professional collaborations.

Executive Functions

The umbrella term executive functions refers to processes such as planning, organizational skills, optimal set maintenance, and selective attention and inhibitory control, for which the prefrontal regions of the brain appear to be specialized (Fuster, 1985; Goldman-Rakic, 1988; Perecman, 1987; Stuss & Benson, 1986). These processes obviously cut across content domains, and are equally important in something as purely cognitive as writing a computer program or in something that is much more social, such as chairing a committee meeting. Our understanding of the function of the frontal lobes is less well-developed than our understanding of the functions of the posterior neocortex, the limbic system, or subcortical structures; and our appreciation of the possible contribution of frontal lobe dysfunction to a wide variety of behavioral pathologies is much newer. At this point, we know very little about the prevalence of executive function deficits in children. From an evolutionary perspective, executive function skills should be subject to more variation than many other domains of brain function, because both the relative and absolute size of the prefrontal cortices has increased dramatically in recent evolution. Thus, like the language areas of the brain, the frontal lobes should be particularly vulnerable to developmental pathologies. Part of the problem in determining the prevalence of executive function disorders is that the behavioral symptoms of executive function deficits overlap considerably with the symptoms of childhood psychiatric disorders, many of which have traditionally been conceptualized as arising from faulty social environments. So executive function disorders have not been studied as extensively by neuropsychologists as has a disorder like dyslexia.

The remainder of this section is divided into three parts, concerned respectively with theories of prefrontal function, the normal development of prefrontal functions, and childhood disorders besides attention deficit hyperactivity disorder (ADHD), which may have a prefrontal basis.

Prefrontal Function

The term *executive function* is broadly defined as the ability to maintain an appropriate problem-solving set for attainment of a future goal. Although this term can be defined in a purely cognitive way, we would like to use this term to bridge two levels of analysis: cognitive and neuropsychological. On the neuropsychological side, considerable evidence supports the broad conclusion that executive functions are mediated by the prefrontal areas of the cortex (Fuster, 1985; Goldman-Rakic, 1988; Perecman, 1987; Shallice, 1982; Stuss & Benson, 1986). Beyond this broad conclusion, no consensus has been reached on a cognitive taxonomy of executive functions or on a neuropsychological theory of how and where these executive functions are localized within the prefrontal areas. A list of possible executive functions includes organizational skills, planning, future-oriented behavior, set-maintenance, self-regulation, selective attention, maintenance of attention or vigilance, inhibition, and even creativity. Obviously, some of these overlap or are redundant with one another.

In terms of neuropsychological theories of prefrontal function, several have recently been proposed that agree on some points but differ in other important respects. Goldman-Rakic (1988) has proposed that an underlying function of all the prefrontal areas is to maintain a representation over time to guide future behavior, but that each prefrontal area differs in the kind of representation for which it is specialized. For instance, the dorsolateral convexity is specialized for maintaining spatial representations, and the orbital area may be specialized for maintaining representations of rewards or motivators, including social rewards. This theory fits well with the differential neuroanatomical connections between specific prefrontal areas and specific portions of posterior and limbic cortices, but it has a hard time accounting for the integration of behavior across different representational modalities.

Fuster (1985), in contrast, has proposed a trichotomy of prefrontal functions—working memory, anticipatory set, and interference control—with different portions of prefrontal cortex subserving each function. For instance, interference control is postulated to be subserved by orbital frontal structures.

Shallice (1982, 1988) has proposed a model of frontal functions that is more cognitive than neuropsychological, but which has the advantage of being much more explicit about cognitive mechanisms. This model makes a distinction between routine and nonroutine selection of actions, with the selection of routine actions handled by nonfrontal contention scheduling, whereas nonroutine selection requires the intervention of a frontal supervisory attentional system. Shallice (1982) tested this model by devising routine and nonroutine variants of a planning task (Tower of Hanoi), which was administered to patients with anterior and posterior lesions. The Tower of Hanoi puzzle requires planning several moves ahead to recreate a given configuration of rings on three posts; because there are constraints on possible moves, planning is required. Patients with left frontal lesions were selectively impaired on nonroutine planning. Moreover, this deficit was not attributable to deficits in spatial reasoning or verbal short-term memory. However, he failed to replicate these results in a second study of a different group of frontal patients (Shallice, 1988).

In summary, at a general level, there is fairly broad consensus that executive functions are dependent on the prefrontal areas and that dysfunction in these areas disrupts the organization and control of behavior, especially on novel or challenging tasks. Different theorists include different executive functions in their lists and have different ideas about how these functions are localized within the prefrontal regions. No theorist has yet solved the fundamental problems of how behavior is integrated across various executive functions, and there is clearly the temptation here to reintroduce the homunculus in one form or another. More than in perhaps any other area of behavior, our common-sense psychology, with its reliance on concepts like "will," "self," and "decide," impedes our neuroscientific analysis of prefrontal functions. Despite these difficult theoretical problems, an awareness of the range of behavioral disorders that are possibly frontal is very important for the child clinician.

Normal Development of Prefrontal Function

We now turn to the development of prefrontal functions, which have been reviewed elsewhere (Welsh & Pennington, 1988; Welsh, Pennington, & Grossier, in press). We will only cover the main points here. These points concern (a) the onset of prefrontal function—early versus late; (b) developmental course of prefrontal function—one versus many stages; and (c) the need for developmentally appropriate measures of executive function.

The development of the prefrontal areas has traditionally been seen as occurring quite late in the course of normal brain development (Huttenlocher, 1979; Yakovlev & Lecours, 1967), and prefrontal functions have been viewed as having a correspondingly late onset (Golden, 1981). However, more recent neuroanatomical (Rakic, Bougeois, Zecevic, Eckenhoff, & Goldman-Rakic, 1986), neuroimaging (Chugani & Phelps, 1986), and neuropsychological (Diamond & Goldman-Rakic, 1985a, 1985b) data all converge on the second half of the first year of life as an early important transition in prefrontal anatomical and functional development. Moreover, findings from developmental research would argue strongly against a late onset for the first emergence of prefrontal functions in behavior, since functions like selective attention, inhibition, and anticipation are observable quite early in life.

Obviously, executive functions do have a very protracted course of development. Much of academic and moral education is focused on enhancing that development, and many of the normal difficulties of childhood (e.g., the terrible twos) can be interpreted as examples of less developed executive functioning. Within this protracted course of development, there could be several stages. Different executive function tasks reach developmental plateaus at different ages (Passler, Isaac, & Hynd, 1985; Welsh et al., 1990). Moreover, there is a rough correspondence between these different ages and the transition ages for different neo-Piagetian (Case, 1985; Fisher, 1980) stages of cognitive development. In fact, these stages of cognitive development can be reconceptualized as changes in the nature and complexity of the executive strategies or mental representations that can be held on-line in working memory to guide behavior. The prefrontal system appears to be crucial for both holding such representations on-line and for developing better representations. A fruitful exchange is possible between research on cognitive development and research on the developmental neuropsychology of executive function. For instance, a recent factor-analytic study of normal adults found that a measure of Piagetian formal operations and several executive function tasks all loaded on the same factor (Shute & Huertas, 1990).

In terms of measures of executive function, the foregoing implies that potential measures exist across a broad age range and it is very important that developmentally appropriate measures be chosen. The classic Piagetian AB̄ task is a measure of executive function in 1-year-olds, but is obviously inappropriate for older children. The best-validated adult executive function task, the Wisconsin Card Sorting Task, which requires sorting by color, form, and number, is obviously inappropriate for preschoolers and early elementary children for whom number is a much less salient dimension than form or color.

It should be noted that much research remains to be done in this area. We do not know if all executive functions are prefrontally mediated or if all prefrontal functions fit existing notions of executive function. There is very little data validating the localization of executive functions to the prefrontal areas in children. The best data comes from the cross-species comparisons of Diamond & Goldman-Rakic (1985a, 1985b) and supports the proposed localization, but much more work is needed.

Executive Function Developmental Pathologies

We next consider possible developmental pathologies of executive functions aside from ADHD, which is discussed later. In several adult psychiatric disorders, dysfunction of prefrontal and closely related limbic structures is implicated; perhaps the best example is schizophrenia (Andreasen, 1988). The same may well be true of some childhood psychiatric disorders. Three possible examples are considered here, Tourette's syndrome, autism, and early treated phenylketonuria (PKU).

In Tourette's syndrome, there are chronic, multiple motor, and vocal tics. Tics are repetitive, simple motor sequences that are not consciously initiated, although conscious control can delay them. Thus, tics can be viewed as a failure of inhibition, one of the executive functions previously discussed. Some evidence supports a basal ganglia localization for the neuropathology in Tourette's syndrome; the basal ganglia have strong reciprocal connections with prefrontal areas. Interestingly, data from encephalitic Parkinson's patients suggest that a wide range of problems with the initiation and inhibition of both simple and complex behaviors and thoughts are possible with basal ganglia pathology (Sacks, 1972). It is noteworthy that obsessive-compulsive disorder, in which more complex acts and thoughts cannot be inhibited, appears to be an alternate manifestation of the same genotype that causes Tourette's syndrome (Pauls & Leckman, 1986).

A frontal theory of autism was proposed by Damasio & Maurer (1978); evidence of frontal lobe dysfunction in autism has been found on neuropsychological tests (Rumsey, 1985) and PET scans (Horwitz, Rumsey, Grady, & Rappaport, 1988). While these data broadly suggest autism is a prefrontal disorder, a more specific prefrontal theory of autism has been proposed and is discussed in Chapter 7.

Our third example of possible executive function pathology is early treated PKU. Although PKU children maintained on a phenylalinine-restricted diet have normal IQs, they appear to have a higher rate of learning and cognitive problems than controls, including impairment on measures of executive function (Pennington, van Doorninck, McCabe, & McCabe, 1985; Welsh, Pennington, Ozonoff, Rouse, & McCabe, 1990). In the latter study, we compared preschool age, early treated PKU children with controls similar in IQ, age, and sex on a battery of executive function (EF) measures and a discriminate recognition memory task. The PKU group's performance was significantly worse than the IQ-matched controls on the executive function composite score, but not on the discriminate task. This pattern of results supported our hypothesis of a specific executive function deficit in PKU. Moreover, we also found a significant partial correlation (0.65) between phenylalanine levels within the early treated PKU group and the executive function composite score, but no significant correlation with IQ or recognition memory. A possible biochemical explanation for this relation is that PKU leads to reduced dopamine levels, because the enzymatic defect in PKU prevents the conversion of phenylalanine into tyrosine, the rate-limiting precursor in dopamine synthesis. It is known that the neurotransmitter dopamine is important for normal prefrontal function. We are further testing this prefrontal hypothesis of early treated PKU with tyrosine supplementation and other studies. Interestingly, as their phenylalanine levels get higher, the behavior of early treated PKU children resembles that of children with ADHD; they become distractible, irritable, and impulsive (Realmuto et al., 1986). Moreover, a large British study found high rates of behavioral deviance in a representative sample of early treated PKU children (Stevenson et al., 1979). So early treated PKU may provide a biochemical model of ADHD. ADHD is a confusing but prevalent childhood disorder, which a number of researchers view as likely arising from prefrontal dysfunction.

Long-Term Memory

Considerable advances in memory research have been made in recent years, as a result of converging results from studies of normal adults, adults with brain lesions, and animal models. This work is reviewed in several recent books (Lynch, McGaugh, & Weinberger, 1984; Squire, 1987; Tulving, 1983). As a result of this work, we have both a clearer functional taxonomy for memory functions and a clearer understanding of the brain structures important for these components of memory. Long-term memory is broadly divided into procedural and declarative memory, each of which is subserved by different neural systems. Procedural memory refers to the memory for skills, like driving a car of hitting a tennis ball, which is not retrievable as specific facts or episodes. We all know how to tie our shoes, but it is unlikely that we recall the first (or the sixth) time we did it, and it is only with a fair amount of effort that we could write down good directions for doing so. Procedural memory is evolutionarily older than declarative memory and less vulnerable to insult. Although the precise localization of the structures that mediate procedural memory are not completely understood, the cerebellum has been implicated as one contributory structure, as have the basal ganglia; the limbic memory structures (hippocampus and amygdala) are clearly *not* required for procedural memory.

Declarative memory, on the other hand, refers to memory that is directly available to consciousness as specific facts and events that can be "declared" as a verbal statement or a visual or other representation. The transfer of information into long-term, declarative memory is mediated by the hippocampus, amygdala, and a few other closely related structures. The actual storage sites for long-term declarative memories appear to be in distributed, cortical networks that initially processed the information (Squire, 1987). So storage is distributed and hard to disrupt (hence Lashley's failure to find the engram), but the mechanism of transfer into long-term memory is quite localized and vulnerable to insult.

Declarative memory can be further divided into semantic memory and episodic memory. Semantic memory refers to knowledge of meanings and facts, whereas episodic memory refers to knowledge of specific events in one's personal past. Defining a word such as "joy" requires semantic memory, whereas remembering particular joyful episodes in one's own life requires episodic memory.

It is also worth noting that the structures that mediate immediate and short-term memory are different from the ones involved in long-term memory, thus short- and long-term memory are each dissociable from the other. In fact, adult amnesics, who have profound long-term memory deficits, perform normally on immediate memory span tasks like the Wechsler Digit Span (Shallice, 1988). Among childhood learning disorders, such as dyslexia or ADHD, problems on immediate and short-term memory tasks are common. Furthermore, both short- and long-term memory for verbal material are dissociable from short- and long-term memory for visual material. Parents and clinicians frequently lump symptoms in these different memory systems as "memory problems," thus failing to make crucial distinctions between short- and long-term or verbal from nonverbal.

In terms of the early development of memory, much work remains to be done and many issues remain unsettled. One point of entry is to examine where we are with the perennial puzzle of infantile amnesia—the phenomenon that we can't recall experiences from infancy. Numerous different explanations have been offered for infantile amnesia by investigators from different theoretical perspectives: from repression (by psychoanalytic thinkers, such as Freud), to radical changes in memory codes (by psycholinguists and cognitive psychologists), to immaturity of memory structures in the brain (by neuroscientists, e.g., Schacter & Moscovitch, 1984). From the perspective of multiple memory systems, the scope of infantile amnesia is significantly reduced. Clearly the procedural or habit memory system must operate early in life; how else would we retain the many motor skills first acquired in infancy? Similarly, there are rapid changes in semantic memory occurring in the first two years of life that are clearly retained. So the amnesia in infantile amnesia applies only to the episodic memory system—why don't we remember the first "chapters" of our autobiographies? Are the relevant neural circuits immature? Do infants lack conscious recognition of past experiences?

Some answers to these questions are beginning to emerge. As in so much of the developmental psychology of infancy, the answer to the question of when episodic memory first emerges depends on which task is used to index it. Since infants cannot tell stories, various recognition memory tasks are used to tap episodic memory. Novelty preference, as measured by the Fagan task (Fagan & Singer, 1983), is present as early as 5 months. Other research using different tasks has found some evidence of recognition memory at birth (Slater, Morrison, & Rose, 1982). Nelson (in press) argues that recognition memory develops rapidly over the first 6 months of life. For instance, in an evoked potential study, Nelson, Ellis, Collins, and Lang (1990) demonstrated recall memory in 6-month-old infants by finding a delayed slow wave only after trials in which an expected event did not occur. However, Schacter and Moscovitch (1984) have argued that the novelty preference task may only tap the procedural memory system, as it is similar to tasks on which preserved performance is found in adult amnesics. Moreover, human infants still perform poorly on the delayed nonmatching to sample (DNMS) task at 12 months (Bachevalier, in press-b). This task has been well validated as a marker for the recognition memory system that is impaired in limbic amnesia. So the behavioral evidence can be interpreted to support different conclusions about when the limbic memory structures involved in episodic memory first begin to function.

Recent lesion studies in monkeys have begun to clarify these issues. Bachevalier (in press-a, in press-b) reports that neonatal lesions of the hippocampus and amygdala impair performance on *both* a novelty preferance task very similar to the Fagan task and on the DNMS task, which is accepted as a marker for recognition memory, while leaving performance on tasks of habit memory intact. This pattern of impaired and preserved memory abilities persisted into adulthood in these monkeys. These results imply (a) that the Fagan task is an early marker for the recognition memory function subserved by the limbic memory structures, and is not a measure of habit or procedural memory; (b) that the limbic memory structures begin to function early rather than late in the first year of life; and (c) therefore, infantile amnesia cannot be readily explained by the immaturity of these structures. Their early maturity is also supported by receptor binding studies, which found a mature pattern of distribution in the limbic areas of newborn monkeys, but not in neocortical areas important in visual recognition. Bachevalier's results also imply that the plasticity of the limbic memory structures is limited even in early life, therefore an early acquired amnesic disorder is likely to lead to permanent deficits.

It is important to note two other points from Bachevalier's work. (1) The monkeys with neonatal limbic lesions have persisting social deficits, some of which are similar to those seen in autism. This raises the striking possibility that the apparent absence of a developmental amnesic syndrome is due to the fact that this syndrome overlaps or coincides with autism; we will return to an amnesic theory of autism in Chapter 7. (2) The difference in the development on the two memory tasks, novelty preference and DNMS, appears to be caused by the greater dependence of the latter task on later-maturing neocortical circuits in the temporal and frontal lobes. For instance, correct performance on DNMS requires the infant to always remember the old object but pick the new object. Inhibiting the response of picking the old object may require frontal mediation, just as does successful performance of the AB̄ task, for which proficiency develops at 9–12 months. It may be that the prefrontal or executive component of the DNMS task is late maturing, rather than the mnemonic component.

The prevalence of developmental deficits in long-term memory is unknown and is an important topic for future research. Unlike other adult neuropsychological syndromes, there is not a recognized developmental equivalent of the amnesic syndrome. There are three possible reasons for this lack of parallelism. One is simply that we haven't looked for it. A second is that developmental amnesia would inevitably present as mental retardation or mental retardation with autism, because a failure of declarative or episodic memory would pervasively undermine cognitive development. A third is that the structures subserving declarative memory may be particularly resilient to developmental insult, perhaps because some of them (i.e., hippocampus) are among the last structures of the central nervous system (CNS) to develop and are still developing postnatally. The usual view is that brain structures are most vulnerable while they are undergoing rapid development, rather than before or after such development. Hence, the hippocampus may be less vulnerable to birth insult. However, Bachevalier's data reviewed above argues against this third possibility. Obviously, more research is needed to answer these questions.

Regardless of whether there are developmental disorders that specifically affect declarative memory, it is clear that acquired insults in childhood can impair long-term memory just as they do in adults. Anoxic insults and closed head injuries are two fairly common causes of amnesic disorders in childhood.

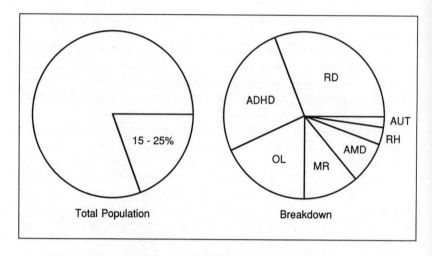

FIGURE 1.2. Prevalence of learning disorders. AUT, autism spectrum disorder; RD, reading disability (dyslexia); ADHD, attention deficit hyperactivity disorder; OL, other language; MR, mental retardation; RH right hemisphere learning disability; AMD, acquired memory disorder.

SUMMARY

These five different cognitive functions—phonological processing, spatial cognition, social cognition, executive functions, and long-term memory—are all separate domains of neuropsychological functioning. Each first emerges early in life, and each is to differing degrees susceptible to developmental perturbation. Figure 1.2 provides a rough idea of the prevalence of the learning disorders related to the different cognitive domains discussed above. The overall prevalence is given on the left and the relative prevalence on the right.

Before discussing these specific learning disorders, we will first consider issues in syndrome validation (Chapter 2) and the clinical process of diagnosing learning disorders (Chapter 3).

C H A P T E R 2

Issues in
Syndrome Validation

The five learning disorders presented in this book represent a nosology for classifying learning problems in childhood (see Table 1.1). In this chapter, the issues involved in validating both a nosological scheme and individual syndromes within a nosology are considered. The concepts of nosology and syndrome imply that the domain of behavior can be divided in meaningful ways; it is not a smooth continuum. Therefore we must ask what validates one division versus others. These issues have been well discussed by Fletcher (1985) and Rapin (1987; Rapin & Allen, 1982); we will draw on their discussions.

The basic goals of a nosology are to identify clusters of symptoms that reliably co-occur and then to identify subtypes of patients who will be homogeneous at the level of either etiology, pathogenesis, or treatment. These two goals concern internal and external validity, respectively.

INTERNAL AND EXTERNAL VALIDITY

Internal validity might also be termed internal consistency or reliability. Fletcher lists five criteria for internal validity: (1) coverage or number of patients classified, (2) homogeneity of the subtypes, (3) reliability of the classification procedures, (4) replicability across techniques, and (5) replication in other samples. Clearly, a sample- or test-specific subtype would necessarily lack reliability.

External validity essentially concerns the explanatory significance of a subtype or its syndrome validity. A subtype may be reliable in terms of the variables used to define it, but not have a distinctive relation to any external variables of interest. Fletcher (1985) lists three possible criteria for external validity: (1) differential response to treatment, (2) clinical significance, and (3) differential relation to processing measures independent of those used to define the subtype, such as neuropsychological measures. To this list, we would add (4) differential etiology, (5) differential pathogenesis, and (6) differential prognosis or developmental course (see Table 2.1 and Figure 2.1).

Fletcher (1985) emphasizes that the search for external validity is essentially a hypothesis-generating and testing affair, much like the search for construct validity (Cronbach & Meehl, 1955). A good subtype or syndrome is a fruitful hypothesis about how to "parse" the domains of both disordered and normal behavior, as well as how to "parse" the various levels of the underlying causes of behavior. If a syndrome is valid, it will satisfy tests of both convergent and discriminant validity across levels of analysis: etiology, brain mechanisms, neuropsychology, and symptoms. The ultimate goal of syndrome analysis is to discover a meaningful causal chain across these different levels of analysis. We would like to know which etiologies specifically cause the subtype in question, what aspects of brain development they perturb, what deficit in neuropsychological processes this leads to, how this underlying neuropsychological deficit leads to the primary (or core) and secondary symptoms of the disorder, how the symptoms and underlying deficit change with development, and how all of this information helps explain the response to treatment. Thus, a valid subtype or syndrome is a construct below the level of observable behaviors or symptoms, which provides a meaningful explanation of why certain symptoms co-occur in different patterns across develop-

TABLE 2.1 Criteria for a Valid Nosology

Internal	External
Coverage	Etiology
Homogeneity of subtypes	Pathogenesis
Reliability	Neuropsychology
Replicability	Developmental course
	Response to treatment

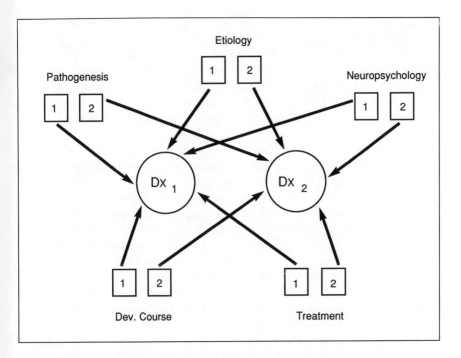

FIGURE 2.1. Convergent and discriminant validity.

ment, as well as a meaningful explanation of why some treatments are efficacious and others are not.

The concepts of convergent and discriminant validity are closely related to the concept of external validity. An ideal nosology would have a complete and unique set of external converging validators for each of its different syndromes, thereby guaranteeing discriminant validity. This ideal situation is depicted in Figure 2.1.

In the scientific description of the five learning-disorder syndromes discussed in this book, we review the evidence for external validity in the areas of etiology, brain mechanisms (pathogenesis), neuropsychology, and developmental course. Evidence for differential response to treatment is included in the clinical section of each chapter. There is at least some evidence for differential etiology, brain mechanisms, neuropsychology, and response to treatment across these five disorders. In general, we know the least about the pathophysiological brain mechanisms for these behaviorally defined disorders, but, in some cases, we know a fair amount about the genetic factors involved in etiology. As we will see, except for a clearly acquired learning disorder such as that produced by closed head injury (Chapter 8), evidence exists for both genetic and environmental factors in the etiology of these disorders. Moreover, for most of these disorders, there is evidence of genetic heterogeneity in etiology: different genetic subtypes of the disorder. It is less certain that subtypes in terms of brain mechanisms or underlying neuropsychological deficits exist. Therefore, instead of a one-to-one correspondence between etiologic and phenotypic subtypes, the correspondence may be many-to-one. Different etiologies may produce similar symptoms by acting on the same underlying brain mechanisms.

A many-to-one situation may turn out to be quite common in the case of complex behavioral disorders generally, and not be restricted to the developmental learning disorders we are considering here. Recent discoveries about the genetics of bipolar illness, schizophrenia, and Alzheimer's disease suggest both major gene effects and genetic heterogeneity in etiology, but it is less clear that the genetic subtypes of these disorders are associated with clearly distinguishable phenotypic subtypes in a one-to-one fashion. It is also important to note that this kind of etiological heterogeneity, by itself, does not invalidate the construct of a behavioral syndrome. If the different etiologies affect the same or similar brain mechanisms and produce the same underlying neuropsychological deficit, then it seems reasonable to retain the concept of the behavioral syndrome and not divide it into subtypes. As discussed by Shaywitz & Shaywitz (1988), there are medical syndromes, such as hypertension and hydrocephalus, that are definitely heterogeneous in their etiologies. A similar point is made by Folstein & Rutter (1988) in reviewing the genetics of autism; while autism is undoubtedly heterogeneous in its etiology, it may not be heterogeneous in its pathophysiology. Thus we may have some deviation from the ideal situation depicted in Figure 2.2 without invalidating a nosology.

SYMPTOM CATEGORIES AND SUBTYPE VALIDITY

Much of the confusion about subtype homogeneity versus heterogeneity arises from the lack of a mature developmental psychology of the domain (e.g., attention) in which the pathology appears to occur. Such knowledge helps us to identify which of the symptoms associated with a disorder are primary and which are not. Subtypes that do not differ

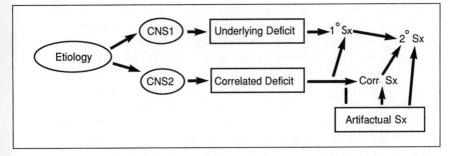

FIGURE 2.2. Relationship among symptom types.

in primary symptoms are not really subtypes. Symptoms associated with a disorder are usually divided into the four categories: primary (or core) symptoms, correlated (or concomitant symptoms), secondary symptoms, and artifactual symptoms (see Table 2.2). This taxonomy of symptoms is similar to that discussed by Rapin (1987).

Primary Symptoms

Primary symptoms are universal, specific, and persistent in the disorder. Most importantly, they are the observable behavioral characteristic that is most directly caused by the underlying neuropsychological deficit. For example, the primary symptom in dyslexia appears to be a deficit in the use of phonological codes to read and spell single words; this primary symptom appears to be caused by an underlying deficit in phoneme awareness. In autism, the primary symptom appears to be a deficit in social relatedness. This primary symptom appears to be caused by an underlying deficit in intersubjectivity or theory of mind—the awareness of minds other than one's own and the ability to stimulate others' mental states. If one assumed that the

TABLE 2.2 Types of Symptoms

Primary	Core symptoms, universal, specific, and persistent
Correlated	Same etiology/affect different brain systems
Secondary	Consequences of primary or correlated symptoms
Artifactual	Appear associated/not causally related

primary symptom in dyslexia were letter reversals or faulty eye movements, obviously a whole different theory of dyslexia would follow. Similarly, if one assumed that the primary symptom in autism were avoidance of eye contact, then a whole different theory of autism would follow. In fact, these different views on dyslexia and autism have been held in the past. As the psychology of normal reading and early social cognition has developed, the theoretical plausibility of letter reversals or avoidance of eye contact as primary symptoms has diminished. Moreover, careful, experimental analysis of the behavior in these two disorders has yielded a clearer view of the primary symptoms in each. This experimental analysis has rested directly on techniques and advances in developmental and cognitive psychology. It is also important to note that both genetic and neurological studies of the disorder can provide additional constraints on which symptoms are primary, and convergent results across levels of analysis provide the clearest evidence about primacy.

Correlated Symptoms

Correlated or concomitant symptoms have the same etiology as primary symptoms, but arise from the involvement of different brain or other organ systems (see Figure 2.2). For instance, the varying etiologies of autism also produce mental retardation in a substantial majority of autistic children, but mental retardation is not a primary symptom of autism because it is neither universal in, nor specific to, the disorder. To take a second example, the varying etiologies of dyslexia also produce other speech and language disorders in many dyslexic children (e.g., articulation problems), but again these concomitant speech and language disorders are neither universal nor specific to the disorder. In both examples, the etiologies involved have likely disrupted other brain systems besides the brain system deficiency in which is necessary and sufficient to produce the disorder.

Secondary Symptoms

Secondary symptoms are consequences of either core or concomitant symptoms. Unusual eye movements during reading by dyslexics are a secondary result of the primary symptom of faulty phonological coding; because they cannot always rely on phonological codes, dyslexics must scan text in a more exploratory fashion to find cues for meaning. Self-injurious behavior, found in some autistic children, is probably a secondary result of the concomitant symptom of mental retardation.

Artifactual Symptoms

Finally, artifactual symptoms are those that appear to be associated with the disorder, but are not causally related. Because the descriptions of most behavioral disorders are based on clinically ascertained samples, and because clinical ascertainment increases the probability of additional, unrelated disorders (Berkson, 1946), an apparent association may result. For instance, it is possible that the apparent association between dyslexia and ADHD, or that between Tourette's syndrome and ADHD, are artifactual. (The co-morbidity between dyslexia and ADHD is discussed in Chapter 5.) There are several ways to evaluate whether an apparent association is artifactual. Perhaps the best way is to see if the association is found in relatives of patients who have both disorders.

Returning to the issue of subtype homogeneity, especially at the level of behavior, confusion about which symptoms are primary can lead to confusion about subtype homogeneity. For instance, there is controversy about whether dyslexia is a unitary disorder or whether there are subtypes of dyslexia. Virtually all of the proposed subtypes of dyslexia are based on cognitive test profiles, that is, on patterns of symptoms found in some but not all dyslexics. For example, it has been found in a variety of studies that there is a language disorder subtype of dyslexia, a visuospatial disorder subtype of dyslexia, and a mixed deficit subtype of dyslexia, with the presupposition being that different underlying deficits and different core or primary symptoms exist in each subtype. However, because these subtypes are based on associated symptoms found in children who read and spell poorly, it is possible that these associated symptoms are a mix of concomitant, secondary, and artifactual symptoms, and that the primary symptom is the same across subtypes. These associated symptoms might affect the expression and course of the disorder; they might even affect treatment. However, if the subtypes do not differ in terms of core symptoms or underlying deficits, then it is hard to assert they are truly different subtypes.

To take a second example, consider the question of whether autism and Asperger's syndrome are the same disorder or different subtypes of social cognitive disorder. They certainly differ in associated symptoms, as autism is associated with mental retardation, whereas Asperger's syndrome is not. Asperger's syndrome is associated with verbal performance IQ (VIQ > PIQ) disparities, whereas the opposite pattern is associated with autism. So, parallel to dyslexia, we could propose both a verbal and visuospatial deficit subtype of autism, with the latter being called Asperger's syndrome. But once again, if these two subtypes do not differ in core symptoms or underlying neuropsychological deficits, then we are just making subtypes out of the cognitive variability associated with any developmental disorder (Chapter 7 presents recent data on the neuropsychology of autism vs. Asperger's syndrome).

It becomes evident that subtyping efforts based on statistical techniques, such as cluster analysis, while admirably empirical, contain no guarantees about either external validity or the causal relations among the symptoms that form the subtype. A subtype or a syndrome is only valuable in terms of its explanatory power, both in terms of ordering relations among symptoms and making differential contact with deeper levels of analysis.

CATEGORIES VERSUS CONTINUA

A possible criticism of the nosology/syndrome approach taken here is that it implies that syndromes are discrete clusters in a multidimensional space, defined by the various levels of analysis discussed here, such as the symptom level, the neuropsychological level, and so on. What if there is just a homogeneous multivariate normal distribution in this multidimensional space, with no discrete clusters? Can we then speak of syndromes? This has been an issue of contention, especially between clinicians and students of normal behavior.

I think the answer to this question depends on the degree of covariation across levels of analysis. If a given region of symptom space covaries with a given region of neuropsychological space and that with a given region of genetic space, then we can still speak of syndromes, although they would have vague boundaries. If there is no covariation across levels of analysis, then obviously syndromes are out. This issue has usually been addressed only at the level of behavior. For example, in the case of dyslexia, there is a controversy over whether there is a hump on the lower tail of the population distribution of reading skill (Rodgers, 1983; Rutter & Yule, 1975; Stevenson, 1988). If there is a hump, then the syndrome of dyslexia is validated. If there is no hump, it is invalid and instead we have continuous variation in reading skill. But what if the distribution is really normal, but different portions of the distribution covary with different etiologies specific to reading skill? Then I would argue we could still talk about a syndrome of dyslexia, although it would have indefinite boundaries at the symptom level.

In the chapters that follow Chapter 3, I will explicitly consider the evidence for internal and external validity of the five learning disorder syndromes presented here. I will also attempt to divide symptoms associated with these disorders into the four categories discussed above (e.g., primary, secondary, etc.). If the learning disorder syndromes prove invalid, then the always difficult clinical task of differential diagnosis becomes impossible. Instead, each case must be considered separately, and diagnosis is reduced to the enumeration of the individual strengths and weaknesses of each patient. Because this is the preferred approach of some clinicians who deal with learning disordered children, we will next consider issues involved in making and communicating diagnoses.

C H A P T E R 3

The Clinical Process:
Differential Diagnosis
and Providing Feedback

The previous chapter provided a scientific perspective on what diagnoses are and how their validity is tested. This chapter reflects on the clinical processes of making and communicating diagnoses, both of which have implications for the clinical utility and "social validity" of the diagnoses we are about to discuss. Teachers, parents, and even clinicians are inherently suspicious of behavioral diagnoses for children. Many have seen examples of the diagnostic process gone awry: a child mislabeled or a diagnosis improperly conveyed. Furthermore, children change so much in such a short amount of time that it may not be appropriate to label them at all. These are important reservations and in what follows I try to deal with some of them.

THE PROCESS OF MAKING DIAGNOSES

The process of making diagnoses has important similarities to the process of hypothesis-testing in scientific research. A good hypothesis or theory accounts for a large amount of observable data in diverse and sometimes unexpected domains. As discussed in Chapter 2, a diagnostic category is a theory or construct; convergent validity for this theory is provided by data from different levels of analysis. Most importantly, a good hypothesis or diagnosis should be more than just a descriptive relabelling of the data and should contain explicit criteria for ruling it in or out. Obviously, one of the main differences between hypothesis testing in research and in the diagnostic process, is that research usually focuses on a group, usually carefully chosen to test the hypothesis at hand, and diagnosis focuses on an individual patient, not chosen but referred. The clinician always deals with an N of one, and cannot exclude confounding factors in an a priori way. In this way, the hypothesis-testing of the diagnostician is inevitably less powerful and precise than that of the researcher.

However, the diagnostician has some important compensating advantages. One is that he or she has a lot more data about one subject than a researcher typically has about an entire group of subjects. This additional data can be used to test for both convergent and discriminant validity of a particular diagnostic hypothesis. If a child is dyslexic, then certain things ought to be true and not true across heterogeneous domains of data, including presenting symptoms, the early developmental history, the school history, the behavior during testing (including kinds of errors), and the test results. A particular diagnosis is supported by a converging pattern of results across these different domains of data and by a diverging pattern of results for competing diagnoses. As will be described, our diagnostic model makes this process of testing for convergent and discriminant validity explicit. A second advantage the diagnostician presumably has is that the diagnostic hypotheses he or she is testing in an individual patient have already been tested on groups of patients in research studies. His or her main task should be to see if a given patient fits an established, well-articulated pattern, not to develop these patterns.

Before presenting our diagnostic model, we should be more explicit about the "medical model" approach to diagnosis advocated here. For some mental health practitioners, this kind of medical model approach is aversive because it does not capture the individuality of the patients' problems. Robin Morris (1984) has said, "Every child is like all other children, like some other children, and like no other children." In other words, some characteristics are species-typical, some are typical of groups within the species, and some are unique to individuals. As diagnosticians and therapists, it is important to have a good handle on which characteristics fall into which category. Some patients have symptoms they feel are unique to them but that are in fact species-typical. Other symptoms are fairly specific to a particular diagnosis, and still others are unique to a given patient. Although a good clinician must be aware of and make use of a patient's unique attributes, scientific progress in understanding and treating mental disorders depends on there being "middle level" variation—differentiating characteristics of groups within our species. If not, mental health work reduces either to just treating the problems everyone faces in living or to recreating the field for each unique individual. On the one hand, we say there are no mental disorders because everyone is "in the same boat." On the other hand, we say there are no mental disorders because everyone is different. A science of mental health is not tenable at either extreme. Although there is much confusion and many limitations in the current state of knowledge about mental disorders in children, that state of affairs hardly means a science of developmental psychopathology is impossible.

Another criticism of the medical model is that it presupposes a single model of physical causality for all behavioral disorders. However, Meehl (1973) has pointed out that within medicine there is no single medical model. Moreover, recent medical research on disorders such as heart disease espouses a multifactoral causal model and acknowledges the contribution of genetic, psychological, and cultural factors in etiology. The medical model that has been castigated by social scientists may increasingly be a straw man. Moreover, our search for the causes of behavioral and learning disorders should be just as broad as the search for causes of "medical" disorders, and not hampered by an a priori assumption of what kind of causes will prove important.

It is important to remember that the patient has the diagnosis rather than the diagnosis having the patient (Achenbach, 1982). In other words, most diagnoses don't provide an explanation for every aspect of the patient's being. A related point is that nosologies classify disorders, not people.

There are several other reasons why diagnoses are important. Diagnoses permit efficient identification and treatment, and research on a given diagnosis can lead to early identification or prevention. As discussed earlier, studies of diagnostic groups can contribute to basic research on human development. Finally, diagnosis itself can be therapeutic for parents and patients, because an accurate diagnosis provides an explanation for troubling symptoms and a focus for the efforts the parents and child are already making to alleviate the symptoms.

A Model of Differential Diagnosis

We view the process of diagnostic decision-making as being similar to the constraint satisfaction problem in cognitive psychology, rather than being similar to an exercise in formal logic. That is, diagnoses are "fuzzy sets," membership in which depends on many soft and a few hard constraints. Not every patient with autism has motor stereotypies or gaze aversion, even though those are frequent symptoms of autism. Thus, these symptoms provide evidence for that diagnosis, but their absence does not violate a hard constraint. On the other hand, a child with an IQ of 100 cannot receive the diagnosis of mental retardation, since IQ level is a hard constraint for that diagnosis. Diagnostic decision-making involves weighing the goodness of fit of different competing diagnoses to the soft and hard constraints provided by the data and deciding which one (or few) fits best. A good fit is determined in part by the convergent and discriminant validity checks previously discussed.

Another important component of the diagnostic process is the recognition that it is a process, and that diagnostic decisions are not possible until there are enough data. Diagnosis is like the process of perception in slow motion. One has to consciously experience the frustrating and sometimes painful intermediate stages of uncertainty. It is important for diagnosticians to be aware of their own sense of uncertainty and not flee from it into a premature diagnostic decision. One's anxiety and confusion about a case is an important signal that more data are probably needed. In the model we present, this uncertainty is illustrated in the early stages of information processing, because many diagnostic options are receiving activation, and so the model is "confused."

Because there are few hard constraints in diagnosis, dual (or triple) diagnoses are possible and even likely. In particular, children with learning disorders also frequently have a second comorbid psychiatric diagnosis, which may or may not be etiologically separate from the learning disorder. In our model, "diagnostic space" is defined by two dimensions, one for learning disordes and the other for psychiatric disorders (Figure 3.1). The goal of diagnosis is to find the point in this 2-D space that best fits the patient's current cognitive and emotional functioning.

Of course, these two dimensions are not completely orthogonal, as some psychiatric disorders, such as schizophrenia and major depression affect cognition in characteristic ways and some learning disorders affect emotional functioning in characteristic ways. Moreover, the assignment of some disorders (e.g., autism) to one axis or the other is somewhat arbitrary. Finally, the two axes are *not* intended to have different etiological implications, with learning disorders being more organic and emotional disorders being more "environmental." In-

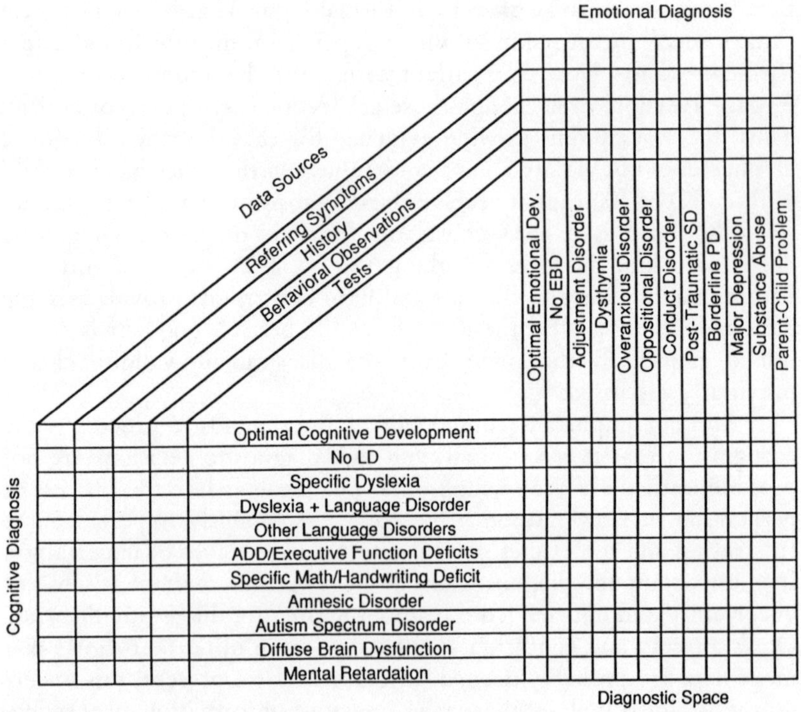

Emotional Diagnosis

Data Sources

Referring Symptoms
History
Behavioral Observations
Tests

Optimal Emotional Dev.
No EBD
Adjustment Disorder
Dysthymia
Overanxious Disorder
Oppositional Disorder
Conduct Disorder
Post-Traumatic SD
Borderline PD
Major Depression
Substance Abuse
Parent-Child Problem

Cognitive Diagnosis

Optimal Cognitive Development
No LD
Specific Dyslexia
Dyslexia + Language Disorder
Other Language Disorders
ADD/Executive Function Deficits
Specific Math/Handwriting Deficit
Amnesic Disorder
Autism Spectrum Disorder
Diffuse Brain Dysfunction
Mental Retardation

Diagnostic Space

FIGURE 3.1. A differential diagnostic model. ADD (ADHD), attention deficit hyperactivity disorders; EBD, emotional or behavior disorders; LD, learning disorder; SD, stress disorder, PD, personality disorder.

stead, all the diagnoses on each axis are conceptualized as resulting from altered functioning of the central nervous system (CNS), with these alterations caused by some mix of genetic and environmental influences, and with environmental influences conceptualized as referring to both neurodevelopmental risk factors, such as head injuries, and to the child's social learning history.

This model is based on connectionist neural network models of cognition, especially models of constraint satisfaction (Rumelhart & McClelland, 1986). The model goes through four iterations, each corresponding to the different sources of data; after each iteration, the "activation values" for each diagnosis node changes. This is obviously not a formal computer model of diagnostic decisions, but such a model could in principle be constructed.

How does this model work? Around the outside of the diagnostic matrix are four "layers" representing the different kinds of data one encounters in a case, arranged in roughly the order one receives each kind of data. So each diagnosis on each axis is preceded by four squares. To model the diagnostic process, one simply puts in "activation values" in these squares as one encounters each kind of data. Somewhat arbitrarily, we have used a range of activation values from –3 to +3. If data in a given domain very strongly suggest a given diagnosis, a +3 is put in that box. Conversely, if it very strongly argues against a given diagnosis, a –3 is put in that box. Lesser degrees of certainty are represented by less extreme values. A zero means the data in that domain are neutral with respect to that diagnosis. The squares record the weighting of the evidence in each domain for each diagnosis. After each level of data have been processed, one can examine which diagnoses are receiving the most activation, as well as which are receiving convergent support across data domains. Both of these criteria are important; a diagnosis that receives consistent positive support across all four levels of data may provide a better fit to the data than one which has a higher final activation total, but inconsistent support. (Obviously, as this is a heuristic model, we cannot provide quantitative criteria for this decision.) So at each level of data, there is a set of diagnoses being considered. Hopefully, this set gets smaller after each successive level of data is processed until the model converges on a best fit solution to all of the data.

If it does not converge, then the data in a given domain have not asked the right questions. Diagnosis has to be an active process of hypothesis-testing. So the list of possible diagnoses suggested by the previous level of data should then be actively tested by the next level of data. If the presenting symptoms suggest dyslexia, then the history-taking should explicitly look for data that will help confirm or deny that diagnostic hypothesis. The diagnostician, like the scientist, must keep careful tabs on what he or she does and does not know; in that way, metacognitive skills are an important part of the diagnostician's armamentarium.

This model can also be used by someone who is listening to a case presentation. In that situation, of course, the listener cannot control which data were gathered at each level. But use of this model can clarify for the listener which critical questions were *not* asked and what impact the missing data have on the diagnostic decision-making process. Our model simulates processes going on in the head of the diagnostician, but it could also be applied to the diagnostic decisions made by a group, such as a clinical team.

Obviously, what is missing from the model is all the content: which data activate (or deactivate) which nodes. To make this determination for the dimension of learning disorders is the task of the subsequent chapters. For each learning disorder, we will review which data at each level are positive, negative, and neutral for that diagnosis as part of the presentation of that diagnosis. Providing the same information for the emotional diagnoses is beyond the scope of this book. Before considering specific diagnoses, we will next consider the process of communicating them.

THE PROCESS OF PROVIDING FEEDBACK

One very important and sometimes neglected part of the evaluation of a learning-disordered child is providing feedback—to parents, other professionals, and to the child patient. The evaluation can be therapeutic; it can dispel unrealistic anxieties and focus energies on the real problem. But these benefits cannot be realized if feedback is not provided in an appropriate manner.

It is important to recognize that the feedback session is a process that is similar in some ways to a psychotherapy process. Because strong feelings and (sometimes) strongly held misconceptions are involved, there needs to be an opportunity for working-through beyond the straightforward transmission of information. Sometimes it is helpful to have two feedback sessions. Without the opportunity for working-through, parents and child patients will often remember little of the new diagnositic information, or worse yet, may distort it. In working with parents, it is important to allow for resistance and denial and to encourage questions and disagreement. Somewhere inside of themselves, most parents already know what you're about to tell them, but they haven't either put it together or faced it. It is also important to allow and respect grief. Some learning disorders (such as autism) have poor prognoses, and so parental grief can be quite profound. More importantly, any learning disorder, however mild, represents the loss of the "perfect child," a fantasy all parents have at some level or another, and so grief is an understandable response in any case. Another important area to address is guilt, as parents often have fantasies about why their child has a problem, and these fantasies frequently focus on something they did. The clinician can often be reassuring that the cause of the problem lies elsewhere, and that in any case, the particular thing they did is very unlikely to be the cause of the child's problem.

Finally, sometimes the parents are angry with the child about his or her learning disorder because they have formulated the problem in motivational terms. "If only Johnny would try harder, he could read (remember, attend, do math, or make friends)." In this situation, it is important to help the parent reframe the problem in nonmotivational terms—in terms of ability strengths and weaknesses, without undermining the importance of the child's efforts. Some learning disordered children are actually trying much harder than their non-LD peers. Other learning disordered children have stopped trying, but it is important to recognize that their lack of motivation is a result, not a cause. To facilitate the emergence and working through of these various emotional reactions, it is important to monitor parents' reactions and be ready to ask questions about how they're feeling and to provide support. It is also important for the clinician to be nondefensive, and available to focus on the parents, rather than on his/her own insecurities.

Of course all of these process issues will go more smoothly if the diagnostician has both done a good job and can communicate their diagnostic formulation *in everyday language.* The most important task is to integrate all the test data into a diagnostic formulation that provides an explanation for the child's presenting problems and points to a plan for their solution, remediation, or compensation. Too often diagnosticians only provide a list of test scores instead of an interpretation, or they hide behind esoteric diagnostic concepts. All of the learning disorders presented in this book can be presented in everyday language, as can the treatment recommendations.

Even in everyday language, the diagnostic formulation may likely require parents to understand new concepts and think in new ways about their child, which is difficult even without emotional interference. Consequently, it is important for the clinician to monitor each parent's comprehension of the feedback. Asking each parent to put the diagnostic statements into their own words can often provide useful information about the extent of their understanding and the degree of mutual communication. To avoid putting parents "on the spot," the clinician can take the blame for possible miscommunication by saying something like "sometimes I do not explain well what I'm trying to say."

To begin the process of providing feedback, it is very important to join with the parents around a focus of mutual concern. As a starting point, I usually restate the symptoms they have already shared with me in their own words. Parents are often the best observers of their children, because they've spent so much time with them; the same can be true of teachers. What they do not always have is the professional training to: (a) recognize which symptoms are clinically important versus those that are developmentally appropriate and (b) construct a coherent explanation for troubling symptoms. You may disagree with the explanation the parent or another professional has adopted to explain troubling symptoms, but you should be able to agree with them on some of the important symptoms.

In the course of discussing the child's problems, it is very important to talk about their strengths as well as their weaknesses, and to show how those strengths can be used to help compensate for the weaknesses that are the focus of discussion. Similarly, it is very important to talk about the child's future in realistic but hopeful terms. Parents may be unrealistically pessimistic about the learning disorder's implication for the future, as when they assume dyslexia precludes going to college. Finally, it is important to leave adequate time to talk about intervention. How to help is what parents are usually most concerned about.

In dealing with other professionals, some of the same issues apply. A clear formulation of the problem that can be expressed in nontechnical language is also crucial for communicating with professionals from other disciplines. If the other professionals have already formed their own diagnostic impression of the child (either because they are the child's teacher or because they have also evaluated the child), then it is certainly important to listen to their impression and look for points of consensus. Sometimes interprofessional communication can be more challenging than giving feedback to parents because: (a) such communication often occurs over the phone rather than in person, and (b) different disciplines may generate competing explanations for the child's learning problems, but lack a means for resolving their differences. If there are persisting differences between professionals, such as between an outside consultant and school personnel, then a meeting is important.

Children with learning problems can quickly become a focus of conflict between groups with different perspectives and interests—parents, school personnel, and outside professionals. Parents often feel the school is not doing enough to help their child. School personnel may feel parents are overly demanding and also resent the opinions of outside "experts" who have different criteria and methods for making diagnoses. A teacher who has had to deal with the problematic behavior of a learning-disordered child may not be too happy to hear that the behavior is not motivated, but rather caused by an ability deficit. Or if there are signs of emotional difficulty in the child or family, the teacher may too readily assume the problem is all emotional, instead of there being two diagnoses. Outside professionals may feel too busy to attend to process issues in dealing with the school. So in providing feedback to schools, it is very important for professionals to try to develop long-term, collaborative relationships, even though most such professionals receive little training in the complicated business of school consultation.

Another area of potential friction between outside professionals and schools is that each uses different criteria for diagnosing learning disorders, with the school's criteria usually being more stringent because they are partly driven by fiscal considerations. Thus outside professionals, following the guidelines in this book, will identify children as dyslexic that the school does not consider learning disabled. This disparity needs to be discussed with the child's parents to help them deal with the school appropriately. If both parents and outside professionals try to maintain a collaborative relation with the school, the school may be more ready to find ways to help the child even when they cannot officially label him or her as LD.

Now we come to the topic of providing feedback to child patients. This is a very important part of the diagnostic process, because the child nearly always has his or her own fantasies about why he or she is having problems at school and why he or she is being evaluated. Older adolescent patients can sometimes appropriately sit in on their parents' feedback session, but most child patients need a separate feedback session, with their parents present.

In talking with a child, begin with his or her understanding of the symptoms. Ask the child why he or she was tested. If he or she does not know, give a reasonable explanation: "Your parents (or teacher) were worried about why you have trouble with reading and wanted to help you. The tests I gave you helped me understand what your problems are and how to help you."

It is important to keep the explanation of the problem simple and developmentally appropriate. It is helpful to begin by discussing the child's strengths. As with adults, it is very important to address the child's own fantasies and explanations for the problems. Many children think they are either dumb or not trying hard enough; few have the concept of a specific learning disability. I often use the analogy of children differing in their talents for specific things, like swimming or football, to explain the concept of a learning disability. If a child cannot provide any answer to the question of why he or she was having a problem, I talk about what other kids with this kind of problem have thought. Then I say that I wanted to make sure the child didn't have the wrong ideas about him- or herself. Once the child has heard the diagnosis, I ask how he or she is feeling about it and then emphasize the plan for help. If a parent has the same problem as the child, I have the parent share that information with the child. The value of this is to emphasize that the child is not the only one in the family with the problem. Most importantly, a parent who has successfully coped with a learning problem provides a role-model and a source of hope for a child who may feel that all of life will be like or her his current struggle to learn to read (or do math, etc.). If the child is in therapy, then the process of understanding the diagnosis and its implications can continue there, as well as in the family.

After the feedback conference, we share our report with parents *before* it is sent to other professionals. In fact, we ask parents to take that responsibility themselves. We encourage parents to recontact us with questions after they read the report; we also suggest other things for them to read about their child's diagnosis. Our overall goal is for parents to be well-informed about their child's diagnosis, so they can be effective advocates for their child with the school and other professionals, and so they can constructively continue to help the child understand and deal with his or her learning problems. Nearly all parents exert a tremendous amount of effort to help their learning disordered children; our goal is to steer that family process in the right direction.

PART II

Specific Learning Disorders

C H A P T E R 4

Dyslexia and Other Developmental Language Disorders

Developmental dyslexia is the first specific learning disorder to be considered because it is the most prevalent and best understood learning disorder in childhood. Thus, it provides a model of what we would like to know about all of these learning disorders.

This chapter and the subsequent ones are divided into two broad sections, one concerned with a research review of the disorder and the other with diagnosis and treatment. The research review section begins with information about the definition, prevalence, and sex ratio of the disorder and then critically reviews what is known about the etiologies, brain mechanisms, neuropsychological phenotype, and developmental course of the disorder. The research review in this chapter also includes information about other developmental speech and language disorders and what is known about their relation to dyslexia.

RESEARCH REVIEW OF DYSLEXIA

Basic Defining Characteristics

Very simply put, developmental dyslexia is unexpected difficulty in learning to read and spell. Unexpected means that there is no obvious reason for the difficulty, such as inadequate schooling, peripheral sensory handicap, acquired brain damage, or low overall IQ. Dyslexia is a prevalent disorder, with prevalence estimates usually ranging from 5% to 10% (Benton & Pearl, 1978), though rates as high as 20%–30% have been reported.

An epidemiologic survey conducted by Berger, Yule, and Rutter (1975) used a regression-based definition of unexpected reading difficulty and found rates of 14.4% in London boys and 5.1% for London girls. On the Isle of Wight, the rates were 5.6% and 2.1%, respectively.

There is currently considerable controversy (e.g., Fletcher & Satz, 1985; Rodgers, 1983; Rutter & Yule, 1975; Stanovich, Nathan, & Vala-Rossi, 1986; Stanovich, Nathan, & Zolman, 1988) over whether traditionally defined dyslexics, those with specific reading disability (SRD) in which reading is unexpectedly poor relative to IQ, constitute a distinct subtype from the larger group of poor readers whose reading is *not* unexpected relative to IQ ("reading backward" children or "garden variety poor readers"). This controversy has mainly focused on two issues (1) whether SRD is statistically distinct within the normal distribution of reading and IQ, and (2) whether SRD is phenotypically distinct in terms of measures of phonological processing skills. The answer to both of these questions could be negative, and the subtype could still be validated by external criteria such as differential etiology, correlates, or developmental course. Because this controversy is unresolved, we follow traditional clinical practice and define dyslexia as SRD. Nonetheless, the appropriate treatment for both kinds of poor readers appears to be similar, which is important for clinicians to know.

If both kinds of poor readers are included in the definition of dyslexia, then of course prevalence estimates are much higher, and reached 22.2% and 15.6% for London boys and girls respectively, and 10.5% and 6.1% on the Isle of Wight (Berger et al., 1975). Urban rates of reading problems among children in the United States have been estimated to be as high as 30% (Eisenberg, 1978).

The commonly cited sex ratio in dyslexia of 3.5–4.0 males to one female is based on clinical samples, but the sex ratio in family samples is considerably lower, about 1.5–1.8 to one. (DeFries, 1989). A recent study (Shaywitz, Shaywitz, Fletcher, & Escobar, 1990) found an equal sex ratio in an epidemiologic sample of young dyslexics. Thus, the sex difference observed in clinical samples of dyslexics may have two components, a possible small component related to the biology of the disorder, and a larger component relating to the sociology of clinical ascertainment. A third explanation is sex differences in the normal means and variances of the IQ and reading tests used to define IQ discrepant dyslexia. In some samples, there appears to be a higher male mean for IQ and a lower male mean for reading. Given these sex differences in means, an IQ discrepant definition based on the mean for both sexes combined will inevitably find a preponderance of male dyslexics, which disappears when the definition is sex specific (Stevenson, personal communication). These sex differences in normal test profiles are interesting in themselves, but are a different issue from the sex ratio among persons with the disorder of dyslexia.

On the biological side, the slight female advantage in some language skills may reduce the rate and/or severity of dyslexia in females. For instance, we have observed a fairly strong female advantage in rates of adult compensation for dyslexia, about 5.1 females per male (Lefly & Pennington, in review). It could be that the sex ratio in young dyslexics is equal, as Shaywitz et al. (1990) have found, and that the slight male preponderance in family samples is due to a sex difference in compensation.

To the extent that dyslexia is genetic, this female advantage in language skills would result in a sex difference in penetrance, the extent to which "dyslexia" genes are expressed in the phenotype. Different genetic scenarios with a sex difference in penetrance include a polygenic model with a lower threshold for males or a major locus model with a sex difference in expressivity. X-linked inheritance is a third possible explanation, but it does not fit the available family data. However, only this third scenario really actually explains the sex difference in penetrance. The other two genetic models rely on an unspecified interaction between the gene or genes for dyslexia and those for sex.

On the sociological side, males with learning disorders may be more likely to come to clinical attention, because they may be more troublesome to parents and teachers when they are having school difficulty. More research is needed on this issue, but the lesson is that apparent sex differences in prevalence rates should not be simplistically interpreted (see also Satz & Zaide, 1983).

Etiologies

Both genetic and environmental factors can cause dyslexia. Because there is more than one etiology in each category, dyslexia is undoubtedly etiologically heterogeneous. On the genetic side, there is evidence for polygenic transmission, recessive transmission, and autosomal dominant transmission. In addition, an abnormal sex chromosome number, specifically 47, XXY, is one rare cause of dyslexia (Pennington, Bender, Puck, Salbenblatt, & Robinson, 1982).

In the following text, the genetics of dyslexia are reviewed in some detail. The purpose of this review is to illustrate the different questions that can be asked about genetic influences on a disorder and the methodologies that are used to answer these questions. Because we know more about the genetics of dyslexia than we do about the genetics of other learning disorders, this detailed review is also presented as a kind of "roadmap" for the genetic reviews presented in later chapters, including what "bumps" in the road are likely to be encountered.

Briefly, current evidence supports the view that dyslexia is familial (about 35%–40% of first degree relatives are affected), heritable (with a heritability of about 50%), heterogeneous in its mode of transmission (with evidence for both polygenic and major gene forms of the disorder), and linked in *some* families to genetic markers on chromosome 15 and possibly in others to genetic markers on chromosome 6.

The data presented below are organized according to these series of linked questions. Familiality (i.e., higher rates of a trait or disorder in relatives of a person with the trait or disorder) is generally necessary for the claim of genetic influence, but not sufficient, because family members share both genes and environment. Twin (and adoption) studies can provide evidence for heritability or genetic influence, but do not generally provide information about the mode(s) of transmission. Some simpler modes of transmission are dominant, recessive, and polygenic inheritance. Segregation analyses can identify the mode of transmission, but do not tell us about gene locations. Linkage analysis addresses gene locations, but traditional linkage analysis does not cope well with genetic heterogeneity, or with oligogenic (several major genes) or polygenic transmission. Newer linkage methodologies deal better with these complexities, which are likely in the genetics of learning and behavior disorders.

In terms of *familiality*, familial aggregation in dyslexia was soon noticed after the disorder was first described by Kerr (1897) and Morgan (1896). It was reported in a number of case studies (Fisher, 1905; Hinshelwood, 1907, 1911; Stephenson, 1907; Thomas, 1905) that children with dyslexia often had affected relatives. Of these, Thomas's (1905) report of two affected brothers and another child with an affected sister and mother was the first to note the familial tendency in dyslexia. Stephenson reported a three-generation family history affecting five females and one male. These early reports documented a number of aspects of the clinical presentation of dyslexia that have been substantiated by subsequent research: early manifestations often include difficulty in learning letter names; affecteds are frequently good at mathematics and spatial tasks; severity varies across affecteds; and the deficit persists into adulthood, either as a problem with both reading and spelling or just spelling.

The magnitude of familial risk for dyslexia had not been measured in a representative population sample until recently. In a selected sample of families, Hallgren (1950) had found the risk to first degree relatives to be 41%, which is considerably higher than the population risk (5%–10%). However, Hallgren's diagnoses of affected family members were not based on testing, and ascertainment biases may have led to the selection of families with higher than normal proportions of affected relatives. Vogler, DeFries and Decker (1985) measured familial risk for dyslexia in the Colorado Family Reading Study (CFRS) sample, which was a representative population sample, and found that sons of affected fathers had a 40% risk of being dyslexic, sons of affected mothers a 35% risk, a five-to-seven fold increase in risk over that found in sons without affected parents. For daughters with an affected parent of either sex, the risk for dyslexia was 17%–18%, a 10- to 12-fold increase over that found in daughters without affected parents. These risk figures are somewhat lower than Hallgren's, but still substantially elevated, and clearly demonstrate familiality.

Similar estimates of familial risk (range 35%–45%) have also been reported by Finucci, Guthrie, Childs, Abbey and Childs (1976), Klasen (1968), Naidoo (1972), and Zahalkova, Vrzal, and Kloboukova (1972). Gilger, Pennington, and DeFries (in press) recently found risk rates generally in this range for three large familial samples, two of which exhibited major gene transmission in a segregation analysis, which is discussed below. The magnitude of familial risk for dyslexia is clinically significant in that family history can be used to help screen for children at high risk for this disorder.

The predictive value of family history was recently demonstrated prospectively in the only longitudinal study of children at high familial risk for dyslexia conducted thus far (Scarborough, 1989, 1990). In this study, family history for dyslexia uniquely accounted for 30%–36% of the outcome variance in reading, with linguistic variables (sound and letter knowledge and discrete trial lexical retrieval—Boston Naming Test) accounting for an additional 7%–8% of the outcome variance. In contrast, a host of other variables including sex, age, socioeconomic status (SES), preschool IQ, nonverbal measures, early education, and exposure to reading and television did *not* contribute significantly to reading outcome. Using a combination of family history and scores on the linguistic variables, 82% of reading outcomes were predicted successfully, which is approaching a level of accuracy acceptable for a population screening test (both false negatives and false positives were under 10%). This study used only a rudimentary measure of phoneme awareness skill, which is the best behavioral predictor of reading outcome currently available, sometimes uniquely accounting for up to 50% of outcome variance (Wagner & Torgesen, 1987). Thus, if family history could be combined with more sophisticated phoneme awareness measures, an even higher rate of predictive success might well be reached. As we will discuss in a later section, further refinement in measuring familial risk is also possible, and will come from identifying genetic loci associated with dyslexia.

The next question to consider is whether this familiality indicates *heritability*. Twin studies have been mainly used to address this question in dyslexia. Earlier twin studies, which indicated substantial heritability for dyslexia, had methodological problems, such as biases of ascertainment, failure to limit the dizygotic (DZ) twin comparison group to same sex twins, and lack of objective diagnostic criteria. Two well-designed twin studies that avoided these methodological problems have recently been conducted.

One study (Stevenson, Graham, Freedman, & McLaughlin, 1986) examined a large population cohort of adolescent twins in London, only some of whom (naturally) were dyslexic. The authors tested for the heritability of both reading and spelling skill in the whole population, as well as specific reading and spelling retardation in a subset of the population. They found only modest heritability for reading ability and disability, but significant heritability for spelling ability and disability. Their results for reading are discrepant from all other twin studies and may be due to the older age of their sample. Moreover, these data were analysed using traditional discrete, concordance analyses.

The second study was conducted by John DeFries and colleagues at the Institute for Behavior Genetics in Boulder. They have developed a new, multiple regression technique for testing heritable and common environmental contributons to extreme low scores on a continuous trait in a twin study. This method assumes that at least one twin in each monozygotic (MZ) or dizygotic (DZ) pair is disabled, as do traditional twin studies. But instead of examining differential (categorical) concordance rates, this technique examines differential regression to the population mean in the co-twin, thus making full use of the information available in a continuous variable, like a reading score. To the degree that the condition is heritable, there should be greater regression to the mean in the DZ co-twin scores (because their degree of relationship is .50, whereas that in MZ twins is 1.00). An expanded version of this model (LaBuda, DeFries, & Fulker, 1986) can estimate both heritability and shared environmental influences (i.e., those environmental influences common to all children in a family, like parental attitudes toward reading). With a large enough data set, this model can also test for major gene effects.

These investigators used this technique to test for the heritability of reading, spelling and related cognitive skills in a sample of 64 MZ and 55 DZ twins, in which at least one member of each pair was reading disabled (DeFries, Fulker, & LaBuda, 1987). The estimate of heritability for a composite reading discriminant score was 0.29, suggesting about 30% of the cognitive phenotype in reading disability is attributable to heritable factors. It is important to note that this result was not simply due to the heritability of IQ, as IQ was controlled in these analyses. With additional data, these heritability estimates have now risen to about .50.

Olson, Wise, Conners, Rack, and Fulker (1989) analyzed the heritability of phonological versus orthographic coding in single-word reading in the dyslexic twin sample studied by DeFries et al. (1987). Quite strikingly, Olson et al. found significant heritability for a phonological coding measure (i.e., oral nonword reading accuracy). In contrast, a measure of orthographic coding skill in single-word reading (picking correct spellings from pairs of phonologically identical letter strings, e.g., rake vs. raik) was less heritable. Moreover, the contribution of phonological coding to the heritability of the reading deficit in these twins was .93 ± .39, whereas the contribution of orthographic coding was essentially zero. Olson and colleagues (Olson, Gillis, Rack, De Fries, & Fulker, in press) have replicated this pattern of results with larger samples, normal twins, different selection procedures (i.e., double entry), and different analytic procedures. Moreover, Stevenson (in press) found similar results in the reanalysis of his twin data. Other evidence argues against problems in orthographic coding being a causal deficit in dyslexia (Olson, 1985; Pennington et al., 1986), whereas the evidence supporting a deficit role for phonological coding is strong. Thus, it is quite interesting that the deficient component is likewise the heritable component.

The next key question is which phonological processing skills at the level of spoken language are a heritable precursor to this heritable deficit in the phonological coding of written language. Olson et al. (1989) found significant ($p < .05$) estimates for the genetic correlation between a phoneme awareness measure, Pig Latin (.81 ± .75) and the heritable deficit in nonword-reading. These investigators pointed out that the large confidence intervals on this estimate meant these results need to be confirmed by future studies. Nonetheless the pattern of results is consistent with the overall argument developing here. We expect that the heterogeneous etiologies leading to dyslexia do not affect reading directly, but instead alter the development of spoken-language skills important for later reading development. These behavioral genetic analyses are consistent with the view that the heritable component in dyslexia at the written-language level is in phonological coding, and the heritable precursor to this deficit in phonological coding is a deficit in phoneme awareness.

While twin or adoption studies are informative regarding the presence of genetic influences, they do not ordinarily address the issue of the mode(s) of genetic transmission. A number of different modes of transmission have been proposed in dyslexia, including autosomal dominant transmission (Hallgren, 1950; Zahalkova et al., 1972), but until recently there has been only one modern complex segregation analysis performed on this disorder (Lewitter, DeFries, & Elston, 1980).

This study included 133 nuclear families, all members of which were tested. Rather than a discrete phenotype definition, a continuous phenotype measure based on a discriminant analysis was employed. Two shortcoming of this study were that adults with a positive history of dyslexia who had normal test scores (compensated adults) were not counted as affected, and the mixed model (a major gene plus a multifactorial background) was not tested.

In the population as a whole, no support was found for a single major locus (autosomal dominant, autosomal recessive, or codominant transmission), but the null hypothesis of no vertical transmission was likewise rejected. These investigators also tested different models of transmission in four subpopulations, including families with probands of a given sex, families with severely affected probands and children considered alone. Autosomal recessive inheritance could not be rejected in families with female probands and codominant inheritance was supported when children were considered alone. The authors concluded that their results likely indicated genetic heterogeneity. This conclusion is similar to that reached by Finucci et al. (1976) in a well-conducted study of 20 extended families, all members of which were tested. This sample was too small to permit a formal, complex segregation analysis.

Pennington and colleagues (in review) recently performed complex segregation analyses on four samples of dyslexic families with a phenotype definition that included compensation. They also tested the mixed model. One of the samples was the Lewitter et al. sample, which was reanalyzed to see if the results would differ using a different phenotype definition and a more powerful segregation analysis program. A major gene model with some degree of dominance best fit the data in three of four samples, including the Lewitter et al. sample, whereas the multifactorial model best fit the fourth sample. In the first three samples, the hypotheses of recessive transmission and a multifactorial background could both be rejected. The gene frequency of the putative major gene was estimated to be about 3%–5%, and penetrance estimates were reduced only in females. Even though the three samples were ascertained quite differently, the results and parameter estimates were quite similar, providing the best evidence yet for dominant transmission in at least some dyslexic families.

In short, the existing data support genetic heterogeneity in the transmission of dyslexia, and the recent analyses provide support for a partially dominant major gene or genes.

To look for *gene locations* affecting dyslexia, we have been conducting linkage studies of dyslexia for about ten years now, and the main results are: (a) significant evidence for linkage between dyslexia and chromosome 15 markers in a minority of families with apparent autosomal dominant transmission (Smith, Kimberling, Pennington, & Lubs, 1983), and (b) significant evidence of genetic heterogeneity (Smith, Pennington, Kimberling, & Ing, 1990). We are currently testing the linkage to chromosome 15 with DNA polymorphisms in the same region as the original marker, and we are looking for a possible second dyslexia locus on another chromosome in the majority of families who are not linked to chromosome 15. A clue about where to look for a second locus has been provided by the association found between dyslexia and immune disorders (Geschwind & Behan, 1982; Pennington, Smith, Kimberling, Green, & Haith, 1987). We are currently testing for a possible second locus on chromosome 6 near the HLA region, which codes for genes affecting the immune system.

In the original study (Smith et al., 1983), which found significant linkage between dyslexia and chromosome 15 markers, one family had a substantial negative LOD score for markers on chromosome 15, arguing against linkage in that family. (A LOD score is a logarithm of the probability of linkage.) However, a test for heterogeneity was not statistically significant. Since then we have doubled the number of families in the sample and more than doubled the N. We now have linkage data on 245 individuals in 21 extended families. When we tested this larger sample for genetic heterogeneity using Ott's (1985) test, the hypothesis of heterogeneity was supported over two competing hypotheses: that of homogeneity and that of no linkage (Smith et al., 1990). It was estimated that dyslexia is linked to chromosome 15, in about 20% of the families. The range of LOD scores in the entire sample of families spans six orders of magnitude, from negative LOD scores less than –3.0 (i.e., 1000:1 odd against linkage to 15) to a positive LOD score around 3.0 (i.e., 1000:1 odd in favor of linkage to 15), which by itself indicates linkage to chromosome 15 in one family.

However, a Danish study (Bisgaard, Eiberg, Moller, Niebuhr, & Mohr, 1987) failed to find linkage between dyslexia and chromosome 15 heteromorphisms. Because only five families were studied, this apparent nonreplication may only be due to heterogeneity (dyslexic families linked to 15 appear to be rarer than those not so linked). In addition, there were other problems with this study. Only nuclear families were studied and the diagnosis of dyslexia was based on questionnaire rather than test data. However, confirmation of our original linkage result by different investigators and different markers on chromosome 15 is obviously important.

The results of the linkage work on dyslexia is similar to the results emerging from linkage studies of other complex behavioral disorders, including schizophrenia, bipolar illness, and Alzheimer's disease. That is, there is evidence for both linkage and genetic heterogeneity. What is currently unclear is how common are the major locus forms of these disorders. Nonetheless, it is certainly true that major gene effects are turning out to be more important in understanding complex behavioral disorders than was previously thought, although the extent of such effects is still controversial (Plomin, 1990).

Both the results of segregation and linkage analyses support the not too surprising conclusion that dyslexia is genetically *heterogeneous*. Additional support for this conclusion is provided by the finding of high rates of dyslexia among boys with a 47, XXY karyotype (Pennington et al., 1982); this sex chromosome anomaly is too rare (about 1/1000 male births) to account for much of the genetic influence on dyslexia.

As discussed in Chapter 2, it is important to note that heterogeneity in etiology does not necessarily imply heterogeneity in pathophysiology; there may not be a 1:1 mapping between etiologic and phenotypic subtypes. In fact, the evidence for discrete phenotypic subtypes in developmental dyslexia is much less compelling than it once appeared. Current evidence supports the view that the vast majority of develomental dyslexics have an underlying problem in the phonological coding of written language. While there are individual differences in this and other component reading processes within the dyslexic population, there is little evidence for discrete subgroups (Olson, 1985). Thus, at the level of behavior, the final common pathway in most of developmental dyslexia is a deficit in phonological coding.

Much less is known about *environmental causes* of dyslexia. Perinatal complications have a weak, nonspecific association with later reading problems (Accordo, 1980), and some authors postulate that infectious or toxic environmental insults may play a role (Schulman & Leviton, 1978). Aside from these kinds of bioenvironmental risks, aspects of the sociological environment, including large family size and low socioeconomic status (SES) (Badian, 1984) very likely contribute to reading problems. Stevenson and Freedman et al. (in press) recently examined which environmental factors affected reading independent of IQ and found significant effects for family size and maternal warmth. In addition, there appear to be large SES effects on phoneme awareness, which is a strong predictor of later reading skill (Wallach, Wallach, Dozier, & Kaplan, 1977). Some lower SES families read less to their children and play fewer language games with them; the lack of these preschool experiences appears to retard the development of later reading skills.

Adams (1990) has reviewed ethnographic research on how different communities and subcultures within and across nations stimulate literacy skills in preschoolers. One of the most striking results is the wide range of variation across subcultures. Many readers of this book came from subcultures in which preschoolers spend thousands of hours being read to, playing spelling games, and watching PBS's "Sesame Street," but there are also subcultures in which adults do not read to children and solitary reading by anyone is frowned upon since the subculture places a premium on social skills and facility with oral language (Heath, 1983). In some of these latter subcultures, there were no storybooks in the home and children received less than four hours of storybook experience per year. Adams emphasized that these subcultural variations are not necessarily a simple function of SES or race, since some poor communities managed to provide good preliteracy experiences. Because reading is a cultural invention and literacy depends on cultural training, these environmental differences in preschool print exposure undoubtedly exert a major effect on individual variation in eventual reading skill. Certainly some children who appear to have dyslexia do not have underlying genetic or neurological differences as a cause for their reading problems. Moreover, all children with reading problems, regardless of etiology, deserve the same intensive efforts to remediate and/or prevent their problems, (Wallach & Wallach, 1976).

Brain Mechanisms

Less is known about the neurology of dyslexia than known about its genetics or neuropsychology, but what we do know converges on the broad conclusion that dyslexia is some kind of a developmental anomaly of left-hemisphere development. Studies using electroenaphalographs (EEGs), evoked potentials, and positron emission tomography (PET) scans are generally consistent in showing differences in left-hemisphere functioning in dyslexics, most importantly on tasks that do not involve reading (see Hughes, 1982 for a review). The results of neuroanatomical studies are somewat less consistent. Some studies using computed tomography (CT) scans have found alterations in the posterior cerebral asymmetry, and others have not. In normals, the posterior left hemisphere is larger than its homologue on the right in the majority of cases, whereas in some studies of dyslexics, either symmetry or an opposite asymmetry (R > L) has been found.

Hier, Le May, Rosenberger, and Perlo (1978) found 10 of 24 dyslexic patients had a reversed occipital asymmetry on CT scan; these patients also had a lower mean verbal IQ than the 14 other dyslexic patients. Handedness was not a significant confound in this result. A similarly high rate of reversed posterior asymmetry associated with low verbal IQ was found in a second dyslexic sample by these same investigators (Rosenberger & Hier, 1979). Because similar results were also obtained in an autistic sample (Hier, Le May, & Rosenberger, 1979), reversed occipital asymmetry is not specific to dyslexia. Moreover, a different set of investigators (Haslam, Dalby, Johns, & Rademaker, 1981) failed to find an increased frequency of this same reversed asymmetry or an association between asymmetry and either verbal IQ or dyslexia subtypes; they did find a higher than normal proportion of dyslexic subjects with symmetry of the occipital widths. In contrast, Roberts, Varney, Reinak, and Parkins (1988) failed to replicate the finding of either reversed or symmetrical occipital width in a sample of 44 adult dyslexic males in which right- and left-handed dyslexics were examined separately. The CT scan data are inconsistent; recent magnetic resonance imaging (MRI) scan data are more consistent.

These MRI studies have focused on the temporal lobes, because evidence of altered temporal lobe structure in dyslexia has been provided by neuropathological studies of the dyslexic brain conducted by Albert Galaburda and colleagues at Harvard Medical School (Galaburda & Kemper, 1979; Galaburda, Sherman, Rosen, Aboitiz, & Geschwind, 1985). Eight autopsies on brains of dyslexic individuals have been conducted by this group. The most consistent finding is symmetry of the planum temporale in all eight cases. The planum temporale is the superior posterior surface of the temporal lobe. In the left hemisphere, it is part of Wernicke's area, which is involved in phonological processing. This neuropathological result is consistent with the extensive cognitive research on dyslexia, which has found that it is essentially a phonological processing problem.

Ectopias and architectonic dysplasias (i.e., malformations in the arrangement of neurons) were also found by Galaburda; their location has been less consistent across cases, but they are more frequent in left perisylvian regions. It is important to note that the size of these ectopias is smaller than the resolution of the MRI (or CT) scan, so the failure to find such anomalies in the MRI and CT scan studies is not a failure to replicate these autopsy findings. While neuropathological studies provide the most detailed neuroanatomical data, it is important to note that extreme ascertainment biases are likely in an autopsy group, so confirmation of the planum temporale findings in a representative sample of dyslexic individuals is important.

There have been three reported studies of neuroanatomical differences in dyslexia using MRI scans. Rumsey and colleagues (1986) studied ten severely dyslexic adult men and failed to find developmental anomalies or pathologic changes, but did find apparent symmetry of temporal lobe volume in nine of ten subjects. However, no measurements of the temporal lobes were reported. Two more recent MRI studies have measured the planum and both have essentially replicated the autopsy finding of altered planum asymmetry in dyslexia. The first study (Larsen, Hoien, Lundberg, & Odegaard, 1990) used MRI to compare left and right planum areas in 19 adolescent dyslexics and controls. They found significant group differences in the pattern of planum asymmetry; 70% of the dyslexics had symmetrical plana, whereas only 30% of the controls did. Moreover, planum symmetry was significantly associated with phonological coding deficits within the dyslexic group. The second study (Hynd, Semrud-Clikeman, Lorys, Novey, & Eliopulus, 1990) measured anterior and posterior width and area as well as bilateral insular and planum length in 10 severely dyslexic, 10 ADHD, and 10 control children. They found that the dyslexics differed significantly from both other groups in both left planum length and in the pattern of planum asymmetry; the dyslexics had shorter left planum length and only one exhibited the typical L > R planum asymmetry, compared to 70% of each of the comparison groups. The dyslexics also had significantly shorter left insular length than normal controls. Both the dyslexics and ADHD subjects had significantly smaller right anterior widths than normal controls, whereas measures of posterior width and area did not differentiate groups.

In summary, these studies indicate that alterations in planum symmetry are specifically related to dyslexia, and more specifically related to phonological-coding skills. It is noteworthy that the neuroanatomical measures used in these studies exhibited excellent reliability, which is important given the difficulty of localizing the planum on MRI scans.

There is another neuroanatomical theory of dyslexia, which has less empirical support. This theory holds that there is a deficit of some kind in the corpus callosum, and as a result, information is transferred less efficiently between the two hemispheres (e.g., Wolff, Michel, Ovrat, & Drake, 1990). This theory implies that both hemispheres are necessary for reading, which may not be true.

Neuropsychological Phenotype

The cognitive psychology of reading is a relatively mature field, consequently our ability to ask and answer refined questions about the underlying deficit in dyslexia is much greater than is true for other learning disorders. We now have a detailed understanding of which components of reading are impaired in dyslexia and what the underlying linguistic influences are on that impairment.

In the vast majority of cases, the underlying deficit appears to be in phonological-processing skills. That is, dyslexia is basically a subtle language-processing disorder, not a disorder of visual or spatial processing as is commonly assumed by the lay public (Vellutino, 1979). There are a variety of other cognitive explanations that have been advanced for dyslexia, including faulty eye movements, vestibular system dysfunction, general problems in rule-learning or conceptual skills, differential sensitivity to certain light frequencies, failure of binocular convergence, problems in foveal vision, and so on. The important point is that none of these other, sometimes esoteric, explanations (or treatments) of dyslexia enjoy anything like the empirical support that the language-processing explanation and corresponding treatments do.

The specificity and nature of the underlying deficit in dyslexia provides important support for the modularity of brain functions. Not all the components of the complex information processing system involved in reading are equally impaired in dyslexia. Reading obviously involves (a) visual perceptual processes to recognize letters, (b) word recognition, and (c) comprehension processes. Research has shown that the locus of difficulty in dyslexia is in word recognition, which Perfetti (1985) has called the central recurrent component of reading.

Dual process theorists have argued that word recognition can be accomplished in two ways, either by "direct" access or through phonological coding. Of these two means of word recognition, developmental dyslexia appears to interfere mainly with phonological coding. A recent review (Van Orden, Pennington, & Stone, 1990) questions the existence of a direct, nonphonological means of word recognition in normals or dyslexics, because there are no positive findings that support the direct-access hypothesis, rather just inferences from null results. In an elegant series of experiments, Van Orden (1987, 1991; Van Orden, Johnston, & Hale, 1988) has demonstrated that normal adult readers mistakenly accept homophonic imposters ("rows" or "roze" for "rose") in semantic judgment tasks, and that this mistake is due to their reliance on phonological coding, rather than to spelling similarity or some other process. This review suggests that a single process handles word recognition and that phonological coding is an inevitable aspect of that process. So phonological coding may be more central to both normal and abnormal reading development than previously supposed.

Thus, dyslexics have a problem with word recognition and this problem is due to a deficit in the use of phonological codes to recognize words. Over and over again when we read, we must translate printed letter strings into word pronunciations. To do this, we must understand that the alphabet is a code for phonemes, the individual speech sounds in the language, and we must be able to use that code quickly and automatically so that we can concentrate on the meaning of what we read (Liberman, 1973; Liberman & Shankweiler, 1979; Liberman, Shankweiler, Fischer & Carter, 1974; Liberman, 1989). The difficulty that dyslexics have with "phonics," the ability to sound out words, makes reading much slower and less automatic and detracts considerably from comprehension. Likewise, poor phonics ability makes spelling considerably less accurate and automatic. We do not simply memorize the spelling of words. If we did, each new word would be completely novel, with no transfer of information from the words already known. Instead, what we already know about the regularities and exceptions of phonological codes in our language helps us learn and remember the spelling of new words. So reading and spelling are very closely related, because both use the same kind of codes, but in different directions. When we read, we go from letters to phonological representations, and when we spell, we go from phonological representations to letters. These codes are probably not represented as explicit rules and exceptions, but instead more implicitly as patterns of regularities. So we know much more than we can say about phonological codes.

As discussed above, the behavior genetic and other evidence suggests there is a spoken language problem that leads to this phonological-coding problem in written language. So we can next ask how specific and modular is this spoken-language problem. First of all, research and clinical experience tell us that dyslexics have a higher rate of spoken language problems, including, early articulation disorders, name finding problems, and problems remembering verbal sequences, (such as phone numbers, addresses, and the months of the year). Even adult dyslexics frequently mispronounce the name of their disorder, calling it "dylexia" or "dyslectia." It is important to emphasize that these symptoms occur in spontaneous speech and *not* in the context of dealing with the printed word. These spoken-language symptoms of dyslexia are easily understood if dyslexia is conceptualized as a phonological-processing disorder; they are harder to explain on a visual or other theory of dyslexia.

Such spoken-language symptoms can be analyzed further to determine which are primary, secondary, correlated, and artifactual, as discussed in Chapter 2. One possibility is that all are primary and are manifestations of a unitary, underlying phonological-processing problem. This is an appealing, parsimonious hypothesis that several researchers are pursuing (e.g., Shankweiler & Crain, 1987). However, recent research indicates that even the seemingly narrow domain of phonological-processing skills has a complex structure, and that different phonological-processing skills have different relations to reading skill and disability. Problems in verbal short-term memory and name retrieval appear to be concomitant and/or secondary symptoms, whereas problems in phoneme awareness appear to be primary, although the relation between reading and phoneme awareness appears to be one of reciprocal causation (Pennington, Van Orden, Kirson, & Haith, in press-b; Pennington, Van Orden, Smith, Green, & Haith, 1990).

In summary, studies of cognitive and linguistic processes in dyslexia have clearly demonstrated that the primary symptom is a deficit in the phonological coding of written language (usually measured by nonword reading) and that the primary deficit underlying this primary symptom is a deficit in phoneme segmentation skills. This result converges nicely with the behavior genetic and neuroanatomical results we have just reviewed. We can summarize all this information as suggesting that the genetic influences on dyslexia affect the development of the planum temporale, resulting in altered planum symmetry. Those alterations in planum structure (and connectivity) lead to phonological-processing problems in both spoken and written language. The phonological-processing problems that are primary in disrupting reading are problems in phoneme segmentation and phonological coding. Undoubtedly, these genetic and neuroanatomical differences can also lead to correlated symptoms in other phonological and even nonphonological cognitive processes.

Supporting this view is research demonstrating that a particular spoken-language skill, phoneme segmentation, is most closely tied to later reading skill (Pennington et al., in press-b; Wagner & Torgesen, 1987). To break a spoken word into phonemic segments, one must be aware that words have a subsyllabic structure of individual phonemes and one must be able to manipulate these segments. For instance, the childhood game of Pig Latin requires phoneme segmentation, because to create Pig Latin translations of real words, one must first segment off the initial sound, then move it to the end of the word and add "ay" ("pig" becomes "igpay"). In our research, we have found dyslexics are specifically deficient at this and other phoneme segmentation tasks (Pennington et al., 1990).

It is important to emphasize here that the development of phoneme segmentation can also be retarded by lack of sociocultural stimulation as was previously discussed. Thus, subcultural variations in early literacy skill stimulation can produce a phenocopy of dyslexia. Across languages and SES levels, poor readers have problems with phoneme-segmentation skills. Some of these problems are due to biological variation, some to deficient early stimulation, and some simply to not reading. As we emphasized in an earlier chapter, phoneme segmentation is a special language skill because it is not necessary for speaking. Better research is needed to measure clearly the independent effects of genes and environment on reading skill and its precursors.

Developmental Course

Recent research has given us a life span developmental perspective on dyslexia, which has traditionally been viewed as a problem in school-aged children. We will first consider the preschool precursors of dyslexia and then its adult outcome.

Dyslexia is not currently diagnosable until school age, usually not before the end of first or second grade. However, it is becoming increasingly clear that precursors of dyslexia are present before school age. Clinically, the preschool histories of some but not all dyslexics contain reports of mild speech delay, articulation difficulties, problems learning letter names or color names, word-finding problems, missequencing syllables ("aminals" for "animals," "donimoes" for "dominoes"), and problems remembering addresses, phone numbers, and other verbal sequences, including complex directions. Asking about each of these possible problems is an important part of taking the clinical history in a case of suspected dyslexia.

Longitudinal studies of reading development beginning at age four and five (for reviews see Pennington et al., in press-b; and Wagner & Torgesen, 1987) have shown that phonological-processing skills are highly predictive of later reading skill, even when the effects of IQ, sex, and age are removed. This predictive and causative relation has been demonstrated most clearly for phoneme awareness and segmentation skills. This research suggests that, as a group, future dyslexics have phonological-processing problems in the preschool years.

Three recent studies have extended the prediction of later literacy downward in age. MacClean, Bryant, and Bradley (1987) found that approximately one-third of a broad sample of normal children showed evidence of some degree of phoneme awareness before age four, and that early phoneme-awareness skill was significantly related to later-reading (but not arithmetic) skill, even when age, IQ, and maternal education were partialled out. In addition, early knowledge of nursery rhymes predicted later phoneme-awareness skill. Similar results were obtained by Stuart & Coltheart (1988). Obviously, these early individual differences in phoneme awareness have both genetic and environmental determinants, but we do not know what proportions of the variance are attributable to each determinant. It is possible that the behavioral precursor to genetic dyslexia might be observable before age four. An early behavioral precursor to dyslexia was found in data from a longitudinal study of children at high familial risk for dyslexia that began when the children were 2½ years old (Scarborough, 1990). The future dyslexic subjects were significantly worse than both siblings and normal risk subjects in measures of natural language production, but not on formal language measures. Nursery-rhyme knowledge or other early measures of phoneme awareness were not evaluated in this study, so we do not know if a deficit in phoneme awareness is detectable this early in dyslexic development.

In summary, these results reinforce the view stressed here that dyslexia is a developmental language disorder. Conceivably, using the right measures, one could find precursors of dyslexia at even earlier ages, but predyslexic infants have not yet been studied.

Turning now to later outcome, the small amount of longitudinal data available indicates the reading gap in dyslexia is fairly constant over time. Thus, the later developmental course of dyslexia in the school years and beyond is clearly *not* one of a developmental lag that catches up, at least for most dyslexics. Most dyslexic children are still measurably dyslexic as adults. In addition, other data suggest an increasing gap over a widening array of cognitive and social skills for some dyslexics as the secondary effects of being dyslexic extract a greater and greater developmental toll. This phenomenon has been termed "negative Matthew effects" (Stanovich, 1986), based on the biblical passage that describes a "rich get richer, poor get porer" scenario. In contrast, some dyslexics, especially females, compensate by adulthood, so that they are no longer diagnosable as dyslexic by standardized tests, though they still report some dyslexic difficulties (Lefly & Pennington, in review).

In summary, there are a range of developmental courses in dyslexia, from compensation by adulthood to an increasing deficit, with most dyslexics falling in the middle and exhibiting a constant lag. We do not understand very well the risk and protective factors associated with these variable outcomes, although sex and quality of early intervention clearly seem important.

It is also important to discuss developmental course in the wider sense of adult outcome. Parents of a newly diagnosed dyslexic child are usually very concerned about what kind of future adult life they can expect for their child. The research data are not as good as we would like, but we do know some things. Most dyslexics finish high school and are capable of going to college, but on average, dyslexics complete fewer years of formal education and are less likely to enter professions such as law and medicine than their unaffected siblings (Finucci, 1986). Some studies also indicate a somewhat higher risk for emotional problems among adult dyslexics (Bruck, 1984; Spreen, 1982) but better data are needed on psychiatric outcome in this disorder.

Nonetheless, some dyslexics are quite successful as adults. In my clinical work, I have encountered several dyslexic entrepreneurs who are far richer than most clinicians or researchers concerned with dyslexia will ever be! One of these men even viewed his dyslexia as an asset, because it freed him from a conventional career track and conventional thinking and allowed him to be more creative in his real estate development business! We hear increasingly about famous dyslexics, and the usual list includes August Rodin, Winston Churchill, and Nelson Rockefeller, as well as the more recent additions of Cher, Bruce Jenner, and Greg Louganis. It is important for dyslexics and their parents to know that dyslexia doesn't preclude talent or success, even though there is no question that it is a risk factor for difficulties in adult adjustment.

OTHER DEVELOPMENTAL SPEECH AND LANGUAGE DISORDERS

As we will see in the case presentations below, dyslexia can be part of a broader developmental language disorder, or it can be a very specific disorder with few or no other accompanying language symptoms. It is important for the clinician who is attempting to diagnose learning disorders to know about other developmental speech and language disorders that may occur with or without dyslexia.

Developmental speech disorders are traditionally divided into three subtypes comprising disorders of articulation, voice, and fluency. In an articulation disorder, speech sounds are mispronounced, because individual sounds are either substituted, omitted, added, or distorted. The normal developmental acquisition of articulatory competence is protracted until about age 8, with some sounds (i.e., /s/ and /z/) exhibiting very wide individual differences in age of mastery. At age five, 15% of children exhibit some degree of articulatory difficulty, but the large majority of these do not have persisting problems (Templin, 1957). A similarly wide range of individual differences was found by Morely (1965) in the age of acquisition for words (6–30 months) and phrases (10–44 months) in children who ultimately had normal language and learning abilities.

There are several possible reasons for persistent articulation problems, including faulty hearing, structural defects in the mouth or tongue (e.g., cleft palate), and neurological dysfunction in the coordination of the speech mechanism (e.g., developmental dysarthia and dyspraxia). The causes of such neurological dysfunction can be genetic or acquired. There is evidence (Ingram, 1959) that articulation disorders run in families, with a higher rate of reading and spelling problems in these same families. Lewis, Ekelman, and Aram (1989) have coined the term "developmental phonology disorders" to encompass this range of phenotypes that run in families. Dyslexics have a higher rate of articulation problems in their histories (Owen, Adams, Forrest, Stolz, & Fisher, 1971), and children with severe articulation disorders have a higher rate of dyslexia. Thus, there is evidence of a real two-way association between the developmental learning disorder of dyslexia and this particular developmental speech disorder. The extent of this overlap is an important area for future research.

The other two broad categories of developmental speech disorders, voice and fluency disorders, do not exhibit a clear association with learning disorders or developmental language disorders. Voice disorders involve problems in either the volume, pitch, rate, or quality (e.g., nasality) of speech; they involve the function of the vocal cords and pharynx in the production of speech, whereas articulation disorders involve the function of the articulators, the tongue, lips, and teeth. Social–emotional factors are frequent causes of deviations in voice volume, and hearing problems are another possible cause. Physical problems in the vocal cords (e.g., laryngitis) or in the nasal cavity (e.g., a cold) can affect pitch and quality.

The one exception to the generalization that voice disorders are not associated with language disorders has to do with the role played by voice in the pragmatics of speech. Pitch, volume, intonation contour, and other prosodic features of speech play important social–communicative functions beyond those carried by the literal message. Children with autism and related disorders of social communication exhibit anomalies in these prosodic features of speech; for instance, they may talk in a robot-like monotone.

The final speech disorders to be considered are disorders of fluency (i.e., stammering, stuttering, & cluttering). In all these conditions, the rhythm of speech is disrupted because sounds, syllables, or words are either repeated, prolonged, or inhibited altogether. Some dysfluency is normal developmentally, but problems past age 5 warrant a referral. The prevalence of stuttering among preadolescent children is about 1%–3%. While the cause of stuttering has traditionally been considered to be emotional, recent work in behavior genetics has demonstrated that the disorder is transmitted in families, and that the mode of transmission is consistent with either polygenic transmission or single gene inheritance with environmental modification and different thresholds by sex (Kidd & Records, 1979).

Why articulation disorders are associated with dyslexia, and stuttering is not, are important research questions, the answers to which would help illuminate underlying mechanisms in all three disorders. One possibility is that the disruption in speech programming that occurs in stuttering is "downstream" from the neural centers that perceive and segment speech and preprogram articulatory gestures. The clinical observation that stutterers do not stutter when they talk either to themselves or to their pets would support this hypothesis. Thus, stuttering may have more to do with the timing of initiation and inhibition of an utterance as a whole action than with the programming of the complex phonemic sequences within the utterance. There is some evidence for the involvement of frontal and basal ganglia involvement in motor initiation and inhibition; these structures are outside the perisylvian language areas. However, direct evidence of the brain mechanisms in articulation disorders or stuttering is lacking.

Developmental language disorders may occur with or without developmental speech disorders, and with or without dyslexia. As is true for dyslexia, the most frequent overlap is with developmental articulation disorders. Developmental language disorders are usually diagnosed with respect both to levels of language processing (phonology, morphology, syntax, and semantics) and to input–output stages (auditory perception, receptive language, and expressive language). Thus, a complete language evaluation examines all four levels of language both receptively and expressively.

Researchers concerned with developmental language disorders (DLD) are struggling with the same subtype issues that are faced by learning disability researchers. There is general agreement that thinking of DLD as a single syndrome is too simplistic, because clinically there appear to be clear subtypes of DLD. Yet how to define and validate these subtypes remains a difficult issue. Two recent efforts give a feel for what some of the possible subtypes look like.

Aram and Nation (1975) used factor analysis to define six different subtypes in children with DLD aged 3–7 years. One subtype was globally impaired across all language tasks, but the remaining five demonstrated interesting dissociations across levels of language processing and between receptive and expressive skills. Two subtypes were relatively impaired on language comprehension, but were better at either repetition alone or repetition and formulation. Another two subtypes had better comprehension and relative impairment in formulation and repetition. Finally, one subtype had a phonologic deficit evident across comprehension, formulation, and repetition.

Rapin and Allen (1982) developed a nosology based on extensive clinical experience with a sample of DLD children followed longitudinally. They described four broad subtypes, some with subdivisions. The four broad categories are: (1) a predominantly expressive disorder, (divided into a phonogic–syntactic syndrome with or without oromotor apraxia, a severe expressive syndrome with good comprehension, and a syntactic–pragmatic syndrome); (2) verbal auditory agnosia; (3) an autistic group; and (4) a semantic-pragmatic syndrome without the severe affective deficits of autism.

This subtyping effort is noteworthy for its attempt to relate functional subtypes to different neuroanatomical defects. For instance, the verbal auditory agnosia subtype results from bilateral temporal lobe lesions that produce a focal deficit in phonetic encoding, which in turn precludes receptive or expressive speech. However, these children can learn sign language and have intact communicative intent and pragmatic functions. The semantic–pragmatic syndrome has hydrocephalus as a frequent etiology, in which the presumed damage to subcortical white matter, sparing perisylvian cortical language areas. Consistent with intact cortical language areas is the sparing of repetition, phonology, and syntax. Instead, what is impaired is the communicative use of language; these children are described as having "cocktail party" conversation-speech that is fluent but empty of content.

DIAGNOSIS AND TREATMENT OF DYSLEXIA

Before discussing the specific diagnosis of dyslexia, we will provide a brief discussion of the *clinical implications* of other speech and language disorders for practitioners who deal with learning disordered children. First, it is important for the clinician to be aware that developmental speech and language disorders occur with a high frequency among children with learning problems. Second, it is important to be sensitive to how such disorders manifest themselves in terms of the child's behavior, symptomatology, history, and test results. In terms of history and test results, children with definite developmental language disorders almost always have a history of some delay in the acquisition of speech and have depressed performances on formal language tests, including the Wechsler Verbal IQ.

Besides learning problems, presenting problems often include difficulty following directions, reduced speech or difficulty expressing themselves, and often problems with peer relations. Language problems interfere with childrens' ability to deal with their feelings verbally, and so such children may be more likely to either act out their feelings physically or to withdraw from interaction.

The observable behaviors that index language problems can be fairly subtle. Many child clinicians (except for speech and language pathologists) automatically and unconsciously compensate for language problems the child may have as they focus on meaning in communication. Because language is a medium for communication, the clinician is more concerned with getting that medium to work rather than inspecting the medium itself. So an important first step is to observe the child's use and understanding of language more critically. If a child isn't talking very much, it may be because he or she has an expressive language problem and not because he or she is shy, depressed, or oppositional. Besides amount of speech, important things to look for are the length and syntactic complexity of the utterances the child uses and understands, the child's vocabulary use and understanding, and the child's use and efficiency in formulating an explanation or story. Some children may seem very articulate, but are actually quite inefficient in conveying information. At the level of phonology, it is also important to look for errors that suggest phoneme discrimination or sequencing problems.

To summarize, clinicians who work with children with learning disorders should be aware of the kinds of speech and language disorders found in these children and be prepared to evaluate such problems and/or make appropriate referrals. We now turn to the diagnosis of dyslexia, beginning with presenting symptoms.

Presenting Symptoms

The key symptoms in dyslexia are difficulty in learning to read and spell, often with relatively better performance in arithmetic. Because some dyslexic children like to read or have good reading comprehension, it is important to ask specifically about reading aloud and learning phonics, two aspects of reading with which virtually all dyslexics have trouble. Similarly, a report of good performance on weekly spelling tests should be followed by a question to determine the quality of spontaneous spelling, as some dyslexic children will work hard to memorize the spelling list, but not spell even simple words correctly in their usual writing. Parents or teachers may also report slow reading or writing speed, letter and number reversals, problems memorizing basic math facts, and unusual reading and spelling errors. These dyslexic errors are discussed below under behavioral observations. Parents or teachers may also report some of the associated language difficulties previously discussed. Table 4.1 organizes the symptoms of dyslexia into the categories of primary, correlated, secondary, and artifactual.

Finally and most importantly, the initial referral may be prompted not by these kinds of cognitive symptoms, but by emotional or

TABLE 4.1 Symptoms in Dyslexia

Primary	Problems in reading and spelling; a problem in the phonological coding of written language
Correlated	Problems in language processes (articulation, naming, verbal short-term memory & long-term memory)
Secondary	Poor reading comprehension, poor math, poor self-esteem, letter reversals, eye movement differences in reading
Artifactual	Problems with attention, delinquency, and visuospatial problems

physical symptoms, such as anxiety or depression, reluctance to go to school, or headaches and stomach aches. It is important to find out if these symptoms happen all the time or only on school days. Even if they happen all the time, the root cause could be dyslexia because of the failures (and fear of failure) dyslexics experience.

History

Most dyslexics do not have high risk events in their prenatal or perinatal histories, nor do they have clear delays in early developmental milestones, although mild speech delays and articulation problems are present in some histories. There are three aspects of the history that are particularly informative—family history, school history, and reading and language history.

Because familial risk is substantial in dyslexia, it is important to take a careful history of reading, spelling, and related language problems in the first and second degree relatives of the patient. Parents will not necessarily know whether they or their relatives are dyslexic, but they are usually able to report accurately on reading and spelling problems, as well as problems with articulation, name finding, and verbal memory for things like phone numbers and addresses. It is a fairly common clinical experience to discover a parent's or relative's dyslexia in the course of the dyslexic child's evaluation.

In terms of school history, dyslexic difficulties should be evident by first or second grade, and may be present by kindergarten as problems with learning the alphabet, letter names, or other prereading skills. It is very unlikely that reading problems with an abrupt later onset are due to developmental dyslexia; acquired etiologies need to be considered in this situation.

If the child is an adolescent when first referred, the pre-school and early elementary school histories may not be readily available, and the presenting symptoms may have changed. The child may now like to read, though more slowly than other children, and the main complaints may involve poor performance on timed tests or difficulty completing homework.

Behavioral Observations

During the testing of the child, it is important to look for subtle language difficulties and reading and spelling errors that are characteristic of dyslexia. For instance, some children are unusually quiet because they have word-finding and verbal formulation problems. These and other language-related problems are observable on the Wechsler IQ scales. For instance, word-finding problems are likely to become apparent on the Vocabulary and Picture Completion subtests.

The most important behavioral observations come from a child's actual reading and spelling errors. There are four main kinds of reading errors to look for: dysfluency, errors on function words, visual errors (whole-word guesses), and lexicalizations when reading nonwords. Spelling errors will be discussed shortly. Dyslexics are usually slow and halting in their oral reading because their automatic decoding skills are weak. However, dysfluency may not be evident in older dyslexics who have overlearned a large, automatic reading vocabulary.

By function word errors, we mean substitutions on "little" words, such as articles and prepositions. Dyslexics will frequently interchange "a" and "the" and misread prepositions. The significance of function-word errors is that the dyslexic is working hard to properly decode the content words in the sentence and is relying more on context than a normal reader would to identify function words. Function-word errors are puzzling to parents and teachers, who remark that if the child can read the big words, why can't they read the little words?

By visual errors, we mean substitutions on content words that are based on a superficial visual similarity to the target word (e.g., "car" for "cat"). The significance of these errors is that the child is using visual similarity rather than the full phonological code to name the word, and so again these errors are reflective of a phonological coding or "phonics" problem. Lexicalization errors when reading nonwords refer to misreading a nonword as a real word, usually one which is visually similar to the target (e.g., "boy" for "bim"). The significance of these errors is essentially the same as visual errors: lacking good phonological coding skills, the child assimilates the target to whatever other schema is available for word recognition.

In terms of spelling errors, we mainly examine the proportion of errors that are not phonetically accurate, especially errors in which consonants have been added, omitted, or substituted (e.g., "exetive" for "executive"). Dyslexics are also weaker at spelling vowels, but normal developmental acquisition of vowel correspondences is more protracted and so many young normal children make vowel errors. In the normal groups we have studied, the mean rates of phonologically accurate (with regard to consonants) errors have been about 70% for children aged 8–12 and about 80% for adolescents and adults (Pennington, Lefly, Van Orden, Bookman, & Smith, 1987). As a rough guide, a phonological accuracy rate for consonant sequences lower than 60% in children and 70% in adolescents and adults would be suggestive of dyslexic difficulties.

The final kind of error to mention is the so-called "reversal" errors in reading and spelling. Although earlier accounts of dyslexia viewed reversal errors as the hallmark of dyslexia, their rate of occurrence in dyslexia is actually quite low and there are many dyslexics who do not make such errors (Liberman, Shankweiler, Orlando, Harris, & Berti, 1971). Nonetheless, the presence of reversal errors in patients 9 years old and older is of some potential diagnostic significance, as normal readers of that age or older virtually never make such errors. By a reversal error, we mean substituting a visually similar letter in reading or spelling (e.g., "bog" for "dog"). These errors most typically involve b/d confusions. Vellutino (1979) has convincingly argued that the basis of many such reversal errors is linguistic rather than visual: *b* and *d* are phonetically as well as visually similar.

Test Results

While all the previous sources of data can suggest a diagnosis of dyslexia, tests of reading, spelling, and related-language skills are necessary to confirm the diagnosis. The test battery we use consists of the Wechsler Intelligence Scale for Children—Revised (WISC-R), the Peabody Individual Achievement Test (PIAT), the Gray Oral Reading Test, the Wide-Range Achievement Test (WRAT) Spelling Test, and the Woodcock-Johnson Word Attack subtest from the Woodcock-Johnson Reading Mastery battery (1972). This battery provides three measures of oral reading (PIAT Reading Recognition, Gray Oral, and Word Attack), one measure of reading comprehension (PIAT Reading Comprehension), two measures of spelling (PIAT and WRAT Spelling), and several discriminant measures (PIAT Math and the Performance subtests of the Wechsler). Some Wechsler subtests (especially

Digit Span, Arithmetic, and Information) tend to be lower in dyslexic profiles, apparently because they measure language skills, such as verbal short-term memory and name retrieval, problems which are frequently correlated symptoms in dyslexia.

We use two operationally defined test patterns to help diagnose dyslexia, a reading quotient (RQ) and a specific dyslexia algorithm (SDA). The RQ was adapted from Finucci (1986). These are explicitly defined in the text that follows. The main idea of each is to look for a significant discrepancy between general ability and reading and spelling skills. Although the nonword test does not enter into the diagnostic formulas, a significant discrepancy (1 SD or larger) between a patient's IQ and nonword score is a converging piece of evidence for the diagnosis of dyslexia.

Reading Quotients

Adults:

$$RQ = \frac{(\text{PIAT Spelling age equiv.} + \text{Gray Oral Reading age equiv.})/2}{(\text{Age for last grade comp.} + \text{PIAT Math age equiv.} + \text{PIAT Gen. Info. age equiv.})/3}$$

Children:

$$RQ = \frac{(\text{WRAT Spelling age equiv.} + \text{Gray Oral Reading age equiv.})/2}{(\text{Chron. age} + \text{Age for grade} + \text{IQ age equiv.})/3}$$

$$\text{IQ age equiv.} = \frac{(\text{Chron. age} \times \text{Full Scale IQ})}{100}$$

Specific Dyslexia Algorithm

The SDA compares oral reading and spelling to other achievement test scores that do not rely (or rely less heavily) on a knowledge of grapheme–phoneme correspondence rules. The oral reading test is PIAT Reading Recognition, and the spelling tests are PIAT and WRAT Spelling. The criteria in the algorithm are as follows:

1. The subject shows normal performance on a nonreading achievement measure: PIAT Mathematics or General Information age Standard score is $\geq$ 93.

2. The subject's performance on the nonreading measure is higher than all their oral reading and spelling scores and significantly higher (age standard score difference ≥ 15) than one of them.
3. The subject's performance on at least one oral reading and spelling measure is delayed (age standard score < 93) OR the discrepancy in criteria 2 (above) is very large (age standard score difference ≥ 30).

If a patient's test results fit either of these patterns, then the test results are considered consistent with dyslexia. Although we weigh test results most heavily in reaching a diagnostic decision, they do not overrule consistently negative evidence in the other data domains; convergent validity is a key diagnostic criterion. We have seen a few patients with either lower IQs and/or attention problems who have a positive RQ, but no other indications of dyslexia. In these patients, there was a better fit to another diagnosis.

Treatment

In terms of remedial recommendations, the single most important step is for the child to receive individualized tutoring in a phonics-based approach to reading. Especially with younger dyslexics, this intervention may need to incorporate training in segmental language skills as well. Some dyslexics fail in traditional phonics programs because they still lack the prerequisite phoneme awareness skills such programs assume to be in place.

It may seem paradoxical to say, on the one hand, that the core deficit in dyslexia is in phonological coding and, on the other, that remediation should focus on this deficient skill—why not teach to strength? The problem is that phonological coding is so central to reading development that it can't be bypassed (see Adams, 1990; Clark, 1988). We have previously argued that recent evidence indicates the reading of even normal adults is phonologically mediated. Although mature readers have automated their recognition of familiar words so that they do not have to "sound out" the different sounds in the word, their achievement of such automaticity depends on a sophisticated understanding of the alphabetic code, not just on thousands of visual learning trials. There is no evidence that I know of to indicate that single-word recognition for a reasonably sized reading vocabulary is automated without an understanding of the alphabetic code. To accomplish this feat, each of about 20,000 words would have to be memorized separately as a unique exemplar, without any transfer from related words.

Even if memorization of single words will not work, could dyslexics use context to compensate for poor word-recognition skills? Several authors (Goodman, 1967; Smith, 1978) have argued that mature reading is essentially a "psycholinguistic guessing game" in which the reader uses redundancy in text to develop hypotheses about upcoming words, and needs to sample only a few visual features to decide which hypothesis is correct. If we could teach dyslexics this guessing game, maybe they could bypass their phonics problem.

Unfortunately, even normal readers show no evidence of making explicit guesses about upcoming words (Stanovich & West, 1983). When they are forced to guess the identities of missing words in continuous text, they are right only about 20% of the time. Therefore, normal readers do not appear to engage in the psycholinguistic guessing game, and it doesn't work very well for them when they are forced to try.

Research on normal eye movements in skilled reading buttresses this conclusion (Just & Carpenter, 1987). Skilled readers fixate about 80% of content words in text, with their fixation times being directly proportional to the number of letters in the word. Information from a fixated word is processed immediately, whereas very little processing of adjacent words occur. Thus, comprehension processes are focused on the word being fixated and its relation to preceding text; the generation of hypotheses about upcoming words would be too effortful and time-consuming to fit well with the rapidity of individual fixations (about 250 msecs). In addition, word recognition appears to depend on abstract letter identities rather than word shape; presentation of text in aLtErNaTiNg case only increases reading time by about 10%. If skilled readers used only a few visual features to guess a word's identity, such as a whole-word visual envelope strategy, then alternating case would be much more disruptive because the visual envelope of each word would be drastically altered. Moreover, if a visual envelope strategy were used, fixation times would not be so tightly related to the number of letters in the word, as it would be with a letter-mediated process. Thus, while many cognitive psychologists speak of visual word recognition and a visual word-form processing center in mature reading, these processes appear to depend intimately on the alphabetic code in some fashion. Instantaneous recognition of visual words as wholes does not occur, even though that is what appears to be happening on introspection.

Additional evidence against the psycholinguistic guessing game is the tight relation (r's up to .80) between isolated word-recognition skill and reading comprehension. If reading comprehension depended on context-based guessing, we wouldn't find these high correlations with context free word recognition.

Finally, a large number of studies have found no differences between good and poor readers in their use of context to aid word recognition. If anything, poor readers are using context more, but for all the reasons previously outlined this strategy does not compensate for their word recognition problems (Clark, 1988; Wise & Olson, 1991).

Therefore, intervention must target directly the faulty word-recognition proceses in dyslexics, and must do so by addressing its root cause, which is a deficiency in phonological coding. While whole language approaches to reading may work well with nondyslexic youngsters, who learn phonological coding regardless of the particular reading curriculum they are exposed to, such approaches do not help dyslexic youngsters. Dyslexics need much more sustained and systematic instruction in phonological coding. Although they have a deficit in this area, it is not an absolute one, and they can learn phonological coding, albeit more slowly.

Programs that are helpful use explicit synthetic phonics approaches, which teach letter–sound relations and blending. Examples are the Orton Gillingham, Slingerland, and DISTAR approaches. Clark's (1988) book presents a description of these and other phonics-based programs. It is a useful book for parents, tutors, and teachers of dyslexics.

In terms of approaches that teach phoneme awareness skills, several are available. These include the Lindamoods' (1969) Auditory Discrimination in Depth program, Bryant and Bradley's (1985) sound categorization program, and the program devised by Ball and Blachman (1988). All of these programs have been tested and found effective in treatment studies.

Older dyslexics may need help with reading comprehension strategies and study skills. Even with treatment, they will likely read somewhat slower than nondyslexic age mates, therefore, they need to deploy their reading time most effectively.

Dyslexics' problems with spelling appear to be less remediable than their reading problems, and we do not make spelling a direct target of remediation efforts. Instead, we recommend compensatory devices such as word processors with spell checkers, or hand-held spell checkers (like the Franklin Ace Spellmaster).

Compensations that can be provided by the school environment include extra time on written tests, marking but not downgrading spelling errors, being excused from foreign language requirements, and oral exams for severely impaired dyslexics. Identification and understanding of the problems by all of the child's teachers is very important: otherwise it is very common for dyslexic children to be pejoratively labelled as "lazy" or even "stupid."

Parents have important roles to play in the treatment of their dyslexic child, as advocates, facilitators of appropriate interventions, and sources of emotional support. Dyslexics are at increased risk for problems with self-esteem and depression. It is important for parents to provide success experiences in areas of strengths, monitor these secondary psychological symptoms, and refer for psychotherapy if necessary.

It is nearly always inadvisable for parents to tutor their dyslexic child for two reasons. A parent is usually not trained to teach reading, especially to dyslexics. Even if he or she is, there is an inherent conflict in the two roles that makes the parent–child tutoring situation too emotionally charged to be successful in most cases. I encourage would-be parent tutors to imagine what it would be like to have their spouse teach them bridge (or tennis or skiing). Moreover, tutoring takes valuable time, time that is needed to provide emotionally supportive experiences to the dyslexic child and to meet the needs of other family members. The parent–child tutoring relationship can easily distort other relationships throughout the family system.

Finally, it is important to mention briefly the many unsubstantiated treatments for dyslexia, so parents and practitioners can avoid them (even if they are touted on network television!). These unproven treatments include various visual therapies: convergence training, eye movement exercises, colored lenses, and devices to induce "peripheral" (as opposed to normal foveal) reading; medications intended to affect vestibular system functioning; chiropracty; megavitamins; and dietary treatments. These various treatments of dyslexia are based on unproven and improbable theories of the underlying processing deficit. Moreover, the efficacy of these treatments has never been scientifically documented. Such documentation requires careful treatment research, which is replicated independently. Reviews criticizing many of these treatments have appeared recently, either in professional journals (e.g., Bishop, 1986; Klein, Berry, Briand, D'Entremont, & Farmer, 1990; Wright, 1989) or in publications of the Orton Dyslexia Society. Many otherwise intelligent parents will spend money on such treatments, because they are desperate to help their child.

In the following text we illustrate the points previously made about the diagnosis of dyslexia with two case presentations. Chapters 5–8 also each have two case examples of their respective learning disorders. Readers interested in improving their skills should compare and contrast their response to case presentations across chapters, using the diagnostic model in Chapter 3.

CASE PRESENTATION 1

Jill is a 10-year-old fourth grader. Her parents sought an evaluation, because she was becoming very resistant to school, seemed angry and depressed, and refused to bring home homework. Teachers complained that she was often off task in school, fidgety, and disruptive to other students. She has made poor progress in reading, her spelling is very poor, and she had considerable trouble in math last year on timed tests.

Jill's birth and early developmental histories appear normal. The only medical history of note is frequent ear infection. Father reports he had problems learning to read, but he is college-educated and has a professional career. Parents became concerned about Jill's development when she had trouble learning to read in first grade. Because of her poor progress, she was given extra academic assistance toward the end of first grade. Extra assistance was continued in second grade, but Jill made little progress, and parents were told that she was slow in developing. In third grade, when reading problems persisted, Jill was staffed into a part-time resource room placement.

Jill became a discipline problem at home during second grade, and began psychotherapy. The therapist felt Jill had significant problems with self-esteem. Parents report that therapy improved her behavior last year, but recently she has seemed more depressed. A summary of Jill's diagnostic testing is found in Table 4.2.

Discussion

Some of the presenting problems in this case are suggestive of either depression, ADHD, or oppositional defiant disorder, but the problems with reading, spelling, written work, and time tests are all suggestive of dyslexia. Moreover, the parents' and therapist's observations of this child did not suggest ADHD. In terms of the history, Father's reading problem and the first grade onset and persistence of the patient's reading problem are noteworthy. Behavioral observations of this

TABLE 4.2 Test Summary, Case 1

WISC-R Full Scale IQ = 108			
Information	9	Picture Completion	9
Similarities	15	Picture Arrangement	14
Arithmetic	7	Block Design	11
Vocabulary	12	Object Assembly	12
Comprehension	13	Coding	10
Digit Span	9		
Verbal IQ = 107		Performance IQ = 108	
Verbal Comprehension = 12.3		Perceptual Organization = 11.5	
		Freedom from Distractibility = 8.6	

	Grade equivalent	Age standard score
PIAT		
Math	5.7	105
Reading Recognition	2.6	80
Reading Comprehension	2.6	78
Spelling	2.2	72
WRAT Spelling	2B	69
Gray Oral	1.5	—
Word Attack	2.0	80
Reading Quotient .66		

child's test performance revealed dysfluency, function-word errors, visual errors, lexicalizations on nonwords, and nonphonetic spelling errors. Thus, these three domains of data are all convergent for the diagnosis of dyslexia.

The test results confirm this diagnosis. Both the reading quotient of .66 and the PIAT disparities between math and both reading recognition (25 points or 1.7 SDs) and spelling (33 points or 2.2 SDs) fit the two operational test criteria. In addition, nonword reading is significantly depressed relative to either Full Scale IQ (FSIQ) or PIAT Math. The WISC-R profile, while not diagnostic, exhibits a subtest profile very commonly found in dyslexic children. The third factor, Freedom from Distractibility (FD) is significantly lower than either the verbal (VC) or perceptual (PO) factors, suggesting a specific problem in verbal short-term memory, a frequent correlate of dyslexia. Moreover, the low Information and Picture Completion scores may be due to other language-processing difficulties, in verbal long-term memory and name retrieval respectively. Behavioral observations on Picture Completion were consistent with this latter hypothesis, since the child frequently had trouble naming the missing part. Low scores on Arithmetic, Coding, Information, and Digit Span have been dubbed the ACID profile. We interpret this ACID profile as arising from the difficulties in various phonological-processing skills that dyslexics have; these phonological-processing problems differentially affect performance on different subtests.

CASE PRESENTATION 2

Jason is a 16-year-old high school junior. He was referred by his parents who wonder whether his academic difficulties are related to a learning disability, a lack of motivation, or some other problem. Parents describe Jason as very bright, but as having difficulties in spelling and writing, in spite of tutoring. He has been depressed and is in psychotherapy. He had already been evaluated by a child psychiatrist for ADHD, who ruled out this diagnosis.

Birth and early developmental history appear normal. Medical history includes milk allergy and hayfever. Jason's father had reading difficulties in school, but has a professional career.

Problems were first noticed in second grade when Jason had difficulty with spelling and written language. Handwriting was poor, and he resisted written work. It was believed he might have a hearing or eye problem, and eye exercises were prescribed. His third grade teacher thought he was bright, but not working up to potential. Problems continued, and when he was tested in fourth grade, his IQ was found to be 145. Reading scores were at grade level, math at grade 7.9, and spelling at grade 3.9. Parents report he got only minimal help at school, because his grades were average. He did have private tutoring during the summer.

Jason received no extra help at school in junior or senior high and generally got B's. He is interested in science and engineering and enjoys inventing things. He has invented household items, contacted manufacturers, and learned about patent laws to get inventions patented. Jason's diagnostic testing summary is found in Table 4.3.

Discussion

The diagnostic issues in this second case are more subtle, because of the later age at referral and the high overall abilities of the patient. This kind of patient is rarely referred or diagnosed in schools because of average grades and grade level performance in reading, even

TABLE 4.3 Test Summary, Case 2

WISC-R FSIQ = 132

Information	15	Picture Completion	13
Similarities	13	Picture Arrangement	12
Arithmetic	13	Block Design	18
Vocabulary	15	Object Assembly	18
Comprehension	14	Coding	12
Digit Span	9		
Verbal IQ = 124		Performance IQ = 132	
Verbal Comprehension = 14.3		Perceptual Organization = 18	
		Freedom from Distractibility = 11.3	

	Grade equivalent	Age standard score
PIAT		
Math	>12.9	123
Reading Recognition	10.6	99
Reading Comprehension	>12.8	109
Spelling	12.4	106
WRAT Spelling	4.8	78
Gray Oral	10.8	—
Word Attack	4.4	86
Reading Quotient .73		

though relative to his other abilities this patient clearly has a learning handicap. This patient also exhibits the unusual talents seen in some dyslexics.

The significant presenting symptoms for the diagnosis of dyslexia are the persistent problems in spelling and written language. The history is noteworthy for the father's reading problem, the early onset of the spelling and written language problems and the marked disparity between IQ and math on the one hand and reading and spelling on the other in the previous testing. The main behavioral observation was a higher proportion of nonphonetic spelling errors and lexicalizations in nonword reading; in contrast, oral reading of text was fluent and there were no visual or function-word errors.

In terms of test results, this patient likewise has a significantly lower FD factor score, with a Digit Span score that is significantly lower than any other subtest score. His PO factor score of 18 (we average Block Design and Object Assembly only) is in the gifted range and is consistent with his talents and interests in engineering and inventions. He does not fit the ACID profile. His Reading Quotient of

.73 fits the criteria for dyslexia, mainly because of his low WRAT Spelling score. It is noteworthy that there is such a discrepancy between the PIAT and WRAT Spelling scores, a not uncommon result in older and brighter dyslexics. PIAT spelling is a recognition test that is heavily influenced by word-recognition skill and print exposure. WRAT Spelling is a spelling production task that taxes phonological-coding skills much more severely. He does not fit the SDA, though there is a discrepancy (>1 SD) between math and both reading recognition and spelling on the PIAT. There is a striking 3 SD discrepancy between his FSIQ and his nonword reading score, indicating a clear deficit in phonological coding. Thus his impaired achievement test scores are not limited to spelling; though he has compensated in some aspects of reading, the compensation is not complete.

C H A P T E R 5

Attention Deficit Hyperactivity Disorder

After one has ruled out dyslexia and other language disorders, the next most common learning disorder is attention deficit hyperactivity disorder (ADHD). We view "true" ADHD as a subgroup, both within the wider group of children now identified as ADHD and within the broader category of executive function deficits; the evidence for and against these hypotheses will be discussed below. Regardless of whether ADHD involves an executive function (EF) deficit, the category of EF deficits is an important one for diagnosticians to understand, as there are reasonably large numbers of children with learning problems whose difficulties are hard to understand without this category.

RESEARCH REVIEW OF ATTENTION DEFICIT HYPERACTIVITY DISORDER

As we will see, issues concerning syndrome validation are more pressing in the case of ADHD than they are for disorders like dyslexia and autism. Some authorities do not view ADHD as a distinct syndrome (Barkley, 1981; Ross & Ross, 1982; Rutter, 1983; Whalen, 1983) because of poor diagnostic reliability, low levels of agreement across different measures of hyperactivity, failure of the cardinal symptoms—hyperactivity, inattention, and impulsivity—to cluster together within samples of ADHD children, lack of differentiation from conduct disorder, and lack of a single etiology or a consistent response to treatment. These are all serious threats to syndrome validity. However, many of these criticisms derive from the likelihood that hyperactivity or attention deficit is too coarse a behavioral phenotype to form the basis of a syndrome, just as poor school performance is obviously not a syndrome nor is obesity. Thus, it is possible that some subtypes of ADHD may possess syndrome validity; if so, future taxonomies will need to parse behavior in this broad domain more precisely, so that the real syndromes are easier to distinguish from the imposters. Conners and Wells (1986) point out that research on ADHD is particularly troubled by the bootstrap problem: A better behavioral definition of ADHD is needed to yield homogeneous subtypes more likely to have a unitary etiology and pathophysiology, yet it is hard to define such subtypes without knowing about etiology and pathophysiology. One solution to this dilemma is to study groups with a well-defined biological risk factor, such as children with early treated PKU or children at high familial risk for ADHD. This strategy has rarely been employed in ADHD research.

In the following text we try to delineate the characteristics of subtypes of ADHD and to discuss which subtypes appear to qualify as a primary executive function disorder and which appear to be secondary to other causes.

Basic Defining Characteristics

As a psychiatric diagnosis, ADHD is defined in terms of problematic behaviors reflecting inattention, impulsivity, and hyperactivity. As in dyslexia, these problematic behaviors must be unexpected and not explained by developmental or mental level, thought disorder, or affective disorder. Attention to confounding conditions is important because the possible causes of the symptoms used to define ADHD are manifold. Beyond those already mentioned, confounding causes include high anxiety, dyslexia, family dysfunction, conduct disorder, and even intellectual giftedness. A gifted child can be so bored by a regular curriculum as to be restless and act impulsively. ADHD is a prevalent disorder, though prevalence estimates vary widely reflecting differences in diagnostic practices. The prevalence in the United States ranges between 4% and 10%, whereas that found by Rutter, Tizard, and Whitmore (1970) in the Isle of Wight epidemiologic survey was only 0.1%. In that survey, a much larger percentage of children were found to be overactive in association with a conduct or neurotic disorder. British criteria for diagnosing ADHD are stricter than those in the United States and require the presence of problematic behavior across settings, whereas problematic behavior in the school setting alone is sufficient to meet American criteria. The latter is very likely a mistaken procedure, because it does not adequately screen out the many possible confounding conditions. In an epidemiological survey of 5,000 U.S. children, 5% were found to be hyperactive by one reporter, either parent, teacher, or physician, but only 1.2% were considered hyperactive by all those reporters (Spreen, Tupper, Risser, Tuckko, & Edgell, 1984). Using parent reports alone, the rates of attentional problems, restlessness, and social immaturity—all symptoms of ADHD—reported for normal children from 4 to 16 years averaged around 30% (Achenbach & Edelbrock, 1981).

The male to female sex ratio is 2:1 to 9:1, but data drawn from family samples are lacking. One worries that the possible biases of clinical ascertainment have inflated these sex ratios or that the diagnostic criteria do not adequately rule out developmentally normal male behaviors at younger ages.

If real, one genetic explanation of the male preponderance is a polygenic model with a higher threshold for girls than boys. If this model were correct, there should be higher rates of hyperactivity and/or psychopathology in general among the relatives of female versus male probands, because female probands require a higher genetic loading to be affected. This model has been tested by two separate groups, both of which found null results (Goodman & Stevenson, 1989; Mannuzza & Gittelman, 1984). Two recent studies have also failed to find differences between ADHD boys and girls in their behavioral and academic profiles (Breen, 1989; Horn, Wagner, & LaLongo, 1989). Thus this particular genetic explanation of the apparent sex difference in the rates of ADHD has not been supported.

Etiologies

Both genetic and environmental factors can cause ADHD, and ADHD is undoubtedly etiologically heterogeneous. There are several genetic disorders, including Turner syndrome (45, X) in females, 47, XYY in males, and fragile X syndrome, which include ADHD in their phenotype (Bender, Puck, Salenblatt, & Robinson, 1987; Hagerman, 1987; Hier, 1980). Attentional problems also appear to be part of the behavioral phenotype of children with neurofibromatosis (Eliason, 1986). As noted in Chapter 1, the behavioral manifestations of early treated PKU bear important similarities to ADHD (Realmuto et al., 1986; Welsh et al., 1990).

Aside from these specific genetic disorders, there is other behavioral genetic evidence that provides some evidence for a heritable component in idiopathic ADHD. First, there is substantial heritability (about .50) for normal variations in temperament, including activity level and shyness (Plomin, 1986). These variations are assumed to be polygenic and multifactorial. Beyond a certain threshold, children with normal variations in activity level will meet the criteria for ADHD. So if the entire distribution of normal variations in temperament is heritable, then these ADHD children will perforce have a heritable component to their ADHD.

Second, behavior genetic studies of abnormal activity levels (i.e., hyperactivity) support the conclusion that ADHD likewise has a heritable component, which may or may not be distinct from the genetic factors contributing to normal variation. Existing behavioral genetic studies of ADHD per se fall into three types—family studies, partial adoption, and twin studies. Thus, we only have data pertaining to the familiality and heritability of ADHD; we lack knowledge about modes of transmission and gene locations.

In terms of "familiality," family studies (Cantwell, 1972; Morrison & Stewart, 1971; Nichols & Chen, 1981; Singer, Stewart, & Pulaski, 1981) have found increased rates of hyperactivity among first and second degree relatives of hyperactive children compared to the rates among relatives of controls, as well as increased rates of alcoholism, sociopathy, and hysteria in the parents of hyperactive children. In the Singer et al. study, the control group consisted of reading disabled (RD) children and their families. The lower rates of hyperactivity in the RD families suggests that ADHD and RD are distinct syndromes that are transmitted separately, a hypothesis that is supported by much of the other data reported here on these two disorders. The finding of increased rates of other psychiatric disorders in the parents of hyperactive children admits of several possible interpretations, the first two of which are nongenetic: (1) the parents' psychiatric problems caused the child's ADHD by contributing to a dysfunctional family environment; (2) maternal alcoholism caused the child's hyperactivity through an intrauterine, teratogenic effect, or (3) these psychiatric disorders are part of the adult phenotype of ADHD.

The converging results of the three partial adoption studies of ADHD (Cunningham, Cadoret, Loftus, & Edwards, 1975; Morrison & Stewart, 1973) help to sort among these hypotheses. Arguing against 1 is the fact that much lower rates of hyperactivity (and the psychiatric disorders already mentioned) were found among the adoptive parents and adoptive relatives of hyperactive children adopted away at birth than among the biological parents and biological relatives of hyperactive children not adopted away. Interestingly, in the Alberts-Corush, Firestone, Goodman (1986) study, attentional problems but not impulsivity occurred more frequently in biological versus adoptive parents of ADHD children. These adoption results are consistent with the third hypothesis previously discussed, but do not fully rule out the second hypothesis concerning fetal alcohol exposure. Unfortunately, these data do not deal with the likely possibility of ADHD subtypes, which vary in adult phenotype. These studies would also be more powerful if data were available on the biological parents and other relatives of the hyperactive adoptees; that is why they are partial, rather than full adoption studies. We lack the critical comparison between biological and adoptive parents of the ADHD probands.

There are two relevant twin studies, one of activity level and hyperactivity (Willerman, 1973), and a recent study of rated hyperactivity and objective measures of attention (Goodman & Stevenson, 1989). Willerman found significant heritability for both normal activity level and hyperactivity. However, the hyperactive twin sample was small, the definition of hyperactivity was broader than that indicated by current clinical criteria, and most importantly, there was evidence for a maternal expectancy effect. Specifically, the monozygotic correlation for hyperactivity was large (.71), whereas the dizygotic correlation was unexplainably small (.00).

Goodman and Stevenson (1989) circumvented such expectancy effects both by using objective attention measures and by comparing recognized versus unrecognized monozygotic (MZ) pairs. After accounting for expectancy effects, they found that half of the explainable variance in hyperactivity and inattentiveness was genetic, whereas common environment accounted for 0%–30% of the variance. Direct measures of possible common environment factors accounted for less than 10% of the variance in hyperactivity, and there was no evidence of an effect of within pair differences in perinatal adversity, one possible specific environment factor.

In summary, this recent study provides the best evidence we have for genetic influence on ADHD. The earlier studies have methodological problems that have recently been examined in more detail by Rutter and colleagues (1990). One point stressed in their review is the inadequacy of phenotype definitions of hyperactivity and ADHD used in most studies, as evidenced by high rates of comorbid disorders in probands and relatives.

In terms of "environmental" causes of ADHD, we have already mentioned fetal alcohol syndrome (Shaywitz, Cohen, & Shaywitz, 1980), although Hesselbrock, Stabenan, and Hesselbrock (1985) did not find this relation. Environmental exposure to lead has been shown to be associated with attention deficit in children (David, Hoffman, Svid, & Clark, 1977), and this may be true of other environmental toxins as well. However, more recent evidence on low level lead exposure suggests the association with ADHD may be partly confounded with social class (Taylor, 1986). Pediatric head injury is a fairly common cause of attentional deficits, but we will defer the discussion of the sequellae of head injuries until Chapter 8.

Historically, an ADHD-like condition was frequently found in children who suffered encephalitis in the epidemic of 1918; thus an infectious insult to the brain appears to be one possible environmental cause of ADHD. Because similar symptoms were found in children who experienced anoxia at birth or head injuries, the unidimensional concept of minimal brain damage (MBD) was formulated by Strauss and Lehtinen (1947), with unfortunate consequences for the field of developmental neuropsychology. It is now clear that the syndrome of MBD was too vague and overinclusive to be clinically useful, and more importantly, that the developing brain is too complex an organ to always yield the same set of symptoms when perturbed.

While discussing environmental causes of ADHD it is important to point out that deleterious social factors, including inadequate environmental stimulation, large family size, and social disability (Rutter, Tizard, & Whitmore, 1970), may produce a phenocopy of ADHD, without there necessarily being a genetic or environmental insult to the developing brain. However, other research by Loney and colleagues indicates that the social environment affects secondary (e.g., aggression and poor self-esteem) rather than primary (e.g., hyperactivity and inattention) symptoms in ADHD (Milich & Loney, 1979; Paterhite & Loney, 1980). In summary, aside from pediatric head injury, no environmental agent emerges as a robust and frequent cause of ADHD.

Comorbidity of ADHD and Dyslexia

The relationship between ADHD and dyslexia provides a fascinating case example of comorbidity and the methods that can be used to understand the basis of comorbidity. Comorbidity is a potential threat to syndrome validity for the two comorbid disorders, because it can mean there are not two distinct disorders. What do we know about the comorbidity between ADHD and dyslexia?

First, it is common to find elevated rates of ADHD in LD populations (Cantwell & Satterfield, 1978; Halperin, Gittelman, Klein, & Rudel, 1984; Holobrow & Berry, 1986; Lambert & Sandoval, 1980; McGee, Williams, & Silva, 1985; 1987; Safer & Allen, 1976; Shaywitz & Shaywitz, 1988). However, at least some of this association may be an artifact of definitional overlap; historically, the concepts of LD and ADHD were both derived from the concept of minimal brain dysfunction. In an epidemiologic sample in which ADHD, dyslexia, and math disability (MD) were defined independently, Shaywitz and Shaywitz (1988) reported that 11% of ADHD children had either dyslexia or MD, and that 33% of the dyslexic and/ or MD children had ADHD. The latter but not the former rate is greater than population expectations. Similarly, in the Halperin et al. (1984) study, the rate of dyslexia (9%–10%) in an ADHD sample was not necessarily greater than population expectations. Moreover, they found 15% of their ADHD sample were unexpectedly *good* readers, since they were at least one standard deviation above age level in reading. In the Dunnedin epidemiologic sample, about 80% of 11-year-old children identified with ADHD had dyslexia or related spelling or written language problems (McGee & Share, 1988). These authors suggest that many of the children labelled as ADHD really have attentional problems as a secondary consequence of their primary learning disabilities.

Finally, one study failed to find an association between dyslexia and ADHD in two different clinical samples, children with reading problems in remedial education classes and children in an outpatient treatment program for attention problems. Dalby (1985) used Diagnostic and Statistical Manual of Mental Disorders (DSM-III) criteria to select 98 dyslexic boys from the first setting and 35 ADHD boys from the second. The questions of interest concerned the rate of dyslexia in the ADHD group and of ADHD in the dyslexic group. Only 8.6% of the ADHD group met the criteria for dyslexia (1½ years below grade level in reading) and only 5.1% of the dyslexia group met the criteria for ADHD (above the clinical cutoff on the Conner's hyperkenesis index). Neither of these comorbid rates is above population expectations.

Overall, these results suggest that there is not a robust two-way association between dyslexia and ADHD. The evidence for elevations of objectively defined dyslexia in ADHD is lacking in several studies, whereas there is support for increased rates of ADHD in dyslexic samples. While children with primary ADHD undoubtedly have school difficulties, they do not necessarily have deficits on objective measures of reading achievement. On the other hand, the commonly found higher rate of ADHD in dyslexic samples suggests either that there is a subtype of dyslexia plus ADHD with a common etiology or that dyslexia leads to ADHD as a secondary symptom (Cunningham & Barkley, 1978; McGee & Share, 1988; Stanovich, 1986). Because the association has been found in an epidemiologic sample (Shaywitz & Shaywitz, 1988) and recently by us in the Boulder dyslexic sample, the third possible explanation, specifically a selection artifact, appears unlikely. The secondary symptom possibility could arise because the school failure produced by dyslexia may lead some dyslexic children to be more inattentive, distractible, and impulsive. If this were true, we would say that dyslexia in some children leads to a phenocopy of ADHD, and we would predict that the rates of ADHD in dyslexia samples would increase with age as the negative effects of school failure accumulate.

We recently found some evidence for this secondary symptom possibility in two different samples utilizing two different converging methodologies. The first study examined the comorbidity of dyslexia and ADHD in the Boulder dyslexic twin sample by examining the genetic correlation between the two conditions. If there is a subtype of dyslexia plus ADHD with a common genetic etiology, we would expect to find a significant genetic correlation between the two conditions in some or all of the sample. There was an elevated rate of ADHD in the dyslexic twins, and ADHD was significantly heritable, but in the sample as a whole there was no evidence for genetic correlation, which implies that the two conditions are genetically independent (Gilger, Pennington, & DeFries, in preparation).

When we examined the subset of probands with both disorders, both the MZ and DZ concordance rates were higher than would be expected if the disorders were independent, and the MZ concordance rate was significantly higher than the DZ rate. This latter result indicated there may be for a small, minority subtype in which the two disorders have a common genetic etiology. There was also evidence that the common family environment (i.e., common within families and differing between families) in some families acts to make some dyslexic twin pairs also concordant for ADHD. This evidence supported the secondary symptom hypothesis: dyslexia is primary, and certain other factors, (such as family environment) influence whether dyslexia leads to symptoms of ADHD. Overall, these results imply heterogeneity in the basis of the comorbidity of dyslexia and ADHD.

The second study examined underlying neuropsychological deficits in children with both dyslexia and ADHD, children with either condition alone, and children with neither, and asked whether there was a double dissociation between the pure ADHD and dyslexic groups on measures of executive function and phonological processing. In a classical double dissociation, two clinical groups differ in opposite directions on two neuropsychological measures; each group is normal on one measure, but significantly worse than the other group on the other measure. This pattern of results permits strong inferences about the independence of both the two measures and the underlying deficits in the two groups. As expected, children with pure ADHD were only impaired on executive functions, whereas children with pure dyslexia were only impaired on phonological processing. This double dissociation provides important evidence for the validity of the syndrome distinction between ADHD and dyslexia.

Of special interest here is the performance of the comorbid, dyslexia plus ADHD group, whose profile addresses three competing hypotheses about the basis of the comorbidity. If one disorder is secondary to the other, then the neuropsychological profile of the comorbid group should be similar to one of the two pure groups, because their secondary diagnosis is a phenocopy at the symptom level only. In contrast, if they are a true subtype with both disorders, then they should be impaired in both neuropsychological domains. We found that the comorbid group's profile was virtually identical to the pure dyslexia group, providing converging evidence for the hypothesis that ADHD in dyslexia is usually a secondary symptom (Pennington, Groisser, & Welsh, in preparation).

More research is needed to provide a definitive picture of the relation between ADHD and dyslexia, but the results presented above illustrate how converging findings from epidemiological, behavior genetic, and neuropsychological studies can be used to answer questions about comorbidity.

Brain Mechanisms

We have already developed the general hypothesis that ADHD is due to dysfunction in the prefrontal areas of the brain. What direct evidence is there to support this hypothesis or the more global hypothesis that ADHD is due to brain dysfunction?

Early attempts to relate ADHD to brain dysfunction utilized

neurological soft signs as the brain measure. The results of these studies were mixed and discouraging in terms of elucidating a brain basis for ADHD (Rutter, Graham, & Yule, 1970; Werry et al., 1972).

There is a weak association between minor physical anomalies (MPAs) and hyperactivity (Burg, Rappaport, Bartley, Quinn & Timmins, 1980; Rappaport & Quinn, 1975), but the association is not specific to hyperactivity and is not clinically useful in a predictive way. The potential neurological significance of observable MPAs is that they may be correlated with less observable developmental anomalies of the central nervous system (CNS). However, this line of research is more likely to bear fruit if specific genetic syndromes with MPAs (e.g., fragile X syndrome) are studied instead of the undoubtedly heterogenous group of all children with MPAs.

In terms of more direct measures of brain structure and function, the best evidence for differences in ADHD comes from measures of function rather than structure, including measures of electrophysiology, regional cerebral blood flow, and catecholamines (dopamine and norepinephrine). No evidence of structural differences has been found in CT scan studies of ADHD children (Harcherik et al., 1985; Shaywitz, Cohen, & Young, 1983). Hynd et al. (1990), however, did find absence of the usual R > L frontal asymmetry in ADHD children using magnetic resonance imaging (MRI) scans.

The electrophysiological measures support the hypothesis of CNS underarousal in at least a subgroup of hyperactive children (Ferguson & Rappaport, 1983). Lou, Henricksen, and Bruhn (1984) found decreased blood flow to the frontal lobes in ADHD children, which increased after the children received Ritalin®. Ritalin treatment also decreased blood flow to the motor cortex and primary sensory cortex "suggesting an inhibition of function of these structures, seen clinically as less distractibility and decreased motor activity during treatment" (Lou, et al., 1984, p. 829). These investigators have recently replicated this result in an expanded sample (Lou, Henricksen, Bruhn, Borner, & Nielsen, 1989); in this second report they emphasize the basal ganglia as the locus of reduced blood flow. In a recent study, Zametkin et al. (1990) used position emission turnography (PET) scanning to study the parents of ADHD children, who themselves had residual-type ADHD, but had never been treated with stimulant medication. They found an overall reduction in cerebral glucose utilization, particularly in frontal areas. Because hyperfrontality of blood flow is characteristic of the normal brain, hypofrontality in ADHD could explain the low central arousal found in the electrophysiological studies.

In terms of brain biochemistry, Shaywitz, Cohen,, and Bowers (1977) found lower levels of homovanillic acid (HVA) (the main dopamine metabolite) in the cerebral spinal fluid of ADHD children compared to controls. Dopamine has a preponderant distribution in the frontal regions of the cortex. Moreover, a well-validated animal model of ADHD involves dopamine depletion (Shaywitz, Shaywitz, Cohen & Young, 1983). However, there is also evidence of depletion of norepinephrine (NE) in ADHD (see Shaywitz & Shaywitz, 1988). Posner and Petersen (in press) have recently reviewed evidence supporting the view that NE pathways are involved in maintaining alertness, mainly by acting on the posterior attention systems of the right hemisphere. So an alternative view of ADHD is that it involves NE depletion in these posterior right hemisphere systems.

In summary, one plausible theory of brain mechanisms in ADHD proceeds as follows. The executive function deficit of ADHD children is caused by functional hypofrontality, which in turn is caused by either structural and/or biochemical changes in the prefrontal lobes, and is detectable as reduced frontal blood flow. Biochemically, the cause would be low dopamine levels, which Ritalin treatment reverses, at least in part. Unfortunately, the story is not that simple. One study found that dopamine agonists were not effective in treating hyperactive children (Mattes & Gittelman, 1979), whereas certain dopamine antagonists did have unexpected beneficial effects in ADHD children (Zametkin & Rappaport, 1986). Both of these results are opposite to what would be predicted by the dopamine depletion hypothesis. So the neurochemical mechanisms may be more complex, although the ubiquitous problem of heterogeneity in ADHD samples is another explanation.

Zametkin and Rappaport (1987) argue that no single neurotransmitter is exclusively involved in the pathogenesis of ADHD, both because stimulant medications always affect more than one neurotransmitter and because of the multiple interrelation among specific catecholamines and their precursors and metabolites. They argue that the combined action of dompaminergic and noradrenergic systems should be considered in the biology of ADHD.

Obviously, much more research is needed, preferably using familial samples that are as phenotypically homogeneous as possible. For instance, as suggested above, one subtype of ADHD children may have hypoarousal of the right posterior hemisphere secondary to NE depletion, whereas others may have the hypofrontal subtype of ADHD discussed here. Although the posterior and anterior attentional systems interact, separate deficits in each system are possible.

Neuropsychological Phenotype

The research here is less definitive than is research on the neuropsychology of dyslexia, but converging evidence supports a set of impaired and nonimpaired cognitive skills in ADHD that differ from those found in either normal or other learning disordered dyslexic populations.

Historically, phenotypic research on ADHD has shifted from a focus on activity per se to research on attentional processes and then to a focus on other cognitive processes that appear to underlie the surface symptoms of restlessness and inattention. Research on activity level in ADHD generally found that it was not the *quantity* but the *quality* of activity that mainly differentiates ADHD children from controls (Cromwell, Baumister, & Hawkins, 1963), a result that is similar to that found in research on eye contact in autism. Research on attention clarified that it was specific aspects of attention that were impaired in ADHD children. For instance, Porges, Walter, Korb, and Sprague (1975) used an ingenious experiment to demonstrate that there were no differences between ADHD children on and off Ritalin in reactive or orienting attention, but there were clear differences in focused or selective attention. Similarly other studies have shown that, contrary to the prevailing belief, ADHD children are no more vulnerable to extraneous stimuli that engage orienting attention than are normals (Douglas & Peters, 1979). In contrast, on measures of vigilance or sustained attention, ADHD children have a clear deficit, especially when prolonged attention is required and time of presentation is experimenter (vs. self) paced (Sykes, Douglas, Weiss, & Minde, 1971; Sykes, Douglas, & Morgenstern, 1973). Interestingly, recent studies of both adult lesion patients and blood flow studies of adult normals support a right frontal localization for the mechanisms involved in sustained attention (Wilkins, Shallice, & McCarthy, 1987).

Later work has expanded the scope of the cognitive deficit from a selective deficit in sustained attention to a more fundamental deficit. Douglas (1988) has summarized this work as supporting the hypothesis that ADHD children have a generalized self-regulatory deficit that affects the organization of information processing, the mobilization of attention throughout information processing, and the inhibition of inappropriate responding and that this self-regulatory deficit is present across visual, auditory, motor, and perceptual-motor modalities. In her formulation, organization of information processing encompasses planning, executive function, metacognition, optimum set maintenance, regulation of arousal and alertness, and self-monitoring.

The arousal/alertness component refers especially to the deployment of attentional resources in relation to task demands, including maintenance of attention over time. The inhibition component refers to controlling interference from irrelevant but sometimes prepotent response patterns, stimuli, and reinforcers. As can be seen, Douglas explicitly uses the term executive functions and her list of impaired cognitive processes includes many of the executive functions we have already discussed.

What are some of the specific cognitive tasks on which ADHD children have been found to be impaired and not impaired? In the impaired list, are monitoring tasks like the Continuous Performance Test, perceptual search tasks like the Matching Familiar Figures Test, logical search tasks, such as Raven's Progressive Matrices, and motor control and visuomotor tasks such as Porteus Mazes, Bender Gestalt, and the Rey Osterreieth Complex Figure. ADHD children have also been found to be impaired on validated measures of prefrontal function, including the Wisconsin Card Sorting test (Chelune & Baer, 1986; Parry, 1973, Groisser et al., in preparation), the Tower of Hanoi planning task (Groisser et al., in preparation), and conflictual motor responding tasks, such as the "go–no go" paradigm (Douglas, 1988). In the unimpaired list are various verbal memory tasks, such as Digit Span, paired associates and story recall, and various nonverbal memory tasks, such as recurring figures and recall of spatial positions. Interestingly, similar tasks can elicit or fail to elicit deficits in ADHD children depending on task conditions such as reinforcement schedule, number of items and distractors, and processing speed. This dependence of deficits on task conditions reinforces the hypothesis that the underlying deficit is not in a particular information processing domain, like verbal memory, but in executive functions that regulate all of information processing.

Another important contributor to our understanding of the neuropsychological phenotype in ADHD is Keith Conners. In an early study (Conners, 1970), he compared neurotic and hyperkinetic children from the same clinic setting on a variety of measures. The hyperkinetic children had significantly lower Verbal and Performance IQs, performed significantly less well on the Porteus Mazes (which may be sensitive to frontal lobe functions), and exhibited deficits in the *voluntary* inhibition of motor responses. The paradigm used to evaluate motor inhibition is worthy of note, as it permitted a distinction between voluntary and involuntary motor responses. With a Luria tremograph attached to both hands, subjects were instructed to make responses to target stimuli with the right hand only; some stimuli were very loud noises (gun shots), which initially produce a startle response in both hands. This startle response habituates over trials. The hyperactive subjects did not differ from controls in left hand performance, either for errors or rate of habituation of startle responses, indicating similar involuntary motor control. In contrast, hyperactives made more errors and habituated more slowly with their right hands, indicating a deficit in higher cortical mechanisms concerned with the inhibition of voluntary movement (see Conners & Wells, 1986, for a summary of these studies). Conners interprets these results as consistent with frontal lobe dysfunction.

In a later series of studies, Conners used a neuropsychological test battery to define six subtypes within a sample of hyperkinetic children. These subtypes exhibited differential drug responsiveness, among other things, and so appear to possess some external validity. Two groups did not give evidence of academic or cognitive disabilities, and their overactivity appeared to be mainly due to anxiety. One group appeared to have attention deficits in the context of learning disabilities; medication did not help this group. Perhaps this third group had ADHD as a superficial secondary symptom of dyslexia or another LD, as discussed previously. A fourth group had an isolated deficit in motor impulsivity, which also did not respond to drug treatment. A fifth group had mainly a visuospatial pattern of deficits, similar to the nonverbal learning disabilities discussed in Chapter 6.

The final group Conners labelled "frontal lobe dysfunction" because of distinctively poor performance on the Porteus Mazes. Although these children had the lowest IQ scores of all the groups, they were not depressed on measures of academic achievement or paired associate learning, both results indicating intact language processing and long-term memory skills. Their cognitive profile is reminiscent of that described by Douglas (1988) in her studies of ADHD children and best fits the executive function deficit definition of ADHD espoused here. Moreover, their response to drug treatment was different from that seen in all the other groups, in that significant changes on teacher ratings well in the areas of defiance, hyperactivity, and overall psychopathology. In other words, medication helped these children inhibit socially inappropriate responses, whereas medication in the other groups was either ineffective or mainly seemed to affect anxiety-related behaviors. This and other work by Conners underscores the clinical importance of distinguishing anxious from nonanxious (and LD from nonLD) hyperactive children, with the nonanxious, nonLD subtype best exemplifying the syndrome of ADHD as we are describing it here. Conners (1975) and Klove and Hole, (1979) both found that nonanxious hyperactives have low autonomic arousal and a significantly greater history of CNS risk events.

Conners' view of ADHD is distinctive for emphasizing the deficit in voluntary motor control in ADHD, which he sees as arising from a deficit in higher cortical arousal, particularly in frontal areas. Thus for Conners, hyperactivity per se remains an important primary symptom of the disorder because it reflects a deficit in the inhibition of voluntary motor behavior. Conners and Wells (1986) highlight a recent study, which unlike earlier research using objective measures of activity, found activity differences between hyperactive and normal boys over a week-long period using a solid-state accelerometer (Porrino et al., 1983). Most importantly, these activity differences persisted during sleep, arguing against the interpretation that they were secondary effects of attentional differences or social contexts. Instead, the sleep differences in activity suggest a cross-situational deficit in the CNS mechanisms involved in motor inhibition.

In summary, studies of the neuropsychological phenotype in ADHD are consistent with the hypothesis of a primary executive function deficit, but hardly provide conclusive evidence for this hypothesis. Of the various converging empirical criteria needed to establish primacy (Chapter 2), only a few have been met. We do not know if executive function deficits are among the most persistent features of the disorder, although adult outcome studies provide indirect evidence for this view. We do not know if executive function deficits are clearly distinctive in nonanxious, nonconduct-disordered ADHD children. We do not know if executive function deficits are coheritable with ADHD. Most importantly, we do not know if executive function deficits in early life predict later ADHD. So there is much research that still needs to be done on the neuropsychological phenotype in ADHD.

As suggested in the section on brain mechanisms, an alternative neuropsychological theory of ADHD involves a primary deficit in alertness secondary to dysfunction of posterior right hemisphere attentional systems. A much more articulated cognitive neuropsychological theory of the localization of different attentional systems in the brain has been recently proposed by Michael Posner (Posner & Petersen, in press; Posner, Petersen, Fox, & Raichle, 1988) and has begun to be applied to various clinical disorders (such as schizophrenia, closed head injury, and ADHD) in which attentional disturbances are prominent. As discussed earlier, research on a given learning disorder depends crucially on basic research on the neuropsychological processes which appear central to that disorder. Research on ADHD has suffered because of the lack of a sophisticated theory of attentional processes. Posner's work will certainly help fill that gap.

Developmental Course

Retrospective reports indicate that the symptoms of ADHD are often present in infancy in the form of high activity levels, emotional lability, irregular sleep patterns, and reduced need for sleep. These same symptoms persist into the preschool years, when additional symptoms, such as short attention span, proneness to tantrums, and difficulties in group settings also appear.

Earlier researchers (e.g., Laufer & Denhoff, 1957) viewed ADHD as limited to childhood, with the symptoms partially disappearing by adolescence. This developmental lag view of learning disorders has repeatedly been shown to be incorrect; the same is true for ADHD. There have since been both retrospective and prospective studies of outcome into adolescence and adulthood, and the general conclusion is that problems such as impulsivity, restlessness, poor self-esteem, and poor social skills are found in a majority of ADHD children on follow-up into adolescence and adulthood. Gittelman, Mannuzza, Shenker, and Bonagura (1985) found that in adulthood symptoms of ADHD were still present in one-third of the ADHD group but only in 3% of controls. Less education, lower SES, and more impulsive lifestyles (as indexed by greater debt and more changes of residence and jobs) appear to be part of the adult outcome of many ADHD children. On the other hand, the large majority are employed and self-supporting. While there is evidence of antisocial personality in about 25% of this group, they do not appear to be at increased risk for other severe psychiatric disturbances. Elevated rates of substance abuse on outcome have been found in some studies, but not in others (Shaywitz & Shaywitz, 1988).

Thus, there appears to be some congruence between the adult phenotype as measured by outcome studies and that found in biological parents of ADHD children, in that both sociopathy and substance abuse are found in each kind of study. A closer comparison of these two kinds of studies is needed to help answer the basic question of how the phenotype in ADHD changes with development.

From an executive-function perspective, what is changing may not be the underlying cognitive deficit, but the differing developmental tasks for which executive functions are crucial. In other words, there may be heterotypic continuity in the manifestation of this disorder across development. Work, especially lower status work, can be highly structured and routine and not tax executive functions too much. Other aspects of adult development that require initiative, planning, and flexibility, such as career development, intimacy, marriage, and parenting may pose greater problems. We lack data on these aspects of later adult development in ADHD samples.

DIAGNOSIS AND TREATMENT OF ADHD

As suggested earlier, the diagnosis of ADHD is difficult because of the number of confounding conditions that must be excluded, because of fundamental disagreements in the field on how to define the syndrome, and because objective tests of ADHD are less well-developed than those for a learning disorder like dyslexia. So clinicians should be duly cautious in making this diagnosis.

Presenting Symptoms

Because the diagnosis is based primarily on symptoms, much of the research on diagnosis has focused on developing lists of critical or primary symptoms and behavioral rating scales for parents and teachers that incorporate these critical symptoms. The critical symptoms described in DSM-III-R fall into three categories: inattention, impulsivity, and hyperactivity.

Other symptoms that demonstrate an association with ADHD, but do not appear to be primary include aggressive behavior, conduct disorder, learning disabilities, depression and poor self-esteem (see Table 5.1).

History

Symptoms of ADHD are usually present from early in life. *DSM-III-R* requires that the symptoms be present by age 7 to make the diagnosis, and some researchers recommend an earlier age of onset criterion. If the symptomatic behaviors are not present before first grade, they may be secondary to reading problems and not reflective of primary ADHD. Therefore, we are more convinced by a history that includes clear examples of inattention, impulsivity, and overactivity in the preschool years.

In infancy, symptoms may include a high activity level, less need

TABLE 5.1 Symptoms in ADHD

Primary	Inattention, impulsivity, hyperactivity
Correlated	Sleep disturbances, emotional lability
Secondary	Poor self-esteem, poor social skills, academic problems, substance abuse, conduct disorder(?)
Artifactual	Anxiety, conduct disorder(?), giftedness, dyslexia(?)

for sleep, colic, frequent crying, and poor soothability—characteristics that overlap with what is called a "difficult" infant. In toddlerhood, the ADHD child often has a low sense of danger, an unusual amount of energy, and a tendency to move from one activity to another very quickly. Parents may notice that the child wears out shoes, clothing, and toys faster than other children (Cantwell, 1975).

ADHD children nearly always come to clinical attention in the early school years because of the behavior-management problems they pose in a classroom setting: frequent talking, getting out of their seats, difficulty keeping their hands to themselves, and problems finishing schoolwork. If a patient does not have a history of these and related problematic behaviors in the early school years, a diagnosis of ADHD (except from acquired causes, such as a closed head injury later in childhood) is unlikely to be correct.

In terms of family history, the family studies previously reviewed indicate a greater risk for ADHD in children of parents who themselves had or have ADHD, or who have antisocial personality, substance abuse or hysteria. Therefore, the psychiatric history of the parents is an important piece of diagnostic information.

Behavioral Observations

Because ADHD children may not manifest their problematic behaviors in a novel or structured situation, the absence of ADHD symptoms in the clinician's office does not necessarily rule out the diagnosis. If such behaviors do occur, they then provide important converging evidence. Fidgetiness, poor attention, difficulty with limits, an impulsive response style on tasks that require self-monitoring and persistence (such as drawing tasks), perseveration, other indications of difficulty in shifting cognitive set, difficulty with new or abstract concepts, concrete responses, and emotional lability are all behaviors in the clinical setting that are consistent with the diagnosis.

Test Results

There is no pattern of test scores on a standard psychometric test battery (a WISC-R, achievement tests, and visuomotor tests) that is clearly diagnostic of ADHD. As previously discussed, some depression in IQ is a typical finding as is impulsive performance on visuomotor tasks. This makes the diagnosis more difficult to make, especially for psychologists, who are more comfortable when their test results confirm clinical hypotheses based on other data. Particularly if behavioral observations during testing are noncontributory, the psychologist is put in the awkward position of diagnosing a behavioral syndrome without actually having observed any of the problematic behaviors!

Some researchers (e.g., Kaufman, 1979) had suggested that the third factor on the WISC-R, called Freedom from Distractibility (FD), measures attention and is depressed in the WISC-R profiles of ADHD children. However, later research provided little evidence to support this claim (Henry & Witman, 1981). Actually, the association of low FD scores with dyslexia is much more robust. This association of low FD with dyslexia arises because all three subtests in the FD factor (Arithmetic, Digit Span, and Coding) tap verbal short-term memory to some extent; we have already discussed problems in verbal STM as a correlate of dyslexia.

To provide direct test evidence of ADHD, the psychologist must move beyond traditional psychometric tests and use measures of executive function that have been shown to be sensitive to ADHD in research studies. Measures for which normative data are available include the Wisconsin Card Sorting Test (Chelune & Baer, 1986), the Continuous Performance Test, and the Contingency Naming Test (Taylor, 1988). I would recommend using at least two of these measures in a child otherwise suspected of ADHD. Diagnoses of ADHD based on behavioral checklists alone run the risk of misdiagnosing children who really have dyslexia, anxiety, and so on. By requiring both a positive history and positve test results, such false positives can be greatly reduced. It is likewise important to rule out dyslexia in a child suspected of ADHD.

Treatment

Most authorities agree that medication alone is not sufficient treatment for most cases of ADHD (Denckla, 1979; Shaywitz & Shaywitz, 1988) and instead recommend an approach that combines educational intervention, medications, and psychotherapy for the child, and education and/or therapy for the parents. Conners and Wells (1986, p. 133) review the treatment literature and conclude that "at a minimum, a combination of stimulant therapy and behavior therapy in the home and school represents the most clinically efficacious treatment." Medication may make the child more available for development in the various areas of his or her life, but it should be remembered that a chronically ADHD child has missed some aspects of normal development and needs remedial training in the strategies necessary for normal educational and social functioning. Learning and experience undoubtedly affect the development of what we are calling executive functions; a chronically ADHD child has both primary and secondary deficits in executive functions.

Stimulant medication for the treatment of ADHD has been and remains controversial, because of concerns about side effects and questions about whether the medication actually improves cognitive and academic performance, in addition to making the child easier to deal with behaviorally. There are also reasonable concerns about the effects on self-concept when a child comes to attribute control of his or her behavior to an external agent rather than to the self. However, it is important to note that beneficial behavioral effects are well-documented in double blind trials, with 70%–90% of hyperkinetic children showing improvement (Barkley, 1977; Conners & Werry, 1979).

More recent research has alleviated the concerns about side effects, which are generally minimal and usually disappear as the child develops tolerance or if the dosage is reduced. Ritalin in high doses can cause growth retardation, but drug-free holidays allow catchup growth. Shaywitz & Shaywitz (1988) discuss the rare but most serious side effect of Ritalin as being the emergence of Tourette's syndrome (TS) in some children treated with the drug. Because TS is a familial disorder, stimulant medication may be contraindicated in children whose families have a history of tics.

In terms of cognition, more recent research indicates the beneficial effects of medication in ADHD children on academic tasks (Douglas, Ball, O'Neil, & Britton, 1986; Pelham, 1988). Some of the confusion regarding this issue in the older literature appears due to the differential effects of dosage levels (low vs. high) on cognition and behavior. Optimal cognitive effects are attained at lower doses than those required for optimal behavioral effects; moreover, the time course of these effects differ (Conners & Wells, 1986). Interestingly, these cognitive effects are most noticeable on the very aspects of those tasks on which ADHD children perform worst and where it is plausible that the executive functions are most important—on later learning trials, motivation, self-monitoring, and correction of errors. Douglas (1988, p. 79) postulates that "the self-regulatory problems of ADHD children create an abnormally large discrepancy between capacity and performance. On some tasks and under some conditions stimulants act to decrease the discrepancy."

Thus, given these recent results concerning side effects and beneficial effects on cognition, stimulant medication is an important component of the treatment of children with ADHD. The possibly deleterious effects on self-esteem can be handled in the course of the accompanying therapy and parental education.

In terms of educational intervention, an emphasis on teaching metacognitve skills may be important, as ADHD children have less experience developing and applying such strategies to academic tasks. Such a metacognitive intervention has shown dramatic success in improving reading comprehension skills among poor comprehenders (Brown & Campione, 1986), and could be very helpful with ADHD children. Other metacognitive interventions would include teaching explicit algorithms and strategies for dealing with complex problems and assignments, whether they be long division problems or term papers.

CASE PRESENTATION 3

Jeff is a right-handed boy of 8 years who is currently in the third grade in a regular classroom in a public school. He was seen in our laboratory as a subject in a study comparing the neuropsychological profiles of dyslexic and ADHD children. He was diagnosed as having ADHD at age 7 when he was in first grade, and was placed on 15 mg of Ritalin per day, which helped improve his behavior, but did not alleviate all his symptoms. Both his parents and teachers have continued to do many extra things to help structure his behavior and to find arenas in which he can succeed. More recently, he was placed on Cylert®, which is working better than Ritalin. There is a family history for ADHD. Jeff's younger brother has been diagnosed as having ADHD; his paternal uncle had similar symptoms as a child, as does his son. There is no family history for antisocial behavior, substance abuse, or other mental health evaluations and treatments.

In terms of his early history, Jeff was the product of a full-term pregnancy complicated by toxemia. There was some transient fetal distress during a prolonged, induced labor, but Jeff's Apgar scores were 8 and then 10, and he did not require any special interventions after delivery. His mother noticed during the pregnancy that he was a much more active fetus than her daughters had been. She recounted one embarrassing episode in which his movements were so noticeable that her abdomen became the focus of everyone's attention during a dinner party. Jeff was a colicky baby; for 3 months he would have episodes of colic lasting about 8 hours nearly every day. His parents tried several medications to ease his colic. Once he was mobile, he was very active and impulsive. He once ran into a coffee table on a dead run blackening both eyes. He had recurrent ear infections requiring the placement of ear tubes. There were no other neurodevelopmental risk factors including no history of seizures, head injury, or major illnesses.

Both as a toddler and later, Jeff has been hard on toys and clothes. He breaks his toys without meaning to, and he wears out his pants and shoes more quickly than do other children. He has had some difficulty with both gross and fine motor coordination, and has had trouble with drawing, writing, and riding a bicycle. Unlike some ADHD children, Jeff has been afraid of physical danger and has not had fractures and lacerations. His preschool recommended more practice at home with coloring books to help his fine motor skills. Unfortunately, Jeff drew on the walls, and for several years the walls had to be repainted yearly. Both dinner and bed times have been a trial. Jeff stood while he ate, and moved about with the result that a lot of food was spilled. Both Jeff and his younger brother who also has ADHD have shared a bedroom, and neither is very tired at night. So they keep each other up, and it often takes 2 hours to get them to sleep. Going to restaurants and church has been difficult for the family because the boys won't sit still. Team sports have also been difficult because Jeff won't pay attention; he had to quit T-ball because he nearly got hit in the head with the ball because of inattention. Board games continue to be very difficult for both Jeff and his younger brother.

In terms of school history, he was tested in first grade because of his problems with attention, as previously mentioned. That evaluation led to a referral to his pediatrician for an evaluation of possible ADHD. During the school testing, problems with attention made it difficult for Jeff to complete some tests. Overall, the school estimated his IQ was average to above average. They did not find speech and language problems, but they did find a 2-year delay in fine motor skills. Because ADHD doesn't qualify as a learning disability, Jeff was not placed in an LD class. However, the school has provided other services, such as a support teacher and group therapy with the school counselor. His mother has had a close working relation with his teachers, and a major focus of their efforts has been to help Jeff organize and complete his assignments. Because of his fine motor problems, he hates written work. In addition, he has had a lot of trouble getting organized to bring home books and assignments. It is impressive how much structure has had to come from the home and school environment to help this child plan and organize his behavior. Although Jeff has occasionally distracted other children in the classroom, he has not been a behavior problem in an acting-out, oppositional, defiant fashion. Rather his main problems at school have been paying attention and getting his work done.

His parents have worked hard to find activities at which he can succeed, and this has been very helpful to him. He likes reading, including poetry, and he likes to read to his younger brother. He also likes Boy Scouts, which has helped him build self-esteem in some of the physical activities of which he used to be afraid.

At the time we saw him, Jeff still met criteria for ADHD on a number of commonly used, parent-report, symptom inventories. For instance, on the Diagnostic Interview for Children and Adolescents (DICA) (Herjanic, Campbell, & Reich, 1982) ADD scale, 17 of 20 items were scored positively. On Barkley's inventory of problem situations (1981), which is a measure of pervasiveness, he was positive on 14/16 situations, with a mean severity rating of 7.1 (on a scale of 1–9) in those situations. Finally on the Achenbach's Childhood Behavior Checklist (CBCL), he scored in the clinical range on the Hyperactive (T score = 80), Aggressive (85), Depressed (77), Obsessive Compulsive (76), and Somatic Complaints (75) scales. In contrast, he did not have a clear history for either conduct disorder or dyslexia. A summary of Jeff's test scores is provided in Table 5.2

Discussion

Jeff's Verbal, Performance, and Full Scale IQ scores all fall solidly in the average range, and there is no significant difference between his verbal and performance IQs. Moreover, there is not a significant difference between his verbal (VC) (10.5) and perceptual (PO) (12.5) factor scores. In contrast, his FD factor score of 7.3 is significantly lower than each of the other two. This low FD score is mainly due to a markedly impaired Coding score, which is probably secondary to his fine motor and attention problems. This poor Coding score is the only clear indication we have on the WISC-R of cognitive dysfunction. In contrast, he does not appear to have a problem with language or spatial cognition.

TABLE 5.2 Test Summary, Case 3

WISC-R FSIQ = 104

Information	8	Picture Completion	15
Similarities	13	Picture Arrangement	11
Arithmetic	11	Block Design	11
Vocabulary	10	Object Assembly	14
Comprehension	11	Coding	3
Digit Span	8		
Verbal IQ = 103		Performance IQ = 105	
Verbal Comprehension = 10.5		Perceptual Organization = 12.5	

Freedom from Distractibility = 7.3

Achievement tests	Grade equivalent	Age standard score
Gray Oral Reading test	5.0	—
WRAT Spelling test	4.8	110
Woodcock-Johnson Word Attack	5.8	113
Reading Quotient = 1.14		

Executive funtions	Raw score	T score
Wisconsin Card Sorting test		
Perseverative responses	95	02
Categories	2	34
Tower of Hanoi planning task (3 ring)	29	41
Matching Familiar Figures Test (MFFT)		
Mean reaction time	15.1	48
Errors	20	36
Continuous Performance Test (CPT)	.30	29
Language		
Phoneme segmentation (Pig Latin)	33/48	55

The reading and spelling achievement test scores in combination with the WISC-R arithmetic score rule out dyslexia or a math disability. In fact, his reading and spelling scores are above grade level, and his (RQ) of 1.14 indicates he is overachieving in reading. These results, in combination with his good performance on a demanding test of phonemic segmentation, indicate he has a strength in phonological-processing skills.

The one clear area of deficit is in executive functions, in which he performed significantly below age and IQ expectations on three of four tasks (all but the Tower of Hanoi, which was low average). He was extremely perseverative on the Wisconsin Card Sorting Test, earning a score nearly *five* standard deviations below his age mean. He was also impaired on both measures of vigilance, the MFFT and CPT.

He has deficits in the executive functions of set-shifting ability and vigilance.

Although we did not directly test for possible deficits in long-term memory or social cognition, the history is helpful in ruling out deficits in these neuropsychological domains. As previously discussed, he clearly meets clinical criteria for ADHD. Moreover, his problems began well before school age. Although he is elevated on both internalizing and externalizing scales on the Achenbach CBCL, his highest scores came on the Hyperactivity and Aggression scales. A lot of the items endorsed on the Depressed scale have to do with self-esteem; as previously mentioned, poor self-esteem is a frequent secondary symptom in ADHD.

It is interesting to compare this case with the next case. Both patients have an underlying executive function disorder, but this underlying deficit has resulted in a somewhat opposite clinical presentation. As we will see, Miguel is docile and passive, with no history of overactivity, whereas Jeff has had problems with overactivity since early life. While Jeff meets the criteria for ADHD, Miguel meets those for attention deficit without hyperactivity, which may be a valid subtype. A similar dichotomy has been described in the clinical literature on adult patients with acquired frontal lesions (Stuss & Benson, 1986), but we really lack a good theoretical explanation for why seemingly similar neuropsychological deficits can lead to what appear to be opposite overt behaviors.

CASE PRESENTATION 4

Miguel is a 13-year-old sixth grader, referred by his adoptive parents. Miguel has had chronic academic difficulty, earning mostly C's in school, although he has recently received some D's on his report card. Parents report that in spite of reminders from his teachers about missing work, he does not follow through in getting in assignments. Parents state Miguel doesn't seem to have much idea about why he is not doing well and that they are frustrated by his lack of organization and carelessness and his inability to take responsibility for himself.

Miguel is a Central American orphan who was adopted at 15 months of age by a couple who both have professional careers. His adoptive parents know little about his natural parents or early history other than that Miguel suffered early developmental delay because of stimulation deprivation, and that he was significantly underweight at 9 months. Developmental milestones were late, with walking around

18 months. Language development was also slow with notable articulation problems.

Miguel was retained in kindergarten because of immaturity. From the beginning of school, Miguel has had academic difficulty, particularly with staying on task and completing homework. He has particular difficulty with reading comprehension and math. After fourth grade, the parents transferred him to a private school where they felt he would receive more individual attention, and where he repeated fourth grade. Previous private evaluation found a Full Scale IQ of 105, a Verbal IQ of 97 and a Performance IQ of 115. Miguel was believed to show a high level of visual–spatial ability and to have deficits in language and sequencing.

Miguel has generally been a cheerful child, who is cooperative about helping with tasks at home. In spite of his academic problems, he has not been a behavior problem at school and teachers have liked him. Peer relationships have been satisfactory. Table 5.3 provides a summary of Miguel's test results.

Discussion

The presenting complaints and history suggest several possible diagnoses, including ADHD, emotional or motivational problems, or specific handwriting problems. The early speech and language difficulty suggest a possible dyslexia or other language disorder, but the school history does not sound like dyslexia. Although problems with staying on task are suggestive of ADHD or an emotional problem, the lack of symptomatic problems in relations with parents, teachers, and peers does not fit with those diagnoses. One telling part of the history is that reading comprehension and math are particularly difficult, which suggest a possible problem with conceptual as opposed to basic skills. Also interesting is the fact that the problems appear to have gotten worse around fourth grade, which is late for dyslexia or a language problem. This late onset makes sense if the main problem is in the conceptual and organizational skills necessary for independent work, which becomes more important around fourth grade. Nonetheless, at this point, this is a puzzling case that weakly suggests a fairly long list of potential diagnoses.

Traditional psychometric testing helps rule out some possibilities, but does not provide positive evidence of what the problem is. The child has an average IQ of 105, and the subtest pattern is not particularly suggestive. Although the VIQ < PIQ disparity of 12 points is statistically significant, there is not a clear difference among factor

TABLE 5.3 Test Summary Case 4

WISC–R FSIQ = 105

Information	9	Picture Completion	15
Similarities	14	Picture Arrangement	11
Arithmetic	9	Block Design	11
Vocabulary	8	Object Assembly	11
Comprehension	10	Coding	11
Digit Span	11		

Verbal IQ = 100   Performance IQ = 112
Verbal Comprehension = 10.3   Perceptual Organization = 11
Freedom from Distractibility = 10.3

	Grade equivalent	Age standard score
PIAT		
Math	5.7	92
Reading recognition	7.0	97
Reading comprehension	10.2	108
Spelling	8.7	103
WRAT Spelling	7B	98
Gray Oral	8.2	—
Word Attack	10.1	104
Woodcock–Johnson		
Math Cluster	4.7	81
Reading quotient: .98		

	Raw score	T score
Executive functions		
Category Test (midrange) errors	30	51
Wisconsin Card Sorting Test		
Perseverations	43	23
Categories	1	16
Contingency Naming Test, Part B		
Time (sec)	126.0	33
Errors	18	10
Long-term memory		
Story		
Trial 1	6	—
Trial 2	13	—
Trial 3	10	—
Trial 4	13	—
Trial 5	17	—
Delayed Recall	17	—
Figure		
Trial 1	13	—
Trial 2	15	—
Delayed Recall	15	—
Language		
Boston Naming Test	64	44
GFW Auditory Discrimination Test		
Quiet	—	41
Noise	—	30

scores. On the achievement tests, it is clear that the child is not dyslexic, since all the reading and spelling scores are consistent with his age, IQ, and grade level. The only hint of a problem is on PIAT Math, on which his standard score is 13 points below his FSIQ. This low score is consistent with the report from the history that math is one of his worst subjects. His handwriting was automatic and well-formed, so we can eliminate the diagnosis of a specific handwriting problem. So our differential diagnosis list has narrowed to ADHD, emotional or motivational problem, conceptual (or executive function) problem, and specific math problem. This child does not appear to have a right hemisphere LD (described in Chapter 6), which is one cause of a specific math problem, because his PIQ is not depressed, his handwriting is fine, and the history does not indicate problems in peer relations or social cognition generally. Clearly more data are needed to make a diagnosis.

Neuropsychological tests of language, long-term memory and executive function were also administered, as well as a second math achievement test (Woodcock Johnson). On this last test, he scored at the 10th percentile, confirming difficulties in math. On the neuropsychological tests, his verbal and nonverbal long-term memory were both excellent as he retained all of the previously learned information over a 2-hour time delay. On the learning component of the verbal memory test, he was impaired, requiring five trials to learn 17 of the 30 units of information in a story. Consistent with this evidence of mild language processing difficulty, were his somewhat lower scores on measures of name retrieval (Boston Naming Test) and phoneme perception (Goldman Fristoe Woodcock Auditory Discrimination Test). So these language problems are consistent with his early history of language delay and likely contribute to his learning problems. It is interesting that he is one of those rare children (at least in our clinical experience) who has a nondyslexic language disorder. However, it is important to consider the possibility that the executive function problems described below contributed to the poor scores on both Story Learning and the noise portion of the GFW Auditory Discrimination Test, as both of these tests require sustained attention.

Most striking was his moderately impaired performance on three measures of executive functions. He only achieved one of six categories on the Wisconsin Card Sorting Test ($z = -3.4$ for his age) and was markedly perseverative, making 43 perseverative responses ($z = -2.7$ for age). On another test of mental flexibility, the Contingency Naming Test (Taylor, 1988), his error score was nearly four SDs below the mean ($z = -3.96$) on part B, which requires set-shifting.

In summary, he had moderate to severe impairments of executive function in the context of normal IQ, achievement scores, LTM, and mildly impaired language skills. These executive function deficits explain his problems with organization, completing work, and the more conceptual aspects of academic tasks. Our emotional evaluation found no evidence of psychopathology in the patient or his family. In particular, he did not meet the DSM-III-R criteria for ADHD, even though his underlying neuropsychological strengths and deficits are similar to those found in studies of ADHD. If we did not have the diagnostic option of executive function deficits and the tests necessary to confirm that diagnosis, this would have remained a very puzzling case.

CHAPTER 6

Right Hemisphere
Learning Disorders

After dyslexia, other language disorders, ADHD or other executive function deficits have been ruled out, the other remaining possible learning disorders occur much less frequently. These include right hemisphere learning disorders, autism spectrum disorder, and acquired memory disorders. This chapter deals with what are sometimes called "nonverbal" or "right hemisphere" learning disabilities (Denckla, 1983; Myklebust, 1975; Rourke, 1989; Rourke & Strang, 1978; Semrud-Clikeman & Hynd, 1990; Tranel, Hall, Olson, & Tranel, 1987; Weintraub & Mesulam, 1983). In these accounts, problems with math, handwriting, and social cognition are all viewed as part of the same right hemisphere syndrome.

Without disputing either the co-occurence of these symptoms in some patients or their possible validity as a syndrome, it is nevertheless conceptually clearer to consider deficits in math and handwriting separately from deficits in social cognition. In our clinical experience, there are certainly children who present with specific deficits in math and/or handwriting without deficits in social cognition. Conversely, there are patients with clearer socal cognitive deficits who do not have math and handwriting problems. Moreover, adult studies in both normals and patients with acquired lesions support the dissociability of spatial and social cognition (Bryden & Ley, 1983; Etcoff, 1984).

Another name for the learning disorder discussed here is developmental Gerstmann syndrome (Benson & Geschwind, 1970; Kinsbourne & Warrington, 1963), which is named by analogy with acquired Gerstmann syndrome, in which there are deficits in calculation, spelling, finger position knowledge, and right–left discrimination. This constellation of symptoms has been considered a left parietal lobe syndrome, but Benton (1977) found these four symptoms did not co-occur with any greater frequency than they did with other left parietal lobe symptoms and questioned the validity of the syndrome. Aside from the dubious parentage of the term "developmental Gerstmann syndrome," it is also problematic because it implies a left hemisphere locus for the difficulties, whereas more recent evidence suggests that specific developmental problems in math and handwriting (but not reading) are more likely due to right hemisphere dysfunction.

Another definitional issue concerns what we mean by specific math and handwriting disorders. We have already discussed the frequent co-occurrence of math and handwriting problems with developmental dyslexia. Although the reasons for handwriting problems in dyslexia are not well understood, it does not appear to reflect a spatial-processing problem but rather a linguistic or motor-sequencing problem. The math problems found in dyslexics are of a different sort than those found in children without reading and spelling problems (Rourke, 1989; Strang & Rourke, 1985b). Briefly, dyslexics have trouble memorizing math facts, and understanding "word" problems because of their reading problem. Sometimes they missequence numbers they write, but usually do not have basic conceptual problems with mathematical understanding. In contrast, nondyslexic children with poor math performance appear to have fundamental conceptual problems in understanding mathematics. In some of these children, these conceptual problems appear to be secondary to a deficit in right hemisphere spatial cognition. Thus, what is meant here by the term "specific math and handwriting problems" is a set of such problems that do *not* occur in the context of dyslexia or some related language disorder. This distinction is also supported by the adult clinical literature, in which math and handwriting deficits are frequent concomitants of acquired aphasia, but can occur as a consequence of lesions in nonlanguage areas that do not produce aphasia (Hecaen & Albert, 1978; Luria, 1966). With these definitional points clearly in mind, let us examine to what is known about nonverbal or right hemisphere LDs.

RESEARCH REVIEW

This section will be much briefer than those in other chapters, because there is much less research to review. Rourke (1989) estimates the prevalence of nonverbal LD within an LD clinic sample to be only 5%–10%, which is considerably less than the prevalence of either dyslexia or ADHD, which together would account for the large majority of such clinic samples. Denckla (1979) found a somewhat lower prevalence: 1% of patients in an LD clinic sample of 484 cases. Assuming a poulation prevalence of 10% for all LDs, these figures suggest a very rough population prevalence between 0.1 and 1.0%. In terms of sex ratio, Rourke (1989) estimates it to be 1:1, which is much different than the sex ratio found in clinic samples of dyslexia or ADHD. In three published studies of right hemisphere LD (Rourke & Strang, 1978; Tranel et al., 1987, Weintraub & Mesulam, 1983), the M:F sex ratios were 2.8:1, 0.6:1, and 1:1, respectively, with an overall sex ratio of 1.2:1. These results are generally consistent with Rourke's (1989) estimate. As we will see, there are some genetic syndromes affecting females that produce these symptoms. Interestingly, the sex ratio in reported case samples of Asperger's syndrome, which may overlap with right hemisphere LD, is very different, ranging from 4.7:1 to 9.0:1, and similar to the sex ratio found in autism (Gillberg, Steffenbury, & Jakobson, 1987; Wing, 1981). If the sex ratios for right hemisphere LD and Asperger's syndrome are indeed different, this is consistent with the view that they are different syndromes.

It must be emphasized that the information about both prevalence and sex ratio of right hemisphere LD is very tentative because no epidemiological studies of nondyslexic math and handwriting problems have been conducted.

Etiologies

Aside from an association with two specific genetic syndromes, Turner syndrome and fragile X in females, little is known about possible genetic or environmental causes of this learning disorder. There are no family, twin, adoption, segregation, or linkage studies of these disorders.

Both math and handwriting problems are found in girls with Turner syndrome, who do not have reading problems (Money, 1973; Pennington, Van Doorninck, et al., 1985). Turner syndrome is caused by nondisjunction during meiosis of the paired X chromosomes, resulting in a gamete with no X chromosome. If such a gamete is involved in a successful conception and birth, a phenotypically female indivdual with only one X chromosome (45,X) is the result.

In terms of cognitive phenotype, individuals with Turner syndrome tend to have depressed Performance IQs and problems with a variety of visuospatial tasks (Alexander & Money, 1966; Cohen, 1962; Garron, 1977; Shaffer, 1962). Although their pattern of deficits is often interpreted as due to selective right hemisphere dysfunction (Christensen & Nielsen, 1981; Silbert, Wolff, & Lillienthal, 1977), several neuropsychological studies have found deficits on a wider range of tasks (McGlone, 1985; Pennington, Heaton et al., 1985; Waber, 1979). These latter studies support the interpretation that the brain dysfunction in Turner syndrome is better described as either diffuse or as predominantly (but not exclusively) nonverbal, rather than as involving focal right hemisphere dysfunction. The same caveat should be borne in mind when considering other examples of "right hemisphere LD."

Interestingly, a recent report described problems in affective discrimination and psychosocial adjustment in girls with Turner syndrome (McCauley, Kay, Ito, & Treder, 1987), which were not simply attributable to short stature. So it is possible that Turner syndrome is one cause of the syndrome called "right hemisphere LD." Moreover, because all individuals with Turner syndrome are female, they would introduce a very slight female bias in the sex ratio for the syndrome. However, as the newborn incidence of 45 X is between 1 and 5 per 10,000, this bias would be small if the true population prevalence of right hemisphere LD is as high as 1%. If it is as low as 0.1%, then this bias would be about ten times greater.

The other genetic syndrome with a phenotype similar to right hemisphere LD also involves the X chromosome, fragile X syndrome in females. Most males who inherit the fragile X locus are retarded, therefore, they are not found in LD samples. In contrast, the large majority of fragile X females are nonretarded. Because this is a fairly frequent anomaly (1/1000), fragile X females would contribute to a female bias in the rates of right hemisphere LD. Nonetheless, the sex ratio among idiopathic cases of right hemisphere LD would still need to be low, less than 1.2:1 for the slight female bias of these two X chromosome anomalies to produce an overall sex ratio of 1:1 (again assuming a prevalence of 1% of right hemisphere LD). On the other hand, if the true prevalence is as low as 0.1%, then Turner syndrome and fragile X in females together could account for a majority but not all of female cases (moreover, not every female with these genetic disorders has the clinical syndrome of nonverbal LD).

The evidence that the cognitive phenotype in fragile X females is similar to right hemisphere LD is less clear than for Turner syndrome, because research on fragile X is newer and because the genetics of the fragile X locus are more complicated. Apparently because of these genetic complexities, there is a very broad spectrum of phenotypic effects in fragile X females, ranging from mental retardation and autism to no effects on behavior or cognition. Nonetheless, across IQ levels there appears to be some consistency in the cognitive and behavioral phenotype. Several studies have found problems with spatial skills in fragile X females (Kemper, Hagerman, Ahmad, & Mariner, 1986; Madison, George, & Moeschler, 1986; Miezejeski, et al., 1986; Veenema, Veenema, & Geraedts, 1987). However, across studies, there is not a consistent finding of VIQ-PIQ differences, unlike Turner syndrome (Pennington, Schreiner, & Sudhalter, in press-a). Among academic skills, problems with math are much more frequent than problems with reading and spelling. Systematic data on handwriting has not been collected. In the social and behavioral domain, there are problems with attention (Hagerman & Smith, 1983), social anxiety, and shyness (Hagerman, 1987), with 33% of female heterozygotes meeting the criteria for schizotypal features and 40% meeting the criteria for some form of depressive disorder (Reiss, Hagerman, Vinogradov, Abrams, & King, 1988).

In summary, both Turner syndrome and fragile X syndrome in females appear to be possible genetic causes of specific math and handwriting problems. It is known that normal variation in mathematics has a heritable component (Plomin, 1986), so there are likely to be other genetic influences on those learning disorders. Obviously, more research is needed on the genetics of these particular learning disorders.

In terms of *environmental* causes, there are also few data. Weintraub and Mesulam (1983) discuss etiology in their 14 cases; they have found evidence for an acquired insult in 9 of these (e.g., infantile hemiplegia, perinatal complication, or early onset nonfamilial seizure disorders). Such acquired insults were only present in 1 of the 11 cases reported by Tranel et al. (1987).

Rourke (1989) lists several other possible etiologies of nonverbal learning disorder, including moderate to severe closed head injury (presumably early in development), unsuccessfully treated hydrocephalus, cranial radiation, and congenital absence of the corpus calosum.

Brain Mechanisms

There are very few data in this area as well; more direct validation of the right hemisphere hypothesis regarding these disorders is needed.

Voeller's (1986) study most directly addresses the issue of brain mechanisms. She studied 15 children with right hemisphere findings on neurological exam and/or CT scan selected from a clinic population of 600 children referred for a pediatric neurological exam. Thus her sample, unlike others in this area, began with patients identified according to a neurological criterion and then studied their behavioral and neuropsychological characteristics, which turned out to be similar to those reported in other studies of right hemisphere LDs. These results provide partial validation of the right hemisphere hypothesis—"partial" because her sample was not an unbiased sample of children in the general population with right hemisphere neurological findings. Quite conceivably, there could be such children who have not come to cliical attention and do not have the social and behavioral difficulties characteristic of this syndrome. Neurologic tests were also reported for the Weintraub and Mesulam (1983) and Tranel et al. (1987) samples. In the former, these were motor signs on the left, especially asymmetrical left arm posturing during complex gait, found in 12 of 14 patients. In Tranel et al. (1987), only 2 of 11 patients had asymmetric motor findings and none had any abnormalities on CT scan. Five of seven EEGs in this study had mild diffuse abnormalities, a finding that does not differentiate these patients from other LD or ADHD groups.

More sophisticated neuroimaging techniques would be interesting to pursue in patients with these disorders, and would provide a better test of the hypothesized right hemisphere localization.

Neuropsychological Phenotype

Analysis of the neuropsychological phenotype in this disorder is complicated by the likelihood of subtypes within the group of children who are selectively poor at math and handwriting. Traditional neuropsychological accounts of acquired disorders of these two academic skills recognize several subtypes, each associated with different lesion locations. These include an aphasic subtype, associated with left perisylvian lesions, a spatial subtype, associated with right hemisphere lesions, and (for math disorders) a planning and perseveration subtype, associated with frontal lesions (Levin, 1979; Luria, 1966). We have already excluded from consideration math and handwriting problems in the context of a language disorder (the first subtype), but that still leaves two possible subtypes—right hemisphere and frontal—to consider. What neuropsychological research there is on specific math and handwriting disorders has been guided by a right hemisphere hypothesis, but has not tested the overlapping but distinct hypothesis of prefrontal dysfunction. In our clinical practice, we have encountered LD patients with each type of developmental math disorder, so similar heterogeneity is likely in published studies.

With this caveat in mind, let us review the evidence for a causal connection between an underlying deficit in spatial cognition and specific problems in math and handwriting. If this hypothesized relation is correct, several converging results ought to be found: (a) normal variation in math and handwriting skill should be substantially correlated with measures of spatial cognition; (b) individuals with deficits in math and handwriting should be deficient in spatial cognition; and, most importantly, (c) spatial cognition skill should precede and predict later math and handwriting longitudinally, after other possible contributing influences (e.g., verbal IQ, executive function, sex, SES) have been factored out. Similar empirical criteria are relevant for the hypothesized relation between spatial and social cognition. We will first review the data relevant to math and handwriting and then turn to social cognition.

With regard to the first point, there are two factor analytic studies of normal math ability that support the hypothesized relation (Battistia, 1980; Fleischiner & Frank, 1979). In the Fleischiner & Frank (1979) study, several visual perceptual measures accounted for more variance in mathematical achievement than did IQ.

Establishing the second point, that deficits in math and handwriting are associated with visuospatial problems, requires care in evaluating control groups and discriminant measures. If subjects with specific math and handwriting problems are only compared to normals of the same age, any visuospatial deficits that are found may arguably be just the result of either decreased math and writing experience or membership in a clinical group.

The studies of Tranel and colleagues (1987), Voeller (1986), and Weintraub and Mesulam (1983) did not include a control group, either normal or clinical. Instead, subjects were compared to norms on the tests utilized. In contrast, Rourke's studies (Rourke, 1989; Rourke & Finlaysen, 1978; Rourke & Strang, 1978; Strang & Rourke, 1983) are exemplary with respect to control groups: children with specific math problems were compared to children with reading *and* math problems, who were similar in age, FSIQ and level of math achievement. The children with specific math problems were significantly worse than the RD + math problem group on measures of spatial cognition, thus supporting the hypothesized causal relation.

With regard to discriminant measures, it is important that the test battery include a range of nonvisuospatial measures, including measures of executive function. All four of these studies used a variety of neuropsychological measures, both verbal and nonverbal, but none explicitly tested executive functions.

The cognitive results from these four studies are very similar. Performance IQ was depressed relative to Verbal IQ; nonverbal memory was depressed relative to verbal memory; performance on visuoconstructive tasks was depressed relative to performance on auditory-linguistic tasks; and motor and tactile perceptual performance was worse on the left side of the body than on the right. In the Strang and Rourke (1983) study, the children with specific math problems were significantly worse than LD controls with reading *and* math problems on the Halstead Category Test, which measures concept formation abilities. The Category Test is sometimes considered to be an executive function task, but is not specifically sensitive to prefrontal lesions. These results provide converging evidence of relative impairment on a variety of spatial cognitive tasks and support the overall hypothesis that specific deficits in math are caused by underlying visuospatial problems. Problems with handwriting were also found in the Weintraub and Mesulam (1983) and in the Strang and Rourke (1983) samples.

The socioemotional results from these four studies are also similar. In the Weintraub and Mesulam (1983) study, problems with shyness, depression, and social isolation were reported by a substantial majority of these adult subjects. The majority of these patients also had deficits in eye contact, gestures, and prosody. In the Tranel et al. (1987) study, all the patients reported significant problems with shyness, depression, and social isolation, and only 2 of 11 were normal on measures of eye contact, gestures, and prosody, with no one subject being normal in all three areas.

The subjects in these two studies were predominantly adults, and one wonders if similar social deficits would be found in children with the same nonverbal LD. The studies by Voeller (1986) and Rourke and colleagues help to answer this question.

In the Voeller (1986) study of patients from 5 to 13 years of age, formal visual and auditory measures of emotion perception were utilized, as well as clinical assessments of socioemotional functioning. She found that her patients were significantly below normative scores on auditory, but not visual, emotion perception. All but one met clinical criteria for ADHD, suggesting a potentially important comorbid relation between right hemisphere LDs and ADHD. The majority had problems with peer relations, shyness, and prosody.

Strang and Rourke (1985a) compared maternal report of psychopathology on the Personality Inventory for Children (PIC) for the LD groups used in the studies already discussed. The specific math group was significantly elevated on the PIC Psychosis scale and generally elevated on the other scales that load on an internalizing factor— depression, withdrawal, anxiety, and poor social skills. Qualitatively, the children in the specific math group had tangential speech, problems with the understanding as well as use of gestures, and other pragmatic cues.

In summary, available evidence supports both a relation between normal variation in visuospatial skills and normal mathematics skill, as well as between deficient visuospatial skills and specific math problems. We lack appropriate longitudinal data to test whether this relation is causal, and we lack studies using executive function measures as a discriminant measure to test whether the relationship is indeed specific to spatial cognition. Clinical observations upport a similar relation between visuospatial deficits and problems in handwriting, but there is little formal research on this topic.

The connection between deficient visuospatial skills and social deficits is less clear. Rourke (1989) argues that the same underlying right hemisphere neurospychological disorder leads to both the cognitive and social deficits in nonverbal learning disorder. In Rourke's (1989) model, the disruption of right hemisphere functioning is caused by early damage or dysfunction in white matter connections, especially long white matter connections important for intermodal integration, for which the right hemisphere is specialized. In contrast, left hemisphre functional development is hypothesized to be less vulnerable to white matter dysfunction, and so will more likely be spared.

On the other hand, the social deficits found in the studies discussed above could be correlated symptoms that are not related in a causal way to the deficient visuospatial skills. Arguing for this possibility are data that indicate that the processing mechanisms in the right hemisphere that mediate spatial cognition are dissociable from those that mediate social cognition. Developmental insults to the right hemisphere may frequently impair both sets of mechanisms, producing the observed correlation between deficits in each area found in the studies we have just reviewed. In at least two of these studies, subjects were selected in part because they exhibited this pattern of correlated deficits, so we really don't know in an objective way what the extent of this correlation is. In our clinical experience, there are certainly children with specific math and handwriting problems who do not have deficits in social cognition.

Developmental Course

There has been only one small ($n = 8$) adult follow-up study of children with nonverbal learning disabilities (Rourke, Young, Strang, & Russell, 1986). In that study, the outcome was poor in that all of the subjects exhibited continuing emotional and social difficulties and were working in jobs below their educational level. Some had been diagnosed as schizophrenic as adults. These results are consistent with the kind of problems found in the adult patients reported by Tranel et al. (1987) and Weintraub and Mesulam (1983). Rourke (1989) reports that although children with nonverbal LD may present with characteristics of ADHD in the early school years, their clinical symptoms switch to internalizing ones later, including a higher rate of suicidal behavior in adolescence.

Because the subjects in all these studies were ascertained clinically, we really do not know what proportion of children with visuospatial deficits have (and don't have) concomitant social and emotional problems and what proportion of each of these groups has social and emotional problems as adults. We do know that the adult outcome of patients with Turner syndrome, who have visuospatial deficits, is quite normal in many cases, so the same dissociation likely holds in idiopathic cases of nonverbal LDs.

In terms of early development, the only data available are from retrospective case histories. Strang and Rourke (1985a) summarized these data, and reported greater delays in motor than in language milestones, decreased exploratory activity, hypoactivity, echolalia, and other pragmatic deficiencies in language usage, hyperlexia in some cases, poor peer relations, and overdependency on parents. This type of early history is reminiscent of that seen in higher functioning autistic children or Asperger's syndrome. Once again we are faced with the issue of the degree of overlap between nonverbal LDs and Asperger's syndrome and autistic spectrum disorder. Rourke (1989) believes that what he calls nonverbal LD and Asperger's syndrome overlap considerably, whereas he views autism as distinct because of the greater language pathology in most autistic children. Again the data on Turner syndrome (Berch & Bender, 1990; Robinson, Lubs, & Bergson, 1979) is different from the early developmental profile on nonverbal-LD children just presented. These girls do not have motor milestone delays, echolalia or other obvious pragmatic deficiencies, or the kind of social problems exhibited by the nonverbal-LD children.

To conclude, much more needs to be known about the developmental course of children with visuospatial deficits and the degree to which they are at risk for social deficit and poor adult outcome. To answer these questions, prospective studies of unselected samples of children with visuospatial problems are needed.

DIAGNOSIS AND TREATMENT OF RIGHT HEMISPHERE LEARNING DISORDERS

Presenting Symptoms

Children with specific math and handwriting problems tend to come to clinical attention later than children with dyslexia, ADHD, or autism spectrum disorder, because their learning disorder does not disrupt school performance as noticeably in the early school years. As the amount of written output required increases in the middle and later elementary grades, such children are more likely to experience difficulty completing assignments and thus come to clinical attention (Levine, Obkerlaid, & Meltzer, 1981). A very typical referring symptom is that the child is not completing or turning in homework assignments, and that the child has become locked into an oppositional struggle with parents and teacher over written work. So the initial presentation may suggest an emotional or motivational problem.

Other presenting symptoms are difficulty with arithmetic in the presence of normal reading and spelling, as well as more general difficulty with quantitative concepts such as time and money (see Table 6.1).

History

Children with these learning disorders often have a history of poor coordination, especially fine-motor coordination. They may have been late

TABLE 6.1 Right Hemisphere Learning Disorders

Primary	Specific problems in math/handwriting/art
Correlated	Problems in social cognition, attention, conceptual skills
Secondary	Opposition to written work, spelling problems, depression, social withdrawal
Artifactual	Dyslexia

to acquire a neat pincer grasp of a pencil, and may still hold a pencil awkwardly. As preschoolers, they are often reported to have been less interested and less skilled at drawing and puzzles. They may have also been afraid of heights, and less adept on the jungle gym. As school-age children, their eye–hand coordination tends to be weak, they are poor at building things, including models, and have difficulty with art. There may also be a history of difficulty with finding their way in new places.

Behavioral Observations

These are divided into observations pertinent to writing and math respectively. With regard to writing, it is very important both to observe the child's writing and to obtain samples of the child's writing, especially under time pressure. Not all children with specific handwriting problems produce messy written output; given enough time, some of them write neatly. But they all write slowly, and under time pressure, the quality of their writing declines significantly. So one important thing to look for is slow and labored handwriting. Many of these children hold the pencil awkwardly and very tightly, thus exerting too much pressure on the page, and producing heavy, dark, somewhat jagged lines. A third thing to look for is the degree of automaticity in the writing—are the strokes fluid, consistent, and continuous or does the child draw each letter using multiple strokes, as if he or she is seeing it for the first time? Finally, the spatial organization of the letters to each other and to the lines of the page can provide important information. Letters often vary in size and spacing, and are placed at varying heights above the line. The placement of words on the page is also irregular, and the left margins may drift to the right.

　　With respect to arithmetic, there are several pertinent things to look for. Strang and Rourke (1985b) have summarized the kinds of errors made by children with specific math problems and contrasted them with the arithmetic errors made by dyslexic children. Dyslexic children may make mistakes because they reverse numbers or do not know basic math facts and have to rely on finger tallies. However, they rarely attempt problems that they know are too hard for them or make errors that are not even approximately correct. In contrast, children with specific math problems make a number of different kinds of errors that reveal a deficient conceptual understanding of: (a) the problem they are undertaking, (b) the subroutines needed to solve it, and (c) what a reasonable answer would be. For instance, they attempt problems that are too hard, produce wildly incorrect answers, missalign columns of numbers, and make other errors that reveal a deficient sense of place value. They also misuse computational algorithms, such as subtracting the individual digits of the larger from the smaller of two numbers (e.g., given 11 − 7, they produce "66" as an answer). Their handwriting problems may also affect their written calculations in terms of the legibility and organization of the numbers on the page.

Test Results

On the WISC-R, these children very often have a significantly lower (12 points or greater) Performance than Verbal IQ. Within the Performance IQ, especially low scores are likely to be found on Block Design and Object Assembly, the two best measures of spatial reasoning on the WISC-R. Low scores are also found on Coding, presumably because it requires visuomotor skills. Among Verbal subtests, Arithmetic is likely to be low because of the specific math problem.

The basic operational definition of a specific math problem is selectively low performance on the mathematics subtest of an achievement test that also measures reading and spelling (e.g., WRAT-R, PIAT-R, Woodcock-Johnson Psychoeducational Battery). As already discussed in the chapter on dyslexia, the criteria for "selectively low" are somewhat arbitrary and vary across researchers. Strang and Rourke (1985b) required that the WRAT Arithmetic grade score be at last two years below both the WRAT Reading and Spelling scores, whereas Siegel & Ryan (1989) required a WRAT Arithmetic score below the 26th percentile and a WRAT Reading score above the 29th percentile. The problem with the former criterion is that a two-grade discrepancy is not equal statistically across age; the problem with the latter criterion is that it will select some children wih essentially equal performance in math and reading, some of whom will be dyslexic. In our lab, we require that the PIAT or WRAT-R Math score be one standard deviation (SD) below both PIAT Reading Recognition and Spelling. (This procedure is not perfect either, since it fails to take into account regression to the mean).

If a child is selectively low in math, it is important to determine whether this appears to be due to spatial cognitive versus executive function deficits, as the remediation suggestions are different in each case. If the child performs normally on the Wisconsin Card Sorting Test or other executive function measures, but gives evidence of selective spatial impairment on the WISC-R, then a conclusion of a specific math problem due to a spatial cognitive deficit is warranted. A reverse pattern indicates the math problem is due to executive function deficits. Obviously, some children have both problems.

Because we lack a good standardized test of handwriting skill, the diagnosis of specific handwriting problems is based on observations and history.

Treatment

The treatment of social cognitive difficulties is covered in the next chapter. Here we focus on the treatment of handwriting and math problems. The treatment of specific handwriting problems is fairly straightforward. The diagnosis itself has some therapeutic value, because it reframes the problems as nonmotivational and helps diffuse the oppositional struggle that has often developed between the child and adults. The main treatments are for the child to learn to type and to be given additional time to complete written work. The spatial and fine motor skills needed for typing are not as great as those involved in handwriting. Especially with a word processor, the child's output rate will come closer to his or her thinking rate. The large disparity between these two is often what has made the child give up on writing in the first place. If the child's visuospatial and fine motor sklls are especially deficient, occupational therapy should be considered, especially for younger patients.

The treatment of specific math problems is more complicated and depends on whether the main deficit is in spatial reasoning or executive functions. In either case, it is unlikely the child will ever completely overcome his or her math difficulty, and so compensation is an important part of the remediation program.

If the main deficit is in spatial reasoning, the child may very likely need remedial work on place value using concrete, "manipulables," such as Cuisenaire rods. Using graph paper to keep columns aligned in written math may also help. The child should also be taught to estimate an answer in advance and to check his or her answer either with a calculator or by hand.

If the main deficit is in executive functions, the child probably experiences the greatest difficulty on complex word problems and multistep calculations (e.g., long division). Such children can benefit from explicit written, step-by-step "recipes" or algorithms to guide them through multistep problems. In addition, these children especially need 1:1 instruction from a tutor who models metacognitive functions for the child by explicitly going through the steps in a problem, including estimates, goals, subroutines, and check procedures. The tutor is in effect making "internal speech" external so the child can hopefully learn to use this kind of internal speech to regulate his or her own problem-solving performance. Such children can also benefit from experiences that make math problems more concrete. Similar suggestions for remediation are contained in Strang and Rourke (1985b).

In terms of more long-term compensation, tailoring the child's course choices and career goals to avoid his or her weakness in math are important. Geometry, trigonometry, and calculus are likely to be extremely difficult for these children, as are physics and possibly the other sciences. In terms of career choice, careers that depend heavily on visuospatial skills (such as art, architecture, and surveying) or on mathematical skills (engineering and science) should be avoided.

CASE PRESENTATION 5

Jenny is a 16-year-old high school junior whose parents sought an evaluation to clarify the reason for the marked discrepancy between her achievement in verbal as compared with nonverbal areas (PSAT: verbal 94th percentile; nonverbal 19th percentile). She has had persistent trouble in math since early elementary school, and states she hates math. Parents wonder whether she has an emotional problem with math, a math "phobia." Most recently, geometry has been her most problematic subject, which she failed last year. Jenny also complains of difficulty with English grammar, especially diagramming sentences.

Birth and early developmental histories appear normal. Medical history includes no major illnesses, but does include a skull fracture at age 3, as the result of a fall. Jenny was comatose for 3 days, and dehydration was required to control brain swelling. The accident was believed to be without sequelae. Pertinent family history includes dyslexia in her father and unspecified learning disabilities in an uncle.

Academic problems were first noticed when Jenny was in first or second grade. She didn't complete assignments, and written language, handwriting, and number skills were weak. She was evaluated for special educational services in fourth grade because of continuing difficulty in math. This evaluation resulted in extra in-class help. Since junior high school, she has not received any special help in school, but parents have supplied private math tutoring.

Jenny avoided recess in first grade and mother was reluctant to send her to Field Days during elementary school because she did so poorly at sports. Mother reports Jenny had difficulty learning to use a knife and fork, as well as a key to open a door. She could not play well with Legos® and easily became frustrated in playing dominoes and board games. It was hard for her to grasp time and money concepts. In learning to drive, Jenny had difficulty learning how to coordinate the gear shift and the clutch. Jenny's peer relationships have been adequate, and she has been active and successful on the school newspaper. A summary of Jenny's test results is found in Table 6.2.

Discussion

The presenting complaints and history are striking for the marked disparity between verbal and nonverbal skills, and the host of everyday activities involving spatial skills on which this child is deficient. The problem with grammar at first appears like a language problem, until one remembers that diagramming sentences essentially requires a spatial representation of grammatical relations. Most important, of course, are the very clear and persistent problems with math. Handwriting problems are also mentioned. The early head injury is potentially significant as a cause of the learning problems. Unlike the cases of right hemisphere LD reported in the literature, social relations were not problematic in this case.

In the test results, there is a strongly significant disparity between VIQ and PIQ, with a particularly low score on Block Design. The Arithmetic subtest is lower than all the other verbal subtests, consistent with the history of math problems. On the achievement tests, math is likewise the lowest score, but there is no evidence of dyslexia.

On the neuropsychological tests, there was evidence of mild brain dysfunction, which was lateralized to the right hemisphere. This lateralization is mainly supported by left-sided deficits on the sensory and motor tasks. The patient was mildly impaired with her nondominant left hand on the Tapping test and moderately impaired with her left hand on the Grooved Pegboard. There was also definite dysgraphesthesia with the left hand only.

It is important to point out that this patient's higher cognitive deficits are *not* restricted to the domain of spatial cognition. There was also mild impairment on the Category task, which may be secondary to the patient's problems with number concepts. The number of perseverations on the Wisconsin is somewhat elevated, although on closer examination it is seen that the errors mainly came on trials dealing with number as a sorting category. This kind of item analysis can be an important part of the diagnostic process. Moreover, the deficits in spatial cognition are mild and do not appear on every spatial task. Performance on design–copying, visual learning, and LTM, and the Tactual Performance Test were all normal.

TABLE 6.2 Test Summary, Case 5

WISC-R FSIQ = 115

Information	13	Picture Completion	9
Similarities	11	Picture Arrangement	16
Arithmetic	9	Block Design	6
Vocabulary	16	Object Assembly	10
Comprehension	16	Coding	8
Digit Span	17		

Verbal IQ = 124   Performance IQ = 100
Verbal Comprehension = 14.0   Perceptual Organization = 8.0
Freedom from Distractibility = 11.3

	Grade equivalent	Age standard score
PIAT		
Math	8.9	95
Reading recognition	>12.9	113
Reading comprehension	>12.8	121
Spelling	12.4	100
WRAT Spelling	12.0	106
Gray Oral	13.8	—
Woodcock-Johnson Word Attack	12.9	105

Reading Quotient = 1.05

	Raw scores	T scores
Executive functions		
Category Test (errors)	54	31
Wiconsin Card Sorting Test		
Perseverative Responses	20	46
Categories	6	55
Trailmaking Test: Part B (sec)	96 (1 error)	−10
Memory		
Story		
Trial 1	16	53
Delayed Recall	16	57
Figure		
Trial 1	15	49
Delayed Recall	15	57
Tactual Performance Test Location	4	47
Language		
Speech Sound Perception errors	6	43
Aphasia Screening Exam errors	0	—
Spatial Cognition		
Constructional dypraxia score	2	—
Tactual Performance Test		
Right hand (min. for 10 blocks)	4.3	42[a]
Left hand	2.8	55
Both hands	1.5	60
Total	8.6	54

(*continued*)

TABLE 6.2 (*continued*)

Sensory Perceptual (finger dysgnosia, graphesthesia, and suppressions)		
Right hand (total errors)	6.5	—
Left hand (total errors)	11.0	—
Motor		
Tapping (*n*/sec)		
Right	51.8	59
Left	41.0	41
Dynamometer (kg)		
Right	47.0	—
Left	44.0	—
Grooved Pegboard (sec)		
Right	76.0	40
Left	98.0	14

[a]Based on adult norms.

In summary, this patient does have a right hemisphere learning disorder in which both mathematics and handwriting are affected, but social adaptation is unimpaired. Her underlying deficit is in the domain of spatial cognition. In contrast, language and LTM functions are well above average.

CASE PRESENTATION 6

Andrew is a boy of 14½ who is in the seventh grade, receiving special education intervention 30% of his day; one major focus of this intervention is Andrew's deficient pragmatic language skills. The main presenting symptoms were problems in math, handwriting, and adaptive behavior. For instance, Andrew requires more supervision than a normal adolescent, because he tends to "wander"; he is also difficult to take to a restaurant or large department store.

Following an essentially normal pregnancy, Andrew was born 6 weeks premature and weighed 3 lbs. 3 ozs. He remained in the hospital until he was 6 weeks of age. With the exception of his language skills, Andrew's mother reports that his developmental milestones were achieved generally within normal limits. He was slightly slow to develop walking skills. His language skills were quite delayed (e.g., 2 or 3 word phrases at 24–36 months; sentences at 36–48 months). Additionally, his speech was extremely nasal and indistinct. His parents report that there was a problem with the development of his hard palate, though it is unclear exactly what the problem was.

Mother reports that temperamentally Andrew was a very difficult infant and toddler. As an infant he had sleeping and eating difficulties, he did not want to be held, and was difficult to pacify. As a toddler he was constantly into things and always on the go. He was diagnosed as having ADHD at 4 years of age, and placed on Ritalin®. As a preschooler, Andrew's language continued to be slow to develop, and he also demonstrated some unusual behaviors. He showed some resistance to change and difficulties with transitions. Mother recalls that a preschool teacher noted his need for maintaining sameness; on the basis of these and other observations, this teacher questioned whether he was mildly autistic. Mother also recollects that as a young child Andrew would recite commercials by rote. Some unusual play focused around the television antenna was also noted. At present, Andrew shows some unusual repetitions in his speech, such as saying the same sentence several times, in spite of being told that he has been understood. Mild stereotyped movements involving the hands were also noted when Andrew was young.

Andrew currently demonstrates some unusual preoccupations and interests. For example, he may sit and read a catalogue of baseball card prices for an hour or more. He has also read through large sections of a telephone book on several occasions. Social relationships are clearly not age-appropriate with Andrew showing little understanding of normal interpersonal relationships.

During the testing, Andrew presented as a child quite a bit younger than his chronological age. He was small in stature, and his relational style was that of a much younger child. He was cooperative and pleasant, and he put forth very good effort on most tests. His voice had an unusual nasality, and he has articulation difficulties that sometimes make him difficult to understand. Significant pragmatic deficits were also noted.

He responded well to the structured setting, but during unstructured time he was very distractible. For example, after one testing session was completed and as the examiner talked with his mother, he left. He did not return but was observed by another person in the building running in circles on a lower floor of the building. It was not uncommon for Andrew to walk to the secretary's desk and begin picking up things from it. He did not seem to realize that this was inappropriate behavior. This type of behavior did not occur in the structured test setting. It should be noted that early in the day, when his medication was most effective, he was much less distractible than he was later. A summary of Andrew's test results is found in Table 6.3.

TABLE 6.3 Test Summary, Case 6

WISC-R FSIQ = 89

Information	10	Picture Completion	8
Similarities	9	Picture Arrangement	15
Arithmetic	9	Block Design	7
Vocabulary	10	Object Assembly	6
Comprehension	6	Coding	6
Digit Span	8		
Verbal IQ = 92		Performance IQ = 88	
Verbal Comprehension = 8.8		Perceptual Organization = 6.5	
		Freedom from Distractibility = 7.7	

	Grade equivalent	Age standard score
PIAT		
Math	6.7	91
Reading Recognition	8.1	95
Reading Comprehension	11.4	107
Spelling	10.4	105
WRAT-R		
Spelling	10.2	103
Arithmetic	<3.0	49
Gray Oral Reading	11.8	—
Woodcock-Johnson Word Attack	12.9	113
Reading Quotient = 1.20		

	Raw scores	T scores
Executive functions		
Category Test errors	34	46
Wisconsin Card Sorting Test		
Perseverative Responses	15	50
Categories	6	55
Trailmaking Test: Part B (sec)	35 (no errors)	47
Tower of Hanoi (4 ring)	4	30
Matching Families Figures Test (MFFT)		
Errors	3	51
Time	74	75
Memory		
Story		
Trial 1	27	47
Delayed Recall	27	51
Figure		
Trial 1	25	29
Delayed Recall	16	19
Tactual Performance Test Location	5	51
Language		
Speech Sound Perception errors	5	48
Aphasia Screening Exam errors	4	—
Expressive One Word Vocabulary Test	38	51

(*continued*)

TABLE 6.3 (*continued*)

Thurstone Word Fluency Test, Part A		28	—
Part B		14	—
Spatial Cognition			
Constructional dyspraxia score		8	—
Visual Motor Integration Test		11	23
Tactual Performance Test			
Right hand (min for 6 blocks)		1.6	60
Left hand		0.9	66
Both hands		0.5	59
Total		3.0	63
Sensory Perceptual			
Right hand (total errors)		13	—
Left hand (total errors)		15.5	—
Motor Skills			
Tapping (*n*/sec.)			
Right		37.1	35
Left		32.5	31
Dynamometer (kg)			
Right		16.8	31
Left		14.5	29
Grooved Pegboard (sec/drop)			
Right		74(1)	41
Left		98(2)	14
Static Steadiness (sec/hits)			
Right		8.8/60	49/55
Left		21.2/116	37/45

Discussion

Andrew's FSIQ places him at the 24th percentile. Although a significant VIQ–PIQ disparity was not seen, he generally performed better on measures of acquired verbal information than on measures of spatial reasoning (Block Design and Object Assembly). In the verbal area, his only impaired score was on Comprehension, consistent with his history of social and adaptive behavior deficits.

The marked discrepancy between the scores on the PIAT and WRAT math tests reflects the different nature of these tests. The WRAT is a mechanical arithmetic test, whereas the PIAT is given and answered orally and has many items that are definitional and therefore verbal in nature (e.g., "Which of these shapes is a polygon?"). Andrew scored much lower on the WRAT math test. His score was at the floor of the test: the norms for the test do not go down far enough to reflect his true performance on this test.

In contrast, he scored above grade level on all reading and spelling tests. In fact, his performance on these reading and spelling tests was strikingly good, fitting our criteria for hyperlexia. Such a discrepancy between his language-based and math computation skills is suggestive of a right-hemisphere or nonverbal learning disability.

Andrew's performance on the Halstead-Reitan Neuropsychological Test Battery for Older Children suggests he has mild brain dysfunction, which is somewhat lateralized to the right cerebral hemisphere. Andrew's overall performance falls within the mildly impaired range (Average Impairment Rating = 1.50; mildly impaired range = 1.36–2.00). Andrew's performance was below normal expectations on a number of tests that broadly assess his spatial reasoning and visuospatial skills. His performance on the constructional dyspraxia test fell in the moderately impaired range. Further, on the Beery Test of Visual–Motor Integration, another design copying task, he obtained an age equivalent of 6.0 years, which falls at the 1st percentile. In contrast, Andrew scored above average on a test of psychomotor problem-solving [Tactual Performance Test (TPT)]. His memory for the shapes and their locations on this task (TPT, memory; TPT, location) was normal.

In the domain of executive functions, most of his scores were normal, including his scores on the Category, Wisconsin, and Trail-making tests. However, he was moderately impaired on the Tower of Hanoi planning task, and unusually slow on a test of vigilance (MFFT), indicating less efficient attentional processes. He was also mildly impaired on another test of sustained attention (Seashore Rhythm Test). These deficits in some areas of executive function are consistent with the history of rigidity and poor adaptability in his behavior. As we will see in the next chapter, similar but more extreme symptoms and underlying executive function deficits are found in both Asperger's syndrome and high functioning autistics, whom this child resembles in other ways.

Andrew's performance on a number of motor tasks was also significantly below normal expectations with relatively poorer performance with his nondominant left hand. His performance on a test of pure motor speed (Tapping) was mildly impaired bilaterally. His grip strength (Dynamometer) was moderately impaired with both hands. On a test of fine motor coordination (Grooved Pegboard), he was within normal limits with his right hand but severely impaired with his left hand. In addition, his performance was moderately impaired on several tests requiring interpretation of complex tactile stimuli (Finger Agnosia; Finger-tip Number Writing). Finally, he showed some tendency to suppress tactile stimuli to his left side (Reitan-Klove Sensory Perceptual Exam).

On a test of verbal and nonverbal learning and memory (Wechsler Memory Scale) Andrew learned and retained the verbal information at a normal rate. However, he was impaired at learning and remembering the nonverbal portion of the test.

In contrast to these areas of difficulty, Andrew's performance was within normal limits on a number of tests of language skills. On a test requiring discrimination among verbal stimuli (Speech Sounds Perception Test) Andrew scored in the average range. Basic expressive and receptive language skills were within normal limits on the Reitan-Indiana Aphasia exam and performance was normal on a test of naming (Expressive One Word Picture Vocabulary Test).

Present behavior and history of behavior with mild autistic features suggest that Andrew has a mild pervasive developmental disorder best described as Asperger's syndrome (see Chapter 7). This is a disorder characterized by impairments in social interactions with a failure to understand many rules governing social behavior. Typically deficits in emotion perception or expression, and poor nonverbal communication skills are seen. Generally, there are also some oddities in speech, including pedantic content and sometimes stereotyped repetitions. Unusual and constricted intellectual interests or preoccupations that depend on rote memory are typically evidenced. Individuals with Asperger's syndrome are often reported to have cognitive ability profiles like those of children with "right hemisphere learning disability." This is a pattern that is clearly shown in Andrew's test results.

We also found evidence of emotion perception deficits in Andrew similar to those seen in children with right hemisphere LDs. Andrew was given a projective story-telling task in which he had difficulty determining the emotions of the characters and the nature of the social interaction. He tended to focus on the concrete, readily observable aspects of the pictures (e.g., what the people were wearing) rather than on the interaction between the people in the pictures. Andrew's performance was also below normal on a test requiring him to infer a person's emotional state from a picture or taped voice.

It is interesting to compare Cases 5 and 6. Both have academic difficulties in math and handwriting, and both have right hemisphere lateralizing patterns on motor and sensory tasks. So at this level of analysis, both have a similar right hemisphere LD. However, Case 6 has additional deficits in nonverbal memory, much worse spatial constuctional deficits on drawing tasks, executive function deficits in planning and sustained attention, and, most importantly, deficits in social cognition. Interestingly, the onset is clearly earlier in Case 6 than Case 5, where the symptoms appear secondary to a head injury at age 3. Although the etiology in Case 6 is unknown, there was very likely a perinatal insult. In addition, the father has a history of some social peculiarity. So differences in the nature and developmental timing of the etiologies may help account for the differences in symptoms and underlying deficits.

CHAPTER 7

Autism Spectrum Disorder

In the previous chapter, we began to consider learning disorders that may affect social cognition in a primary way. Several valid subtypes of this broad family of disorders may exist. For instance, most researchers regard Asperger's syndrome as part of autism spectrum disorder (Schopler, 1985; Volkmar, Paul, & Cohen, 1985; Wing, 1986), yet the IQ profiles of many reported cases of Asperger's syndrome are unlike those for autism. In autism, verbal IQ is relatively depressed, whereas the opposite is often true in Asperger's syndrome. In this respect, Asperger's syndrome is more like the nonverbal learning disorders discussed in Chapter 6. Because early social cognition is itself not a unitary domain, it would not be surprising to find subtypes in its pathology, with each subtype reflecting a primary deficit in a different aspect of early social cognition.

The following section presents a scientific description of both autism and Asperger's syndrome, without prejudging the issue of whether they are separate disorders or represent different degrees of severity on the same continuum.

RESEARCH REVIEW

Basic Defining Characteristics

Both autism and Asperger's syndrome are rare developmental disorders in which the main symptom is a severe deficit in social contact that emerges early in life and persists into adulthood. Whereas at least two-thirds of autistic samples are mentally retarded, most reported cases of Asperger's syndrome have nonretarded IQs. Prevalence estimates for autism are in the range of two to five per 10,000 with a M/F sex ratio of approximately 3 : 1 (Smalley, Asarnow, & Spence, 1988). This sex difference appears to be reliable in autism and may be informative about etiological mechanisms. Two studies (Konstantareas, Homatidis, & Busch, 1989; Tsai, Stewart, & August, 1981) have found a greater degree of cognitive and social impairment in autistic females, and the latter study found a higher rate of affected relatives in the families of female probands. These findings would be consistent with a multifactorial threshold model with a more extreme threshold for females.

There have been two epidemiological studies of Asperger's syndrome. Wing (1981) reports a prevalence of 1.7 per 10,000 based on a study of all children with mental and physical handicaps in one area of London, but stresses this figure is an underestimate, because it excludes mild cases of Asperger's that had not come to clinical attention. A more recent study (Gillberg & Gillberg, 1989) reported an estimated prevalence of 10–26/10,000 among nonretarded children. Estimates of the male : female sex ratio in Asperger's in these two studies range from about 4 : 1 to 9 : 1.

Etiologies

Considerably more is known about etiology in autism than in Asperger's syndrome. Both Wing (1981) and Gillberg, Steffenbury, and Jakobson (1987) report some evidence for familiality of Asperger personality traits. Gillberg (1985) described one case of Asperger's syndrome with cyclical depressive features in which there was a strong family history for manic–depressive illness. Evidence for an environmental cause is provided by the fact that half of Wing's cases had significant perinatal complications that may have caused acquired brain insults. Rourke's (1989) list of acquired causes of nonverbal LD (see Chapter 6) is also relevant here.

Obviously, much more research is needed on the etiology of Asperger's syndrome. Such research would be very helpful in clarifying the issue of syndrome validity. For instance, a comparison of the rates of Asperger's personality traits and bipolar illness in the relatives of Asperger's versus autistic probands would be interesting. In fact, a study of Asperger's and bipolar illness in autistic families has been reported recently. DeLong and Dwyer (1988) found that first and second degree relatives of autistic probands had rates of 4.2%

for bipolar illness and 2.0% for Asperger's syndrome, both of which are considerably higher than population rates. The association with Asperger's syndrome was much greater in the relatives of nonretarded autistic probands, whereas the rates of bipolar illness did not differ significantly for retarded versus nonretarded probands, 79% of which were also diagnosable as having Asperger's. These results argue that nonretarded autism and Asperger's are largely equivalent and familial.

The genetics of autism were recently reviewed in three excellent articles (Folstein & Rutter, 1988; Rutter, et al., 1990; Smalley, Asarnow, & Spence, 1988); this section summarizes information contained in these articles. Briefly, existing evidence supports the conclusion that autism is familial, heritable, and genetically heterogeneous. Among the possible genetic subtypes are multifactorial inheritance, autosomal recessive inheritance, X-linked inheritance, and nonfamilial chromosomal anomalies. Among known genetic disorders, autism is specifically associated with fragile X syndrome, untreated phenylketonuria, and possibly two neurocutaneous disorders: tuberous sclerosis and neurofibromatosis (Folstein & Rutter, 1988).

To date there has been one segregation analysis of autism (Spence, et al., 1985). The segregation analysis studied 46 multiplex families and found support for autosomal recessive transmission. However, the preponderance of autistic males in this and other samples cannot be explained by this mode of transmission, since an autosomal gene by itself should affect both sexes equally. Other limitations of this segregation analysis include the assumption of genetic homogeneity, restriction of the phenotype to autism per se (even though there is evidence for familiality of a broader phenotype—see below), and failure to adjust for "stoppage rules," the marked tendency of parents to stop having children after the birth of an autistic child (see Rutter et al., 1990 for a discussion of this segregation analysis).

The linkage analysis of a subset of these same families did not find significant evidence of linkage with any of the 30 markers tested. There was a suggestion of genetic heterogeneity such that families with only affected males versus families with at least one affected female differed in their pattern of linkage results, with the latter group exhibiting a nonsignificant trend toward linkage with the blood-type markers (ABO) on chromosome 9. A separate family study found low plasma dopamine beta hydroxylase (DBH) in some but not all autistic families. Since the gene for DBH is linked to the ABO blood group, Smalley et al. (1988) conclude that further investigation of this region of chromosome 9 in autism is indicated.

In the following section we will focus on attempts to understand what behavioral phenotype is genetically transmitted in autism, as a better understanding of the phenotype will aid future linkage studies.

Both genetic and environmental factors have been implicated in the etiology of autism, and it appears possible that a genotype–environment additive or interactive effect may be involved in the etiology of autism. Although gene–environment interaction effects appear to be rare for normal traits (Plomin, 1986), they may be important for some forms of severe psychopathology. The basic idea of a gene–environment interaction effect is that what is transmitted genetically is a diathesis, but that an additional environmental insult greatly increases the likelihood of the disorder over what would be found for either risk factor taken separately (or additively). A similar situation may be seen in the etiology of several psychiatric disorders, including schizophrenia (Meehl, 1973; Siegel, Waldo, Mizner, Adler, & Freedman, 1984). Such interaction effects would complicate efforts to understand the genetics of these disorders, as the optimal phenotype for behavior genetic studies would be broader than the diagnosis itself. We will use this idea of a genotype–environment effect to organize what is known about a possible genetic autistic diathesis and the environmental risk events that may compound it.

Minimum requirements for an autistic diathesis are that autism itself be familial and heritable. In addition, it must be shown that autism is cofamilial and coheritable with cognitive and/or social abnormalities that might reasonably constitute an autistic diathesis. Smalley et al. (1988) recently reviewed the evidence for familiality of autism and found the rate in siblings to be 2.9%, which is 50–100 times the prevalence rate in the general population, indicating clear familiality. In two new family studies, Rutter et al. (1990) found a very similar rate of 3% in siblings. Adoption studies of autism are virtually impossible, so only twin studies have been used to address the issue of heritability. Unfortunately, biases of ascertainment have contaminated the results of most twin studies of autism (Pauls, 1987), in that both MZ pairs and concordant MZ pairs were overrepresented, and opposite sex pairs were included. These methodological problems were avoided by Folstein and Rutter (1977), who studied 21 twin pairs with at least one autistic member in each pair. They found a concordance rate of 36% in the MZ pairs, but 0% in the DZ pairs, indicating heritability for autism. Moreover, when they examined the relative concordance rates for language or cognitive impairment (a possible autistic diathesis), they found it was 82% in MZ pairs but only 10% in DZ pairs. They also found a higher rate of perinatal problems in autistic probands in MZ pairs discordant for autism but concordant for cognitive or language disorder. This latter result suggests that the autistic diathesis is a genetically mediated cognitive/language disorder, which when combined with an early environmental insult, produces autism.

However, other results argue against the autistic diathesis being only in the cognitive/language domain and instead suggest it is also or only in the social domain. First, a follow-up of the Folstein and Rutter (1977) twin sample has found that the nonautistic MZ co-twins now have definite social disabilities as adults, and a later replication study also found social disabilities in nonautistic MZ co-twins (Rutter et al., 1990). Second, Freeman et al. (1989) recently reported psychometric testing results on a large ($n = 175$) sample of first-degree relatives of an epidemiologic sample of 62 autistic probands. The rate of cognitive and academic problems in these relatives was very similar to population expectations, arguing against familiality of cognitive/language problems in autistic families. Familiality for autism was replicated in this sample; approximately five percent of the siblings were autistic. Third, Smalley & Asarnow (1990) found evidence for subtle anomalies in the processing of emotional faces in the siblings of nonretarded autistic probands. Similarly, Wolff, Narayan and Moyes (1988) found a higher rate of mild schizoid personality traits in the parents of autistic children (especially fathers), relative to parents of children with other handicaps, who were matched to the autistic children on sex, age, IQ, and father's occupation. Finally, a large family genetic study of 78 autistic and 22 Down syndrome probands found substantially higher rates of both cognitive (mainly specific speech and language disorders) and social abnormalities in the siblings of autistic probands, most of whom had normal intelligence (Rutter et al., 1990).

Although some would argue that the apparent familiality of cognitive/language problems in autistic families, such as those studied by Folstein & Rutter (1977), is produced by genetic influences on mental retardation rather than on autism per se (Baird & August, 1985), the last set of results suggests that the diathesis involves both specific cognitive/language problems and social abnormalities.

In summary, it appears clear that autism is familial and heritable, and that the diathesis includes social abnormalities, but much more work is needed on precisely what behavioral deficits are genetically transmitted in autism. As we will see, recent studies of the neuropsychological phenotype in autism have provided promising candidates for this diathesis, which now need to be evaluated in studies of the relatives of autistic probands.

Brain Mechanisms

The neurological basis of autism has been and remains puzzling, partly because we lack good analogies from classic neuropsychological studies of adults with acquired lesions. Such analogies have made the search easier for brain mechanisms in dyslexia and other developmental language disorders. Moreover, confusion over what is the core behavioral deficit in autism has contributed to confusion in attempts to identify its neurological basis. Different brain regions need to be considered depending on whether the core deficit is in language, social cognition, attention, arousal level or executive functions. So the search for brain mechanisms in autism has not been driven by theoretical considerations and has been less constrained than attempts to understand brain mechanisms in the other learning disorders considered thus far. Neurological theories of autism have variously focused on the brainstem, the cerebellum, the limbic system, the thalamus, the left hemisphere, and the frontal lobes. We will argue in the next section that current evidence best supports the view that the core behavioral deficit is in early social cognition, although there is recent evidence for core deficits in executive function, or perhaps a combination of social cognitive and executive function deficits. If this is true, dysfunction in the limbic system and certain portions of the frontal lobes might provide an explanation. There is some research support for anomalies in these brain regions in autism, but there is also evidence for other anomalies, including those in the cerebellum. Because there are no group studies of brain mechanisms in Asperger's, the following review is restricted to autism.

Of the many neurological abnormalities reported in autistic populations, only a few are fairly consistent across studies. One of the more consistent findings is lateral ventricular enlargement, which has been found using pneumoencephalography (Aarkrog, 1968; Hauser, DeLong & Rosman, 1975); CT scans (Herjanic, Campbell, & Reich, 1982; Damasio, Maurer, Damasio, & Chui, 1980); and MRI scans (Gaffney, Kuperman, Tsai, & Minchin, 1989). These findings of ventricular enlargement suggest developmental atrophy in adjacent limbic and associated frontal structures. However, ventricular enlargement is not found in all studies or all autistic subjects (Creasey, Rumsey, & Schwartz, 1986; Harcherik et al., 1985). Moreover, ventricular enlargement is not specific to autism, as it is found in other psychiatric disorders, such as schizophrenia.

Another fairly consistent finding is atrophy of the cerebellum, especially the vermis (Courchesne, Yeung-Courchense, Press, Hesselink, & Jernigan, 1988; Ritvo et al. 1986). Although these cerebellar lesions could be primary and causal in autism, they could also be correlates of the primary cause, because parts of the limbic system, such as the hippocampus, undergo late neurogenesis at the same time as the cerebellum. Neuronal migration is still occurring postnatally in both structures, unlike the rest of the brain, and thus both structures would be similarly vulnerable to a late-acting embryonic insult, whether genetic or environmental (or both). In two careful autopsy studies of autistic individuals, structural anomalies were found in both limbic and cerebellar areas (Bauman & Kemper, 1985).

There has been one recent PET scan study of autism (Horwitz, Rumsey, Grady, & Rapoport, 1988). These investigators found significantly lower correlations in autistics versus controls between frontal and parietal regions, as well as between certain subcortical structures (thalamus, caudate nucleus, and lenticular nucleus) and frontal and parietal regions. Correlated brain activity among brain centers such as these can be thought of as reflecting the integrated function of a distributed processing system; hence, lower correlations would indicate less integrated function. The key question is: *which* function is less integrated? Horwitz et al. (1988) interpreted their results as indicating dysfunction in a distributed system that subserves directed attention; because of the complexity of frontal lobe functions, other interpretations are possible.

Neuropsychological Phenotype

Over the last 20 years there has been considerable progress in defining the core behavioral deficit in autism. When autistic individuals are compared to controls similar in mental age, only a few behavioral deficits are found across studies. These include deficits in imitation, emotion perception, intersubjectivity (or theory of mind), pragmatics, and symbolic play (Rogers & Pennington, in press). Other candidates for the primary deficit have been ruled out, including deficits in basic language processes, intermodal integration, spatial reasoning, and some social processes, including self- and other-recognition. Thus, most remaining candidates for the primary deficit in autism fall into the domain of early social cognition. However, another related possibility is that the primary deficit is in frontally mediated, executive function skills and that this deficit undermines both social and nonsocial adaptation. Rumsey (Rumsey, 1985; Rumsey & Hamberger, 1988) found deficits in high-functioning autistic men on the Wisconsin Card Sorting Test, but no differences relative to controls in language, memory, spatial, or motor skills. The following text discusses our recent study in which executive function and social cognition were examined in the same high-functioning autistic population.

Other current, competing neuropsychological theories of the primary deficit in autism include a deficit in attention/arousal modification (Dawson & Lewy, 1989a; 1989b) or a deficit in long-term, episodic memory (Bachevalier, in press-a; Boucher & Lewis, 1989). We will not attempt an exhaustive review of these theories, but the reader is alerted to the fact that there are possible alternatives to the theoretical view presented below. Because autism is such a profound and puzzling disorder, which disrupts basic aspects of personhood, it would not be surprising either for there to be multiple primary deficits or for the primary deficit to cut across the grain of our current taxonomy of neuropsychological functions in unexpected ways. Our current concepts about brain functions could be misleading about underlying mechanisms (Churchland, 1988); perhaps we need a different conceptualization to understand disorders like autism or schizophrenia.

With these caveats in mind, we will review in more detail the evidence for a primary social cognitive deficit in autism. Because formal studies of social cognition are just beginning to be completed in Asperger's syndrome, our comments on the comparability of deficits in the two disorders will be limited. Pragmatic deficits are noteworthy in Asperger's, and their stilted, pedantic speech could be consistent with a deficit in theory of mind, although it could arise in other ways.

Interestingly, theorizing about the nature of the primary behavioral deficit in autism has recently come full circle. Kanner (1943 p. 42), in the original description of the autistic syndrome, suggested the possibility that autistic children were born "with an innate inability to form the usual, biologically provided affective contact with people." But he also suggested that some of this "disturbance of affective contact" might be due to inadequate social stimulation from parents. Over the next two decades this psychogenic hypothesis prevailed in psychoanalytic accounts of autism (e.g., Mahler, 1952).

Then, as evidence for an organic etiology of autism accumulated, researchers concerned with the primary behavioral deficit shifted their focus to various possible cognitive deficits, neglecting Kanner's original insight that the disorder might represent a primary social deficit of constitutional origin. Various possible primary cognitive deficits were investigated, including deficits in arousal, language, symbolic thought, memory and cross-modal processing. However, when autistic children were compared to nonautistic retarded children similar in mental age, few reliable differences were found in these various cognitive processes. Even when reliable differences are found, there are other reasons why the apparent deficit in these areas is unlikely to be primary (Fein, Pennington, Markowitz, Braverman, & Waterhouse, 1986). Specifically, most of these cognitive processes develop after the onset of autistic symptoms, are theoretically inadequate to explain autistic aloofness, cannot be found in all autistic children, and may be the very cognitive abilities that depend most heavily on normal social functioning. Other reasons for regarding the social symptoms as primary in autism include: (a) the dissociability of social and cognitive impairments both within and across developmentally disabled populations, (b) the special difficulty autistic children have with social stimuli, and (c) the combination of the rarity of social relatedness deficits in even severely damaged babies and its resistance to change in autism.

Research published subsequent to our review has refined our understanding of which social processes are impaired and intact in autism. We have reviewed this work in later papers (Ozonoff, Pennington & Rogers, 1990; Rogers & Pennington, in press) and will summarize it here. Somewhat surprisingly, some early social cognitive processes have proved to be *not* specifically impaired in autism compared to mental age controls. These include attachment behaviors, self-recognition, person recognition, and differential social responsivity. Other early social cognitive processes are specifically impaired and these include imitation, emotion perception, joint attention, theory of mind, pragmatics, and symbolic play. At a very general level, each of these impaired processes requires representation of another person's underlying mental state (motor intentions, feelings, attentional focus, belief, and knowledge), although the complexity of that mental state obviously varies across these different processes, which also vary in their time of onset in normal development. Following Stern (1985), we can construe each of these early social cognitive processes as aspects of developing intersubjectivity and thus recast the primary deficit in autism as an underlying deficit in intersubjectivity, which will manifest itself as failures on these different social tasks at different ages. Autistic children have been described as "behaviorists," whereas normal children are "mentalists," even from a fairly early age (Baron-Cohen, 1989; Bartsch & Wellman, 1989). That is, autistic children's understanding of behavior is based on observable consequences and instrumental contingencies; therefore, we would expect that social behaviors that can be mediated by such an understanding would be relatively unimpaired in autism. In contrast, social behaviors that require an understanding of mental states are impaired.

The intriguing discovery that autistic children are specifically impaired in theory of mind was made by a group of British researchers (Baron-Cohen, Leslie & Frith, 1985; 1986). They have since replicated this result with different tasks and different autistic samples (Baron-Cohen, 1989; Perner, Frith, Leslie, & Leekam, 1989). Perhaps the most convincing demonstration of this deficit involves the use of a false belief task. Children were shown a box of a well-known candy, "Smarties" (essentially equivalent to "M&Ms"), and were asked "What's in here?" All subjects answered "Smarties" or "sweets." They were then shown (and told) that in fact the box contained a pencil. After the pencil was put back in the box, they were asked to predict what the next subject would say was in the box, as well as to say what was really in the box. Similar to previous results on other theory of mind tasks, about 80% of the autistic children failed the prediction task, whereas over 80% of the younger language-impaired children (with somewhat *lower* verbal mental ages than the autistic children) passed it. In other words, the autistic children were unable to correctly predict another's false belief that was different from their own belief; from this behavior it was inferred that the autistic children lacked a theory of other minds. Normal young children master this false belief task at around age 4 (or even earlier, given different experimental conditions), whereas the mean age of the autistic children in this study was around 15 (Perner et al., 1989). At this point, a deficit in theory of mind appears to be specific and primary in autism and is a deficit that fairly readily explains many other symptoms of the disorder.

There is still theoretical disagreement, however, about whether this deficit is social or cognitive in nature and how it relates to the other deficits in imitation, emotion perception, and symbolic play. Three competing theories have been proposed, a metarepresentation theory (Leslie, 1987), an intersubjectivity theory (Rogers & Pennington, in press) and an affective theory (Hobson, 1989).

Leslie's (1987) metarepresentation theory ties the development of both theory of mind and symbolic play to a hypothesized milestone in the second year of life, the development of metarepresentation, the ability to "decouple" primary, veridical representations from their objective referents so they can be used in pretense. This theory nicely accounts for the theory of mind and symbolic play deficits in autism, but it does not account for the imitation and emotion perception deficits except by claiming these are characteristics of minor subtypes of autism. Joint attention deficits in autism also present some difficulty for this theory, because joint attention emerges in normal development well before the appearance of metarepresentation or theory of other minds (Mundy & Sigman, 1989). This theory can be modified by viewing the joint attention deficits as the earliest precursors of the theory of mind deficit, but then the primacy of the metarepresentation deficit is threatened.

The metarepresentational theory is also problematic, because it posits a discontinuity in the development of intersubjectivity. According to this theory, normal infants only have primary representations and thus should be as deficient as autistics in dealing with mental phenomena. However, research indicates a fairly continuous development of intersubjectivity in the first year of life (Stern, 1985); intersubjectivity is likely a precursor to theory of mind, although not everyone agrees with this view. Moreover, the metarepresentational theory also has trouble explaining the onset of autism in the first year of life, which occurs in a substantial minority of cases, and which is *before* the onset of metarepresentation.

To address these problems in the metarepresentational account, we formulated an intersubjectivity theory (Rogers & Pennington, in press). In this theory, the development of theory of mind is continuous and its precursors are observable very early in the first year of life in the infant's capacity for imitation. Our theory is based on Stern's theory of the development of intersubjectivity, which traces a continuous line of development from imitation, emotion peception, and joint attention in the first year of life to theory of mind and pragmatics in the second and later years of life. This theory accounts for all of the social deficits in autism and their secondary consequences (e.g., deficits in symbolic play).

The third theory, that of Hobson (1989), regards the deficits in emotion perception or affective contact as primary. This theory has been criticized (Baron-Cohen, 1988) for failing to account for the deficits in symbolic play and theory of mind.

Fortunately, these competing theories are testable, because they make specific predictions about the associations and dissociations that should occur among imitation, emotion perception, joint attention, theory of mind, symbolic play, and pragmatics in both normal and autistic development. Longitudinal and cross-sectional studies of these early skills in both autistic and normal children will help sort among theories. As previously mentioned, it is also important to study the relation between social cognitive and executive function deficits in autism.

We recently completed a study of executive functions and social cognition in high functioning autistics, who were compared to controls similar on verbal IQ, performance IQ, age, sex, and race (Ozonoff, Pennington, & Rogers, in press). As expected, the autistics were significantly worse on measures of social cognition, including measures of theory of mind and emotion perception. What was surprising was that the autistic group was even more consistently impaired on a cognitive measure of executive function, the Tower of Hanoi planning task, in that this task alone better discriminated autistics from controls than the other tasks. We also found the autistic sample to be impaired relative to controls on a second executive function task, the Wisconsin Card Sorting Task, which replicates the results of other studies of high functioning autistics that found deficits on this task. Together, these results suggest that either: (a) there may be two primary deficits in autism, one in theory of mind and the other in executive function, or (b) the executive function deficits are primary and the theory of mind deficits are secondary, or (c) both deficits derive from some more basic deficiency in prefrontal functions, for which we currently lack a satisfactory formulation in terms of cognitive processes.

Interestingly, half of this high functioning autistic sample also met diagnostic criteria for Asperger's syndrome. When we compared the deficits in these two subgroups, we found that both had clear deficits in executive functions, but only the autistic group had deficits on theory of mind tasks. The Asperger's group, in contrast, performed similarly to the controls on theory of mind tasks, but were deficient on an emotion perception task (Ozonoff, Rogers, & Pennington, in press). These results provide external validation of the distinction between high functioning autism and Asperger's syndrome.

To summarize, current evidence supports the view that the primary underlying behavioral deficit in autism is in the domain of early social cognition and more specifically in the area of intersubjectivity or theory of mind—the understanding that people have mental states and that communication requires bringing mental states into coordination. However, recent results indicate a possibly related primary deficit in executive functions. Moreover, deficits in theory of mind do not appear to be primary in Asperger's syndrome, whereas executive function deficits do. Thus, across both autism and Asperger's syndrome, executive function deficits appear to be more central.

This behavioral work provides the beginnings of a more precise definition of the behavioral phenotype, which should be helpful in both genetic and neurological investigations of autism. As we said earlier, recent evidence suggests that the genetically transmitted behavioral phenotype in autism is an impairment in social cognition, or both social cognition and specific cognitive/language skills, but behavior genetic studies of autistic families have so far not studied measures of theory of mind (or executive functions).

In terms of brain mechanisms, we know very little about the neurological basis of intersubjectivity or theory of mind, although it is known that limbic and orbital–frontal structures play a special role in social behavior. Price, Daffner, Stowe, and Mesulam (1990) recently reported on two patients with bifrontal lesions acquired early in life. The lesions included paralimbic and heteromodal portions of the frontal lobes, as well as underlying white matter and possibly the basal ganglia. These patients had deficits on role-taking tasks that require theory of mind, as well as deficits in moral reasoning and formal operations. They were not autistic, however. These authors speculate that the frontal lobes may be uniquely important in these kinds of social and cognitive behaviors. If correct, this view would provide support for viewing both theory of mind and executive function deficits as manifestations of prefrontal dysfunction. Moreover, at a more abstract or deeper level of cognitive analysis, both theory of mind and some executive functions may involve similar neural computations, which as far as the brain is concerned are not specifically cognitive or social.

Developmental Course

In most cases both autism and Asperger's syndrome are lifelong disorders, and the adult prognosis is usually poor. In Asperger's syndrome, there appears to be a significant risk for depression and suicidal behavior in adolescence and adulthood (Wing, 1981). Again, much more is known about the developmental course of autism, on which we will focus here.

As noted earlier, the onset of autism can be at birth and usually occurs within the first 3 years of life. Early symptoms are avoidance of eye contact, motor stereotypies, peculiarities of speech (such as echolalia and pronominal reversals), loss of speech, and greatly diminished social interest. Some of these classic autistic symptoms (such as avoidance of eye contact) change with age, which can be confusing for clinicians who may exclaim that the child can't be autistic because he or she made eye contact (or didn't have stereotypies, pronominal reversal, etc.). Instead, what persists across autistic development are the problems with social understanding and pragmatics, which may be more subtle in older, higher-functioning autistic children.

In adolescence, a small number of autistic individuals show marked improvement, whereas a substantial minority (10%–35%) regress significantly in behavior. About 20%–30% develop seizures in adolescence, with seizure risk being inversely correlated with IQ (Paul, 1987). These late-onset seizures are distinctive to autism, since seizures in other developmentally disabled groups usually have an earlier onset.

In terms of adult outcome, a large majority need sheltered living and work situations, since two-thirds to three-fourths of autistic individuals are mentally retarded. About half of autistic adults were found to be in residential care on follow-up, and about two-thirds were unable to live independently, with only about 15%–20% gainfully employed (Paul, 1987). Both IQ and useful speech before age 5 have been found to predict later outcome.

Only recently has adult outcome been studied in high-functioning nonretarded autistic individuals (e.g., Rumsey, Rapoport, & Sceery, 1985; Szatmari, Bartolucci, Bremner, Bond, & Rich, 1989). Rumsey et al. reported on 10 men who represented the upper 5%–15% of the autistic population in terms of level of functioning. All but one completed high school, and two had completed some years of junior college. Three lived in an apartment with some supervision, the rest lived with their parents. Four were employed independently, one was still a junior-college student, and the rest were either unemployed or in sheltered employment. Although this group was generally normal in intelligence, academic achievement, and in most areas of neuropsychological functioning, they continued to have definite social and behavioral abnormalities. As mentioned previously, they were impaired on executive function task, the Wisconsin Card Sorting Test.

In the Szatmari et al. study, 4 of 16 (25%) nonretarded autistic individuals had a very good outcome on follow-up and might be considered recovered. In this group, all had a university degree, and lived and worked independently. Most interestingly, one was married and the other three were dating regularly. The remaining 12 subjects had much less optimal educational, vocational, and social outcomes. Performance on the WAIS-R and Wisconsin Card Sorting Test were highly correlated with outcome ($r = .60$ and $.68$ respectively).

In summary, in a small minority of autistic individuals (roughly 5%) a good adult outcome appears possible (although even in these cases, social oddities remain), whereas the large majority have persisting handicaps that affect employment, independent living, and social relations.

DIAGNOSIS AND TREATMENT OF AUTISM SPECTRUM DISORDERS

Currently, the diagnosis of autism and Asperger's syndrome is based primarily on symptoms and history. To date a definitive neuropsychological test profile for either disorder does not exist, in part because typical neuropsychological test batteries do not evaluate social cognition. There are cognitive test profiles that would be consistent with either disorder, however, and cognitive testing is important to identify strengths and weaknesses in children whose everyday performance may present a confusing picture of their underlying abilities.

Presenting Symptoms

These children are often referred for failures to meet language and cognitive milestones in the preschool years. A loss of speech or other developmental attainments is particularly telling, though only true in a minority of cases. In addition, other important symptoms may be mentioned. These include social aloofness or social peculiarity; motor rituals, such as rocking, spinning, hand-flapping; unusual responses to sensory stimuli, including decreased response to pain; nonsocial attachments (such as to pieces of string or orange peels) and unusual interests (such as in timetables, calendars, meteorology, and astronomy); and preserved or enhanced areas of function, such as precocious reading or excellent rote memory.

History

As discussed in the previous section on developmental course, these disorders typically begin in early life. Onset before 30 months was required for the diagnosis in DSM-III, but recent studies have questioned the usefulness of this cutoff, since children with later onset can have very similar symptoms. Nonetheless, it would be very unusual for symptoms in autism to not be noticed before school age (Szatmari, Bartolucci, & Bremner, in press).

Rimland (1971) developed a history questionnaire for parents that is of some value in discriminating autism from other severe developmental disorders, including mental retardation, aphasia, and childhood schizophrenia. This questionnaire includes sections on motor, language, and social development, as well as on appearance, physical disorders, and responsivity.

Behavioral Observations

Evaluating a child with autism spectrum disorder places a heavier than usual burden on the examiner, because the very nature of the disorder can significantly disrupt the relationship with the examiner. It may be very difficult to complete some procedures; thus, behavioral observations will play a greater role in the diagnostic formulation. These are usually abundant and clinically rich.

The examiner should look for any of the unusual behaviors discussed previously. The examiner should also bear in mind that children with autistic spectrum disorders are poor at adapting to new situations, and so the examining situation itself is likely to be particularly stressful and elicit unusual behaviors. We have seen autistic children who read everything in sight as a way of coping with this anxiety, as well as children whose reactions are even more rigid and ritualized in this new situation.

There are several behavioral checklists based on clinician observations of the patient that can be quite useful in the diagnosis of these children. One is the Childhood Autism Rating Scale (CARS), developed by Schopler and colleagues (Schopler, Reichler, DeVellis, & Day, 1980). Such checklists provide a standardized way of assessing behavior relevant to the diagnosis of autism spectrum disorder and are thus a useful adjunct to diagnosis. However, such scales do not cover some of the low probability, but pathognomic, behaviors that might emerge in the clinical situation. For instance, a child may bring a "pet rock" to the session, repetitively sniff pencil shavings or magic markers, or ask if the test manual is asking him questions. These rare, but highly deviant, behaviors provide a great deal of diagnostic information. An overview of symptoms seen in Autistic Spectrum Disorder is found in Table 7.1.

Test Results

In studies of performance on the WISC-R, reviewed by Sigman, Ungerer, Mundy, and Sherman (1987), it has been found that autistic children generally perform worse on the Verbal than the Performance scale. Their best verbal subtest is Digit Span, which measures verbal short-term memory; this result helps to explain the delayed echolalia seen in many autistic children. Their worst performance is on Comprehension, which assesses knowledge of social conventions, among other things. Even relative to children with developmental language disorders, autistic children perform worse on Comprehension, Sim-

TABLE 7.1 Symptoms in Autistic Spectrum Disorder

Primary	Problems in social contact and social understanding
Correlated	Mental retardation, other cognitive/language deficits, self-injurious behavior, and seizures
Secondary	Pragmatic deficits, echolalia, stereotypies, splinter skills, symbolic play deficits
Artifactual	Higher SES, physical agility, and attractiveness

ilarities, and Vocabulary (Bartak, Rutter, & Cox, 1975). We have noticed that autistic children may perform better on language tests such as the Peabody Picture Vocabulary Test or the Boston Naming Test, which require less social interaction, than they do on WISC-R Vocabulary or Similarities, which require explaining a verbal concept to another person. A deficit in theory of mind would certainly affect the role-taking skills necessary for constructing a coherent explanation, whereas it would not affect naming pictures or matching words to them. Thus, it is important to bear in mind that the language deficits found in the standardized test results may not reflect language competence per se, but instead be informative about social and communicative competence.

On the Performance subtests of the WISC-R, autistic children tend to perform best on Object Assembly and Block Design, both of which measure spatial cognition. In fact, autistic children generally outperform either retarded or dysphasic children similar in mental or language age on Block Design (Sigman et al., 1987). In contrast, reported cases of Asperger's syndrome (Wing, 1981) tend to perform worse on the performance IQ.

On tests of academic achievement, autistic children tend to exhibit a more pronounced deficit in math and reading comprehension, both of which require conceptual skills, than they do on oral reading and spelling. Their profile on achievement tests like the PIAT is opposite to the dyslexia profile and in fact, a substantial minority of autistic children are hyperlexic, with unexpectedly good reading skills. These precocious reading skills can mislead parents and teachers into thinking the child is generally able at academic tasks.

As implied earlier, tests of executive function can be useful in the evaluation of autism. Recent studies have found impairments on tests of executive functions even in autistic children with normal IQs, although obviously children with other disorders (e.g., ADHD) also exhibit executive function deficits.

Treatment

In discussing treatment, it is important to mention that a child with autism or Asperger's syndrome needs to be assessed for possible organic causes of the disorder. These include fragile X syndrome, chromosome anomalies, neurocutaneous disorders, and metabolic disorders.

Although the prognosis is poor for the majority of autistic children, intensive treatment efforts can make a difference and appear to be a factor in the relatively good outcome found in a minority of cases (Lovaas, 1987; Rogers & Lewis, 1989; Szatmari et al., 1989). It is important for treatment to begin early, in the preschool years, when a great deal of normal social development is taking place. An atypical social adjustment is more resistant to change the longer it is pursued.

More than any other learning disorder described in this book, autism requires long-term, multimodal treatment. Such a treatment plan includes special preschool and school placements, work with parents, and potentially, medication. Although earlier treatment efforts focused first on insight-oriented psychotherapy, and then on operant and behavioral techniques, more recent approaches have focused on treating the core communicative-social deficit (Rogers & Lewis, 1989).

Rogers and Lewis (1989) documented significant treatment effects of a developmentally based, preschool, day-treatment program. This program utilized play, interpersonal relations with a specific adult (who provided changed affective experiences and scaffolding to introduce the child to new activities and peer relations), and pragmatics-based language therapy. Lovaas (1987) documented impressive gains from a long-term, intensive, mainly behavioral-modification program, which also included some social skills training. There is still much to be known about the treatment of autism. For instance, there is a paucity of rigorously designed treatment evaluation studies.

Medication treatments for autism have recently been critically reviewed by Gualtieri, Evans, and Patterson (1987). They conclude that neuroleptics, such as haloperidol (which is a dopamine antagonist), have been found to be clinically useful in a subset of autistic children to reduce problematic behaviors such as hyperactiviy, aggression, severe disorganization, agitation, or insomnia. Even this treatment is preferably short-term and should be monitored carefully for side effects. Although there has been much publicity about fenfluramine and megavitamin treatments for autism, these authors do not find research support for these treatments. Stimulant medication is also contraindicated in some cases of autism, as stimulant medications are dopamine agonists that worsen some autistic symptoms, such as stereotypies, in some patients.

CASE PRESENTATION 7

Jim is a right-handed boy of 12 years who was seen in our laboratory as a subject in a research project on high-functioning autistic children. At the time, he had been in a group home for autistic children for one year and recently entered individual psychotherapy; both treatments were pursued because of angry physical outbursts at both his mother and the staff at the group home. He has been on 20 mg/day of Mellaril® for the last year and a half to help control these angry outbursts, which become worse when he is off medication. Although he is more social now, his eye contact can still be intermittent and he doesn't engage very much in spontaneous conversation. He answers questions with a word or short phrase, and sometimes will not share particularly important information, such as the fact that other adolescents regularly physically threaten him on the school bus. It is still very hard for him to construct a coherent narrative of an event, even one that is very important to him. At his junior high school he is placed in a self-contained program for children with emotional and behavioral problems.

Jim comes from a supportive middle-class family and there were no reported major social–environmental risk factors that contributed to his problem. His parents were separated and divorced when he was three because of his father's drinking problem and other issues. His mother soon remarried and the stepfather is supportive of Jim. The biological father has been recently diagnosed as having bipolar illness and is being treated with lithium. Although the biological father is very gifted intellectually and musically, he has had a great deal of trouble finishing things and making a living. He also has a photographic memory. He is socially isolated, eccentric, and has a hard time relating to people. Like his son, he can have a vacant look, and can "tune out" as if he were deaf. Jim's mother reports a lot of similarities between father and son—in appearance, mannerisms, and social skills, the difference being that the son's social problems are much worse.

In terms of early developmental history, there were no problems in Jim's pregnancy, delivery, or neonatal course. He was a very quiet baby, who showed little interest in exploration or manipulation. He was also a cuddly baby, who molded well and enjoyed affection. He reportedly walked unassisted and spoke in single words at 13 months, which is completely normal. Stranger anxiety did not develop until 2 years, which is markedly late. As an infant and toddler, he had great difficulty separating from his mother. His parents first became concerned about his development at age 2 when they tried to leave him with a babysitter. He had an extreme tantrum when separated from Mother and couldn't relate to the sitter or the new situation. His parents did succeed in placing him in a preschool a year later, but the preschool staff also noticed separation problems, long bouts of screaming and crying, social isolation, self-stimulation, and occasional aggression towards other children. These problems led to a referral for a comprehensive interdisciplinary evaluation.

That evaluation found he had constricted play, which consisted of lining up toys, and engaging in the stereotypic behaviors of arm and hand flapping. Formal assessment was difficult, because he reacted to most test items with crying, screaming, and refusal. However, he did not appear to be mentally retarded, because both his receptive single-word vocabulary and his ability to complete form- and peg-boards were at age level. His receptive language for sentences was estimated to be at a 24-month level, about a 15-month delay, but hardly explaining his lack of expressive language. Interestingly, precocious reading skills were already in evidence, and Jim continued to be hyperlexic in subsequent evaluations. The pediatric evaluation found both some soft signs, including hyperreflexia and probable Babinski reflexes, and some minor physical anomalies, including epicanthic folds, a broad nasal bridge, and a suggestion of hyperteliorism. Because of these dysmorphic features, he was referred for a genetic evaluation, the results of which were negative. This initial evaluation diagnosed him as having atypical pervasive developmental disorder.

A year later he was enrolled in a therapeutic preschool for children with autism and other pervasive developmental disorders. As part of that placement, he received several psychological and speech/language evaluations from age four to six.

At about age 4½, his receptive single-word vocabulary was still in the average range, but his receptive comprehension of longer utterances was still delayed, at about a 28-month level. His expressive language, which was infrequent, often consisted of pronominal reversals, echolalia, and nonsense words. It was noted he could use and understand some American Sign Language. His IQ on the Stanford Binet fell in the range 67–75, but he only had a 6-month delay on the Vineland adaptive behavior scale. He was highly distractible, oblivious to his success or failure on tasks, and resistant to eye contact with adults besides his mother. He showed affection to her by kissing and hugging and still cried on separation from her. His single-word reading skill had continued to progress.

A year later, he was still difficult to test, but tantrums could be averted by giving him words to read. His word decoding skills were now at a third grade level, but his reading comprehension remained poor. Similarly, he could count but not conceptualize about number relations. More generally, he had poor conceptual and verbal reasoning skills, and could not use language to describe past experiences or to synthesize and express ideas. His IQ was in the borderline retarded range. He still avoided interaction and eye contact with adults and children, and his play was still ritualistic and perseverative. However, if someone else took the initiative, he could be cuddly and affectionate. He still had considerable difficulty with transitions and new situations, which often would result in either intense tantrums with aggression or in stereotypies—hand flapping, tapping, or repeating nonsense syllables. A strength had emerged in drawing skills, even though he had delays in gross and fine motor abilities. In terms of speech and language skills, his articulation and verbal STM were both at age level, indicating (along with the hyperlexia) that his phonological-processing skills were normal. Receptive vocabulary also remained an isolated strength, but receptive language was still delayed and at the same level as IQ.

After 2 years of treatment in this special preschool, he was placed in a full day, self-contained public school program for children with severe emotional and behavioral problems. This program has worked hard on developing his social skills, and he has made gains in eye contact, language, and peer social skills. He developed a relationship with another developmentally delayed boy who had been in his special preschool and was in his elementary special program. They began to have simplified conversations, but had trouble regulating affect in their relationship. For instance, they would hug inappropriately or wrestle playfully, but then escalate quickly into a serious physical fight that appeared to have no real cause.

Reading is still an area of strength for Jim, and he can decode practically anything. His comprehension, which is at about a second or third grade level, still lags markedly behind his decoding skill. He prefers books for much younger children. He can understand the stories in these books, and will sometimes read the same book or series over and over again. He can add, subtract, and divide, but has difficulty with story problems. He has recently become remarkably good at Nintendo™, which is the first toy in his life he has really been "turned on" by. He also has a special interest in older cars and books about cars. He still engages in hand flapping if he hears a song he likes, or if he is seeing a part of a movie he likes. He no longer has pronominal reversals, and there is no evidence of delusions, hallucinations, or bizarre themes in his conversation.

Social skills are still very problematic. Mother feels he hasn't changed at all over the years in his inability to read or express affect. He has little affect in his own face and voice; when he does express affect (except for rage attacks), his intonation is a stereotyped copy of something he's heard and does not seem genuine. He still has a poor understanding of personal space, and gets close to another's face or touches them inappropriately. When angry, he moves in very close and can be quite threatening. Now that he is in junior high, peer relations are even more of a problem, and he is frequently teased about the ways he is different. He is concerned about being teased and will talk some about it, again having trouble recreating the whole story. He has a fixed routine of questions he asks when he meets a new person, which includes asking them about the type of car they drive. A summary of Jim's test results is found in Table 7.2.

Discussion

Although Jim did not receive the diagnosis of autism in his early evaluations (because of the apparently late onset and his attachment to his mother), both his later course and his score on the CARS scale justify that diagnosis. His persisting symptoms of social isolation, limited use of language for communication, motor stereotypies, and rigidity in the face of change all are consistent with that diagnosis. In terms of etiology, the most suggestive piece of evidence is Father's bipolar illness and social peculiarity. These are noteworthy because of recent research documenting a family association between autism and both bipolar illness and social peculiarity. So we have a clinical suggestion of a genetic diathesis operating in this case. In contrast, the history does not provide evidence of any clear environmental risk factors, either biological or social.

The early and later histories of social development are interesting because not all aspects of social development are equally disrupted. As an infant and toddler, there is certainly evidence of attachment behaviors, as there is in the research literature on autism. In contrast, by history, both emotion perception/expression and the understanding of others' mental states appear to be severely and persistently impaired.

TABLE 7.2 Test Summary, Case 7

Prorated WISC-R FSIQ = 81

Information	4	Block Design	4
Similarities	5	Object Assembly	13
Vocabulary	3		
Prorated Verbal IQ = 70		Prorated Performance IQ = 93	

	Raw scores	T scores[a]
Executive functions		
Wisconsin Card Sorting Test		
Categories	0	30(−10)
Perseverative responses (errors)	124(96)	02(−01)
Tower of Hanoi planning task (total for 3 & 4 ring problems)	6	14(−40)
Long Term Memory		
Buschke Selective Reminding Task		
Long-term storage	8.5/10	43
Consistent long-term retrieval	2.6/10	18
Trials to criterion	10	—
Spatial Cognition		
Children's Embedded Figures Test	12/25	37
Social Cognition		
Childhood Autism Rating Scale	37/60	—
Theory of other minds		
Appearance reality	2/4	−10
Mental physical	4/8	22
Picture sequence (Intentional condition)	2/6	40
False belief	Fail	—
Imitation	11/25	35
Emotion perception	24/34	51

[a]T scores are based on a nonautistic LD group similar in IQ. T scores in parentheses for the WCST are based on age norms.

Another persisting impairment is in Jim's very poor ability to adapt to new situations, which continues to lead to catastrophic rage reactions. This feature of the case is reminiscent of patients with documented frontal lobe impairment, and is an aspect of autism that has been very clearly discussed by Damasio and Maurer (1978).

There is also a hint of some impairment in episodic memory in the history because of Jim's persisting difficulty in telling a coherent story about important things that have happened to him. However, this problem may be secondary to other deficits in language, executive function, and/or social cognition and not a primary episodic memory problem.

His language development is interesting because it is certainly *not* globally impaired. Early speech milestones were normal, as were the early development of articulation, verbal short-term memory (STM), and lexical knowledge. He was also clearly hyperlexic, developing word recognition and phonological-coding skills well before school age. In contrast, the comprehension of sentences, whether read or heard, has consistently been delayed, as has been the ability to engage in verbal reasoning or to use language to organize and synthesize experience. Again these deficits are in the more abstract and complex levels of language processing, and may be secondary to deficits in other domains, either executive functions or social cognition or both.

Although Jim has some specialized interests (e.g., automobiles), these are not as overdeveloped as is seen in Asperger's syndrome (see Case 8 below). Finally, it is noteworthy that drawing skills are well-developed despite some persisting motor impairments.

In terms of the test results, Jim's FSIQ is now in the Low Average range and there is a marked VIQ < PIQ disparity, consistent with his persistent limited use of language. The striking split between the usually correlated subtests of Block Design and Object Assembly probably indicates a deficit outside the domain of spatial cognition, such as in executive functions. The history of good drawing skills, argues against a primary deficit in spatial constructional skills. Although not completely normal, the score on the Children's Embedded Figures Test is better than the Block Design score, and again argues against a severe deficit in spatial cognition.

Although academic skills were not evaluated in this testing, previous test results and history argue against a traditionally defined learning disability in reading or math. There are, however, conceptual problems in both of these academic skills, which are once again likely secondary to deficits in other domains.

On the neuropsychological tests, there were consistent and striking impairments in two domains, executive functions and theory of other minds, even relative to LD controls similar in IQ. Jim was incredibly perseverative on the Wisconsin; 124 of 128 trials consisted of perseverative responses to the dimension of form, despite negative feedback on every single trial. He simply could not break out of this response set. Arguing against the interpretation that this poor result simply represents his obliviousness to social feedback is his nearly equally impaired performance on the less interactive Tower of Hanoi task. Moreover, within that task he performed perfectly on the initial two-move problem, but had great difficulty with the subsequent three-move problem, which is the first problem to require a counterintuitive move, or, in other words, a shift in response set. His performance on the Tower of Hanoi was well below that of a normal 3-year-old. Jim's profound deficit in executive functions, specifically in shifting mental set and planning ahead, help explain many of his persisting clinical features, including his very poor ability both to adapt to novel situations and to reason and conceptualize—whether in language, math, spatial, or social tasks.

The second main area of deficit was on theory of other minds tasks, all of which were markedly impaired except the Picture sequencing task. Jim is deficient in the understanding of mental states, both in himself and in others. Lacking this understanding, the basic social tasks of coordinating, comparing, and influencing mental states must be foreign and difficult for him. As discussed in the research section of this chapter, it is intriguing to think about how executive function and theory of mind deficits might be related.

Two other areas of social cognition, imitation and emotion perception, are much more intact, at least on these particular measures. The emotion perception results do not fit with the history of persisting deficits in this domain. It is always possible that these more static measures of imitation and emotion perception don't capture problems that would arise in the more dynamic arena of real social interactions.

Finally, some aspects of the long-term verbal memory task were impaired. Although Jim eventually learned most of the items in the task, he was inconsistent across trials in which items he retrieved, suggesting problems in either components of memory itself or in related cognitive processes, such as executive functions.

CASE PRESENTATION 8

Roger is a right-handed boy of 12½ years who was seen in our laboratory as a subject in a research project on high-functioning autistic children. He has received several clinical evaluations for language and social problems, beginning in the preschool years. One of the interesting aspects of this case is how his clinical presentation has changed with development. Early on he was similar in many ways to a classically autistic child; his language development was delayed, he talked little, didn't play with toys or other children, had motor stereotypies and self-injurious behavior. Now many aspects of his language functioning are normal, and he engages readily in conversation, even though he has pragmatic problems. At the time of this study, he met draft criteria for Asperger's syndrome.

The family psychiatric history is informative, but does not include other relatives with Asperger's syndrome, or autism or definite social pecularity. Mother has had several psychiatric diagnoses, including depression, anxiety disorder, and panic disorder. At times, she has been agoraphobic and has needed much encouragement to get out of the house. Father was an alcoholic who was sometimes abusive to Mother; Mother divorced him around the time Roger was four. Because of her affective illness, Mother was sometimes less emotionally available to Roger. Somewhat later, Roger was sexually abused by one of his mother's boyfriends. So, in addition to possible genetic risk factors, there are also social–environmental risk factors. These social–environmental risk factors are very unlikely to have caused Roger's Asperger's syndrome, because most of them occurred *after* its onset, but they certainly have affected its course and expression. Nonetheless, many of his earlier clinical records implicitly assume that most of his symptoms are due to these emotional traumas.

In terms of early developmental history, Roger was the product of a normal pregnancy and delivery with Apgar scores of 9 and 10. His development in early infancy was also apparently normal, but by 9–10 months of age he had developed inconsolable crying spells that sometimes lasted 8–9 hours. Because of these, Mother felt she couldn't take him out of the house. His language development began normally, but then fell behind, and by age 3 he was receiving twice weekly speech therapy. By age 4, he spoke in broken and often nonsensical sentences, was echolalic, and rarely initiated language in the social setting of the preschool. His overall language development at age four was at about a 2½–3-year-old level. In the social domain, his eye contact was inconsistent, he sometimes "blocked out" other people, did not play with other children at preschool, and was indifferent to toys. At the same time, there were some indications that he enjoyed human contact, but in a somewhat indiscriminate way. For instance, he would approach teachers and peers and say "love me a hug," or kiss them. Although he was not an overt behavior problem at preschool, he was overactive and moved around a lot. Mother continued to have problems with him at home in terms of bad temper tantrums and problems with toilet training. Both at home and at school, he exhibited a number of unusual behaviors, including rocking, flapping his hands, repeated humming, biting, head banging during tantrums, and smelling things. Fine motor and visuospatial development was very immature with very poor fine motor skills, no established handedness, and very little ability to draw. Gross motor development also appeared delayed in that he was unable to ride a tricycle. In contrast to all these problems, a clear area of strength had emerged by age 4. Roger was fascinated with music, would listen to the same records and tapes over and over again, and could distinguish the work of the major classical composers when listening to them.

Upon entering public school, Roger was placed in a special classroom for children with emotional and behavioral problems and received occupational therapy for his motor problems. He was still isolative, echolalic, and showed motor stereotypies. At age 7½, the school found evidence of sexual abuse of Roger by one of Mother's boyfriends, and he was placed in a child inpatient psychiatric hospital, followed by 2 years in a residential treatment facility. After that placement, he returned home and continues in outpatient psychiatric treatment. Like other sexually abused children, he initially showed a preoccupation with sexual themes. However, more than many sexually abused children, he also acted out sexually by "flashing" and making overt sexual gestures toward his therapist, possibly because he had less ability to organize and inhibit. In the early part of the hospitalization, he was also more out of control in general and engaged in tantrums and assaultive behavior toward staff. These sexual preoccupations and problems with behavioral control diminished over the course of residential teatment.

Several symptoms characteristic of pervasive developmental disorder or Asperger's syndrome were noted during this period. He had a preoccupation with mechanical things, such as helicopters, robotic toys, clocks, and antennas, in addition to his preoccupation with music. He played alone frequently and had clear problems both in understanding his own or others' affect and in communicating affect. His intonation and pragmatics were inappropriate. He tended to be rigid in his reactions to the environment, especially to change. When stressed, he made bizarre noises and talked in nonsensical sentences. He still had motor and language delays, but within the language area a strength had emerged in reading words and phonics, in spite of poor reading comprehension. In other words, he was hyperlexic. His IQ at 7½ was in the mildly mentally retarded range on the Stanford Binet, but in the borderline range on the Leiter, which depends less on language skills.

Over the course of residential treatment, his echolalia and stereotypies diminished considerably, and his ability to engage with peers increased, even though he continued to show a preference for solitary play. Around the time of discharge, at age 9½, his scores on the WISC-R were a Verbal IQ of 78, a Performance IQ of 71, and a Full Scale IQ of 72, documenting some improvement in language skills.

As we will see, both areas of IQ have continued to improve, with the greatest improvement in verbal IQ. So, despite both regression in language development and a marked delay in language from preschool into latency, certain aspects of language have reached normal developmental levels. Other interesting changes in symptoms include increases in conversational engagement and marked decreases in echolalia, stereotypies, and other autistic-like behaviors. His preoccupation with music has continued, and he has developed into a very accomplished pianist. Amazingly, Roger can listen several times to a complex classical piece, such as a Chopin etude, and then play it quite well without sheet music. So like other Asperger's cases, he has an area of expertise that is based in part on extremely good memory skills. Although several recent accounts of Asperger's syndrome insist on preserved language throughout development, this case illustrates that there can be marked early language delays in a child who otherwise later meets criteria for Asperger's syndrome.

Roger has continued in individual psychotherapy. His current therapist describes him as being surprisingly connected and verbal with her, despite problems in social skills. These social skills problems consist of problems labelling his own and others' affect, a poor sense of personal space, and a tendency to run on conversationally. He also assumes his therapist should automatically know how he's feeling and gets mad at her when she asks about it. He does have some awareness of his pragmatic problems, and will sometimes ask, "Am I talking too much?" In terms of personal space, he gets too close physically and will bring his face 6 inches away from the therapist when talking. When they walk together, he has trouble not walking diagonally into her. Again he is able to have some self-awareness about this problem, and she is helping him ask himself whether he is too close.

A number of his specialized interests are frequent themes in therapy, including classical music. In addition to being very familiar with classical compositions and being able to play them quite well, Roger is also an expert on classical instruments and their history. He draws very well and draws detailed pictures of classical instruments for his therapist. He also knows a lot about snakes, spiders, fungi, and mushrooms, including the names and characteristics of different species. He is still obsessed with helicopters and has developed an obsession with the parking structure near where his outpatient therapy takes place.

In addition to these obsessive interests, he will still talk vividly about his past sexual abuse; his therapist feels he still has a secondary diagnosis of post-traumatic stress disorder in reaction to this abuse. He will also talk about concerns with puberty and sexuality. On the other hand, he is not able to use therapy to talk about being teased by junior high peers; he does not understand why he is teased but does express sadness and anger about it. He does not have more extreme depressive reactions, including no suicidal ideation. Likewise there are no hallucinations, delusions, or bizarre verbalizations. Therapy has proceeded on mostly an even keel, but Roger still can get very upset by even minor changes. In the course of this treatment, he has had four or five catastrophic reactions to minor changes in routine; on these occasions, he has cried and yelled and been somewhat threatening physically. A summary of Roger's test results is seen in Table 7.3.

TABLE 7.3 Test Summary, Case 8

Prorated WISC-R FSIQ = 92			
Information	10	Block Design	8
Similarities	12	Object Assembly	6
Vocabulary	8		
Prorated Verbal IQ = 100		Prorated Performance IQ = 85	

	Raw scores	T scores[a]
Executive functions		
Wisconsin Card Sorting Test		
Categories	2/6	40(11)
Perseverative responses (errors)	67/63	29(19)
Tower of Hanoi planning task (total for 3 & 4 ring problems)	24/60	37(07)
Long Term Memory		
Buschke Selective Reminding Task (Children's)		
Long-term storage	9.3/10	56
Consistent long-term retrieval	9.0/10	58
Trials to criterion	5	—
Spatial cognition		
Children's Embedded Figures Test	13/25	39
Social cognition		
Childhood Autism Rating Scale	30/60	—
Theory of other minds		
Appearance reality	4/4	53
Mental physical	7/8	47
Picture sequence (Intentional condition)	4/6	51
False belief	Pass	—
Second order task	Fail	—
Imitation	19/25	58
Emotion perception	25/34	54

[a]T scores are based on a non-autistic LD group similar in IQ. T scores in parentheses for the WCST are based on age norms.

Discussion

There are interesting similarities and differences between this case and the previous one. In terms of similarities, there were early language delays and hyperlexia with echolalia and nonsensical speech; problems in social relatedness outside the family, despite an affectionate attachment to Mother; persisting problems in perceiving and expressing affect; persisting problems with understanding personal space; rigidity and resistance to change, with occasional catastrophic reactions in response to minor changes; marked distractibility; early motor delays but eventually good drawing skills; and strong, specialized interests in nonsocial objects (e.g., cars and helicopters). In terms of differences, there were more environmental risks in this case, but a better overall outcome to this point; much better eventual development of language and the conversational use of language; less persistent problems with the avoidance of eye contact and the use of stereotypies; less severe catastrophic reactions, especially those involving physical aggression; much more highly developed specialized interests; greater participation in the psychotherapy process; and much more developed, but still very delayed, self-monitoring abilities.

In terms of test results, there is an opposite profile on the WISC-R, with a significant VIQ > PIQ disparity. As in the previous case, the overall IQ has increased over time compared to preschool levels, but the increase in this case is greater having reached the low end of the Average range, with solidly average verbal subtest scores. Similar to the previous case, there is no evidence for a learning disability in reading. Clear data on math skills are lacking.

Unlike the previous case, the only clear and consistent area of impairment is in executive function skills, which are three to four standard deviations below age-expected levels and about two standard deviations below IQ-expected levels. The performance on both executive function measures is at about a 5–6-year level. These scores are significantly better than those in the previous case, but still markedly impaired.

Roger performed much better on the theory of other mind tasks than Jim, although he did fail the second order task. So he has some understanding that others have mental states, but he is nonetheless not very skilled in social perspective taking. His better theory of mind skills would help explain his greater degree of social engagement, his greater participation in psychotherapy, and his emerging self-monitoring skills.

Another difference is that Roger showed no impairment in verbal memory, a result that is consistent with his average VIQ. As in the previous case, there were no deficits on formal tasks of imitation or emotion perception. The latter result is clearly inconsistent with the history and may be due to the insensitivity of this static emotion perception measure.

C H A P T E R 8

Acquired Memory Disorders

This chapter deals with acquired memory disorders in children, which is the fifth and final type of learning disorder considered in this volume. By memory disorder, I mean a disorder in long-term memory, specifically explicit or episodic long-term memory (LTM), not implicit or procedural memory (see Chapter 1). We could call this disorder amnesia in childhood. This is an important category of learning disorder for clinicians, especially as long-term memory impairments are easily missed by traditional psychometric batteries and usual child clinical procedures. As we said earlier, there is very little research on the question of whether a syndrome of nonacquired or developmental amnesia exists, especially in nonretarded children. Consequently, we will focus here on acquired causes of amnesia in children. These etiologies all affect brain functions in other ways, so they do not specifically and selectively produce amnesia, but long-term memory problems are a prominent part of the symptom constellation produced by these etiologies.

RESEARCH REVIEW

Basic Defining Characteristics

Epidemiological data on LTM disorders in children is lacking; all that can be provided here is prevalence data on the more common risk factors for acquired memory disorders, specifically closed head injury (CHI) and seizure disorders.

About one million children per year suffer closed head injuries in the United States or 1.6% of the population, with one-sixth of these being hospitalized (Eiben et al., 1984). The sex ratio in pediatric CHI is between 2:1 to 3:1 males to females (Levin, Benton, & Grossman, 1982). Interestingly, the survival rate from severe CHI in children is about 90%, in contrast to 50%–70% in adults with severe CHI, a difference possibly attributable to different causes of injury in adults versus children (high speed motor accidents vs. falls or pedestrian accidents) and to greater skull flexibility in children (Levin et al., 1982). Despite their greater survival rate, it is not clear that children are at lower risk for neurological sequelae, especially cognitive sequelae, or that younger children are at less risk than older ones (Goldstein & Levin, 1985).

Seizure disorders have a population prevalence of 1%–2%, with a sex ratio of 1.5 to 2.0:1 males to females. Approximately 90% of all patients with seizure disorders have an onset of initial symptoms before age 20, so seizure disorders, like CHI, are definitely an important risk factor in childhood. While it is generally accepted that a large proportion of patients with seizure disorders have no neuropsychological deficits, we were unable to find studies reporting on the specific proportion of seizure disordered patients who *do* have neuropsychological deficits. Patients with temporal lobe epilepsy (TLE) would be expected to be particularly at risk for memory problems, because the seizure focus is near or in the limbic memory structures. Patients with TLE scheduled for temporal lobectomy were found to have an abnormal P300 [a positive peak occuring at about 300 msec in the averaged, evoked electroencephalographic (EEG) waveform] and memory problems on the Wechsler Memory Scales (Nelson, Collins, & Torres, 1991). The P300 component is regarded by some as indexing declarative memory processes. Of course, TLE patients needing surgery are an extreme group; we do not know the rate of memory problems in unselected TLE patients. A second, overlapping risk factor for neuropsychological dysfunction in patients with seizure disorders is the effect of seizure medications themselves (Dodrill, 1981).

Etiologies

Besides the two most common etiologies mentioned above, there are a host of other medical conditions that can affect memory in children.

These include infections (e.g., herpes simplex encephalitis; Reye's syndrome [Quart, Buchtel, & Sarnaik, 1988]), midline tumors, anemia (e.g., associated with sickle cell disease), medications (e.g., high steroid levels in asthmatics [Bender, Lerner, & Kollasch, 1988]) and strokes. In addition, some chronic diseases of childhood, such as diabetes and asthma (Dunleavy & Boade, 1980), appear to carry some risk for neuropsychological impairment in general, including LTM dysfunction.

Another risk factor which is important to mention here is perinatal anoxia. On theoretical grounds, this risk factor might produce amnesia, but research has not yet clearly related perinatal anoxia to that outcome. Perinatal anoxia is perhaps the single greatest cause of perinatal neurological difficulties (Spreen et al., 1984) and is known to cause cerebral palsy, mental retardation and seizures. Yet many children who have suffered this risk factor appear cognitively normal on long-term followup. Memory has not generally been carefully studied, but if amnesia were present, it would be expected to impair IQ.

Two recent follow-up studies of children who suffered antenatal hypoxia and birth asphyxia found cognitive deficits, including lower IQs (Naeye & Peters, 1987; Robertson, Finer, & Grace, 1989), but neither study examined LTM specifically. In the first study, the relationship was only found for chronic antenatal hypoxia, not for acute perinatal hypoxia. In the second study, only birth asphyxia leading to moderate to severe encephalopathy was associated with later cognitive deficits. These studies suggest more cognitive effects from chronic versus acute hypoxia, as well as possibly suggesting protective factors in the birth process itself. Postnatal chronic hypoxia in infancy secondary to cardiac defects is also related to cognitive deficits at school age (O'Doughtery, Wright, Loewenson, & Torres, 1985). In summary, chronic hypoxia, whether before or after birth, appears to cause long-lasting cognitive deficits; we do not know if these include LTM deficits. The animal studies of amnesia reviewed in Chapter 1 indicate that the limbic memory structures are vulnerable in early life and that damage to them can lead to permanent LTM deficits. So their plasticity is less than might have been supposed. If the same holds for humans, we would expect early, chronic hypoxia to lead to LTM deficits. This is an important issue for future research.

In summary, it is important for clinicians who work with learning-disordered children to be aware of these various medical risk factors for memory disorders. Children with clinical complaints who have one of these risk factors need to be referred for a neuropsychological evaluation that includes LTM assessment.

Brain Mechanisms

Very little research is available on clinico-anatomic correlations in pediatric patients with LTM disorders, so evidence is lacking validating that the same brain structures are involved as those important in adult amnesia. However, primate studies utilizing infant monkeys indicate that the hippocampus and amygdala are crucial for recognition memory early in life. Intact infant monkeys exhibit normal recognition memory on certain developmentally appropriate memory tasks. This ability is impaired by bilateral amygdala–hippocampus lesions to chance levels, just as in adult monkeys (Brickson & Bachevalier, 1984; Nelson, in press). Nelson argues that the medial-temporal structures that support recognition memory develop quite rapidly between birth and six months.

Because acquired memory disorders are defined by neuropsychological test results, rather than by symptoms, it doesn't make sense to discuss their neuropsychology. Consequently we will next discuss developmental course.

Developmental Course

Although there is little research on this topic, clinical observations suggest a declining cognitive trajectory for children with acquired LTM disorders. Because they learn new information much less efficiently than their still developing age-mates, their relative standing on measures of intelligence declines with age. One child victim of a near drowning we followed longitudinally had IQ scores that continued to decline over the 5-year follow-up period into the borderline retarded range (see Case 10 below).

DIAGNOSIS AND TREATMENT OF MEMORY DISORDERS

Presenting Symptoms

These may include misplacing things, becoming lost, especially in new situations, word-finding problems, difficulty learning new information in school or forgetting such information overnight, and failure to remember everyday information, such as what happened earlier in the day. Because of the generalized effects of etiologies that cause acquired memory disorders, these symptoms of memory impairment will likely be interspersed with symptoms of other neuropsychological deficits, such as problems with attention, language, spatial cognition, and conceptual skills. As a result, memory symptoms may not be a salient part of the initial referral, and it is important to inquire specifically about them. Table 8.1 lists symptoms in acquired memory disorders.

History

Because these are acquired disorders, the most important pieces of history are: (a) the presence of one of the risk conditions previously discussed under etiologies and (b) a change in cognitive and academic function after the occurrence of the risk event.

Behavioral Observations

Valuable information implicating memory dysfunction often emerges during testing. Patients with memory disorders may show more distess on memory tests, may only be able to remember isolated details of more complex input, such as a story, or may recall information in the wrong context (e.g., mix up geometric designs from two different parts of the testing). This last behavior may be described as a form of confabulation and is pathognomic of memory problems in that it virtually never occurs in children without memory disorders. If testing takes several hours, memory problems for incidental information may emerge, such as what tests have already been taken, where the bathroom is, or what the patient had for lunch.

Results of Testing

Obviously, the most crucial piece of diagnostic information is the patient's performance on formal memory tests. Traditional psycho-

TABLE 8.1 Symptoms in Acquired Memory Disorders

Primary	Memory problems
Correlated	Inattention, lability, impulsivity, other cognitive/language problems
Scondary	Declining IQ, school failure, confabulation, poor self-esteem
Artifactual	Premorbid ADHD/LD

metric instruments, such as the Wechsler IQ scales and achievement tests, are not very helpful in detecting an acquired memory disorder, which generally spares previously learned information.

There are several long-term memory tests currently being used by neuropsychologists who work with children, including the Wechsler Memory Scales-Revised (WMS-R), the Buschke Selective Reminding Task-Children's Version, the California Verbal Learning Test, the Rey Ostereith Complex Figure, and the Rey Auditory Verbal Learning Test. Unfortunately, most of these tests have not been normed for use with children, making detection of more subtle memory impairments impossible. For instance, the LTM deficits found by Quart et al. (1987) in children recovered from Reye's syndrome were subtle enough that they could easily escape detection by child neuropsychologists using current measures, even these deficits were highly significant relative to IQ-matched normal controls.

Another problem with many currently available measures concerns construct and discriminant validity, issues discussed by Loring and Papanicolau (1987). For instance the Visual Reproduction (nonverbal) subtest of the WMS is also influenced by both visuoconstructive ability and fluid intelligence, as well as nonverbal memory. The Buschke Selective Reminding Task also requires strategic processes and its various component scores are highly correlated. In contrast, these authors describe the California Verbal Learning Test as being well-grounded theoretically in contemporary cognitive psychology and thus having fewer construct validity problems. In our lab, we have used the Story and Figure Memory Tests, which are an adaption of portions of the Wechsler Memory Scale developed by Heaton (unpublished). As in the Wechsler Memory Scales-Revised, complex stimuli are used (a story and complex designs), and there is both a learning and a delayed recall component. But, unlike the WMS-R, there are up to five learning trials, so that efficiency in learning new information can be evaluated, as well as immediate and delayed recall. In our clinical experience, normal children as young as 9 perform similarly to adults on all three components of this task (immediate recall, learning, and delayed recall). Their performance is especially similar to adults on delayed recall. Delayed recall of 80% or better is considered normal for both children and most adults. As we will see in the case examples below, amnesic children perform much worse on this test.

Clearly, it would be very helpful to have well-normed, theoretically derived measures of both verbal and nonverbal LTM for children.

Work is underway to norm some of the measures listed above for children, including the promising California Verbal Learning Test.

CASE PRESENTATION 9

This patient suffered a severe CHI in an auto accident when he was nearly 13; he was tested two and a half years later. After the accident, he was comatose for approximately four months and hospitalized for six months. He underwent neurosurgery to relieve brain swelling. CT scans showed evidence of bilateral frontal and left temporal lobe injury.

Before the accident, the patient was an honors student who loved sports and had no history of emotional or behavioral problems. Since the accident he as been placed in a special education classroom; more recently, he has been mainstreamed with a light academic load and special education assistance.

Recent testing at school found a FSIQ of 81 on the WISC-R with little difference between VIQ and PIQ. There are two previous post-accident WISC-Rs, one at 8 months and another at 11 months. The patient's VIQ has been very stable across all three occasions, whereas the PIQ increased from 67 to 81 from the first to the second testing; it was also 81 on the last evaluation.

On recent achievement tests, his scores were somewhat higher, with standard scores on tests of reading, math, and written language all being similar and averaging approximately 88. Because of the similarity between IQ and achievement test scores, the school did not perceive the patient as having serious cognitive problems. They said his ability and achievement appear to have recovered substantially since his accident, and that he is learning and achieving at an expected level; thus he did not meet state criteria to qualify as either learning disabled or mentally handicapped.

The mother reported a number of behavioral changes in the patient post-accident. She said the patient was more emotionally labile, somewhat tangential in his conversation, had engaged in socially inappropriate sexual behaviors (e.g., dropping his pants in front of a female aide in school, asking nurses in the hospital to take their clothes off), lacked nuances in his interpretation of things, and tended to be rigid and moralistic in his interpretation of rules. He also tended to get lost in new places and had memory problems. Finally, he suffered motor and speech deficits as a result of his CHI, and he still had a right-sided motor weakness, "breathy" speech with poor volume control, and word-finding difficulties. He has always been left handed.

During the neuropsychological evaluation, the patient exhibited some socially inappropriate behavior, such as making comments about the marital status of the examiner. He was also tangential in his conversation, had limited frustration tolerance, and needed numerous breaks, especially on tasks that were more difficult for him. His frustration was greatest on the learning and memory tasks. His learning of new information was fragmentary in that he could only recall a small part of the story and only one of four figures despite repeated learning trials. A summary of this patient's test results is found in Table 8.2.

Discussion

The length of coma, hospitalization, and positive findings on CT scan all indicate that this patient suffered a severe CHI. The research literature indicates persisting cognitive deficits are very likely after such an injury. Because the patient was a good student with no premorbid LDs or social–emotional problems, it is much clearer that the current problems are acquired ones. Although we do not have a measure of premorbid IQ, his grades and the education level of his parents would suggest a premorbid IQ at least in the Bright Normal range (110–120). Thus, his IQ has declined by at least two standard deviations. The postmorbid trajectory of IQ is also interesting and fits the research literature; his PIQ was most affected initially, but showed recovery in the 1st year after the accident. Both VIQ and PIQ now appear to have reached a plateau. Although his standard scores on achievement tests are somewhat higher than his IQ, these scores very likely represent premorbid levels of knowledge and not new learning. Thus, the school's impression that he is achieving at ability level is misleading. Using traditional psychometric tests alone, it is very easy to overestimate the extent of this young man's recovery.

The history and behavioral observations are consistent with both executive function and memory impairment. His disinhibition, emotional lability, tangential speech, and concreteness all suggest frontal lobe dysfunction. His getting lost in new places and other memory problems suggest an amnesic disorder. Notice, however, that the memory symptoms were much less salient to observers at home and school than were the disruptions in social–behavioral functions.

TABLE 8.2 Test Summary Case 9

WISC-R FSIQ = 81

Information	7	Picture Completion	8
Similarities	8	Picture Arrangement	10
Arithmetic	8	Block Design	6
Vocabulary	8	Object Assembly	5
Comprehension	6	Coding	1
Digit Span	6		
Verbal IQ = 84		Performance IQ = 81	
Verbal Comprehension = 7.3		Perceptual Organization = 6.5	

Freedom from Distractibility = 5.0

	Raw scores	T scores
Executive functions		
Category test errors	74	17
Wisconsin Card Sorting Test		
Perseverative responses	40	29
Categories	5	47
Trailmaking Test: Part B	139 sec (1 error)	−50
Memory		
Story		
Trial 1	2.0	—
Trial 2	2.5	—
Trial 3	4.0	—
Trial 4	4.0	—
Trial 5	3.0	—
Rate of Learning	0.6/trial	12[a]
Delayed Recall	0.0	23[a]
Figure		
Trial 1	1	—
Trial 2	3	—
Trial 3	3	—
Trial 4	3	—
Rate of learning	0.8/trial	12[a]
Delayed recall	0	23[a]
Tactual Performance Test Location	0	—
Language		
Speech Sound Perception errors	9	29
Aphasia Screening Exam errors	11	—
Spatial Cognition		
Constructional dyspraxia score	5	—
Tactual Performance Test (blocks/min)		
Left hand	5/10	<−50
Right hand	6/10	<−50
Both hands	9/10	<−50
Total	20/30	<−50

(*continued*)

TABLE 8.2 (*continued*)

Sensory Perceptual (finger dysgnosia, graphethesia, and suppressions)		
Left hand (total errors)	18	—
Right hand	22	—
No suppressions or gross visual field disturbance		
Motor		
Tapping (#/10 sec)		
Left	30.0	9
Right	20.0	23
Dynamometer (kg)		
Left	26.5	—
Right	8.8	—
Grooved Pegboard (sec/# dropped)		
Left	110/1	9
Right	900/50[b]	<–50

[a]Based on adult norms.
[b]Prorated from performance on 5 pegs.

On the neuropsychological battery, there was clear evidence of generalized neuropsychological impairment that was somewhat lateralized to the left hemisphere. This lateralization was indicated by his markedly worse motor performance with his right hand; this lateralization was consistent with the CT scan results, which indicated a left hemisphere injury, as well as bifrontal injuries. Because the patient has familial left handedness, his language lateralization may be atypical, which would help explain why he is not more impaired in language skills despite documented left hemisphere damage.

Of greatest importance, is the fact that the patient was densely amnesic. Despite a Digit Span of 6 (which indicates a low average verbal immediate memory span), his retention of new complex information was extremely impaired. He did not learn new information over time, exhibiting essentially a flat learning curve. Moreover, he lost *all* of the little verbal and nonverbal information he learned after a four-hour delay. A normal 15-year-old would acquire at least 15 "bits" of both verbal and nonverbal information after two trials and would retain at least 80% of it after the delay. Finally, on delayed recall, the patient confabulated. On the verbal test, instead of recalling the story of two hitchhikers named Henry Hooker and Jim who were arrested for vagrancy, he told a story about Eric Christopher and another person who travelled through a desert and died. On the nonverbal memory test, he produced completely unrelated geometric forms. Converging evidence of amnesia is provided by complete lack of incidental memory for the Tactual Performance Test form board (TPT location score = 0). Although the patient's other deficits certainly contributed to encoding difficulties on the memory testing, his learning and LTM were much more impaired than were other areas of neuropsychological function.

Tests of executive function, especially the Wisconsin Card Sorting Test, documented that this patient had frontal lobe dysfunction. His combined deficits in LTM and executive functions represent a severe mental handicap that will very likely preclude independent employment or living. Thus the school's conclusion (based on psychometric testing) that the patient does not have an LD or mental handicap is profoundly misleading.

CASE PRESENTATION 10

The second case involves an amnesia caused by near drowning. The patient is a right-handed boy, who was 11 at the time of testing and who nearly drowned 4 years previously. He was anoxic for about 30 minutes during the drowning episode. He was hospitalized for 2 months after the near drowning, during which time he received occupational and physical therapy for motor deficits, especially on the left side. At the time we saw him, he was placed in a regular fifth grade class and was receiving extra tutoring in math. It was also noted that he worked much more slowly than other students. There was no history of premorbid learning or emotional problems.

During the testing, the patient was a pleasant and socially appropriate child, who appeared to have a large vocabulary and talked readily about his interests in spiders and other pets. No problems in language, attention, or motor skills were readily apparent. However, during the Story Memory test his learning was fragmentary; he never got the idea of the whole narrative, often just gave names or words he remembered from the story, and missequenced events. On the third learning trial, he actually lost information, and acted as if had never heard the story before. A summary of his test results is seen in Table 8.3.

Discussion of Test Results

This child's Verbal, Performance, and Full Scale IQs on the WISC-R all fall in the Average range. There is a statistically significant difference (16 pts) between his Verbal (107) and Performance IQ (91), but this difference is mainly attributable to his impaired Coding subtest score

TABLE 8.3 Test Summary Case 10

WISC-R FSIQ = 100			
Information	13	Picture Completion	12
Similarities	13	Picture Arrangement	8
Arithmetic	9	Block Design	8
Vocabulary	12	Object Assembly	11
Comprehension	6	Coding	5
Verbal IQ = 107		Performance IQ = 91	
Verbal Comprehension = 11.0		Perceptual Organization = 9.5	

Freedom from Distractibility = 7.0

	Grade equivalents	Age standard scores
Peabody Individual Achievement test		
Mathematics	6.0	98
Reading recognition	10.3	116
Reading comprehension	9.5	112
Spelling	10.7	120

		Raw scores	T scores
Executive functions			
Thurstone Word Fluency Test:	Part A	15	—
	Part B	04	—
Midrange Category test errors		26	58
Wisconsin Card Sorting Test			
Perseverative errors		5	55
Categories		6	55
Trailmaking Test: Part B		50 secs 0 errors	—
Memory			
Story			
Trial 1		2.5	—
Trial 2		8.0	—
Trial 3		3.0	—
Trial 4		8.5	—
Trial 5		10.0	—
Rate of Learning		2.0/trial	25[a]
Delay Recall		13.0	57[a]
Figure			
Trial 1		15	—
Rate of Learning		15/trial	45[a]
Delay Recall		8	30[a]
Tactual Performance Test			
Location Component		5/6	—
Language			
Speech Sounds Perception Test (errors)		1	64
Aphasia Screening Exam (errors)		11	—

(continued)

TABLE 8.3 (continued)

Spatial Cognition		
Constructional dyspraxia score	2	—
Tactual Performance Test (min) (6 block version)		
Right hand	2.2	55
Left hand	1.3	58
Both hands	0.5	57
Total	4.0	58
Sensory Perceptual Errors		
Right hand total	6.5	—
Left hand total	6.0	—
Motor		
Tapping test (#/10sec)		
Right	32.6	33
Left	26.2	27
Dynamometer (kg)		
Right	16.5	42
Left	11.0	27
Grooved Pegboard (sec)		
Right	62	58
Left	71	51

[a]Based on adult norms.

of 5, which falls at about the 5th percentile. There was not a significant difference between his Verbal Comprehension (VC) and Perceptual Organization (PO) factor scores of 11.0 and 9.5, so the VIQ–PIQ split does not appear due to a relative problem in nonverbal problem solving or spatial reasoning. Because the Coding (called Digit Symbol for adults), subtest is the most sensitive subtest to brain dysfunction in children and adults, this low Coding score is the most clinically significant aspect of the WISC-R, which is otherwise quite normal.

The achievement test scores confirm a relative difficulty in math, which is consistent with the presenting complaints. Interestingly, his reading and spelling scores are higher than his IQ scores, which could suggest a higher level of premorbid intellectual function. Even though math is relatively low, he does not have a clear-cut learning disability. Similar to the previous case, traditional psycmometric tests do not reveal a definite cognitive or learning disability in this near drowning victim.

On the extended Halstead neuropsychological evaluation for older children, his overall level of impairment likewise falls within normal limits. However, there were several distinctively impaired performances, which are unlike those seen in normal or LD children. Most important were his performances on the Story Learning and the Figure

Memory tests, both of which were moderately impaired. He was very slow to learn new verbal information, never encoded the entire narrative structure, and actually lost more than half of the previously learned information on the third learning trial. His learning curve was very atypical, not only because of this regression but also because it was relatively flat and began with so little information encoded on the first trial. His delayed performance for verbal information was surprisingly better than his last learning trial, indicating consolidation in long-term memory. While he has a marked verbal learning problem, he does not have a verbal LTM problem on this test. This kind of inconsistency is sometimes seen in patients with milder amnesia. His pattern of performance on the Figure Memory test was the opposite. He was above average on the learning portion of this test, acquiring the criterial 15 bits of information on the first trial. However, after a delay, he lost nearly half of this information, which is a very abnormal performance and indicates a nonverbal LTM deficit. He completely forgot the first two of the four designs and could retrieve no part of them even with cues. The patient was also impaired on the Thurstone Word Fluency Test, especially Part B, which could also be due to his memory deficit.

The other main area of impairment in this child's results was a consistent pattern of left-sided motor impairment on the tests of motor speed (Tapping) and grip strength (Dynamometer). These results indicate a slight residual hemiparesis, and like the last case, demonstrate the vulnerability of the motor system to acquired insult.

The patient's memory difficulties are fairly selective and occur in the context of normal performance on measures of intelligence, academic function, language, executive functions, attention, and spatial reasoning. Thus, we cannot attribute this patient's memory problem to attentional or strategic difficulties that would affect encoding. His memory problems would help explain his problems in learning and doing mathematics.

On follow-up 4 years later he was having even more severe problems in school, and he continued to be unable to retain new information. Strikingly, his IQ had fallen into the borderline retarded range, indicating that his memory problems had interfered significantly with his intellectual development.

Treatment

Amnesic disorders are particularly depressing for the clinician, because there is so little we can do about them. There is a beginning research literature on the cognitive rehabilitation of memory disorders, using mnemonic strategies. Wilson (1987) reviews research on the rehabilitation of memory in a recent book. One general conclusion is that the use of a story mnemonic appears to work better than other mnemonics, such as visual imagery, method of loci (imagining items to be remembered in different places in one's home), or first letter cueing. Although amnesic patients did show experimental evidence of memory gains using these strategies, their improvements were not always clinically significant and their memories were still impaired.

Besides trying to rehabilitate the amnesic child's memory, it is very important for the clinician to communicate the nature of the problems clearly to parents and teachers, so that the patient's behavior can be better understood and so that caretakers can help provide compensations in the environment. For instance, if the child can read, written instructions may be needed to supplement oral instructions because the patient can refer back to them. It is easier for an amnesic child to work on a task uninterrupted, as all the necessary materials are in view. Memory problems interfere with finding needed materials or restarting a task after interruption. Parents and educators also need to be alerted to the possibility that a severely amnesic child will likely need sheltered living and work situations as an adult.

PART III

Conclusion

C H A P T E R 9

Implications for Research and Practice

One of the implicit themes of this book has been that we cannot draw a sharp line between research and practice issues. Obviously there is a reciprocal relation between research and practice, as each informs the other. Practical decisions can be misguided if they are unaware of research, as when a school system decides to treat reading problems with unproven and nonstandard remedies, such as colored lenses or auditory training to strengthen middle ear muscles. Research can be misguided if it is unaware of clinical complexities, particularly the problems of heterogeneity and comorbidity within patient groups defined by traditional clinical criteria. Moreover, rare clinical cases can sometimes test the validity of cognitive associations and dissociations derived from group studies. For instance, in Chapter 4, we emphasized the primacy of phonological coding deficits in dyslexia. Suppose a clinician encounters several adult developmental dyslexics who still have reading problems, but who are not impaired on phonological coding measures. Such a clinical observation can lead to new research that examines how phonological coding deficits change in dyslexic development. The goal of this chapter is to encourage a healthy dialectic between research and practice by summarizing the implications for each that are suggested by the preceding chapters. We begin with implications for research.

IMPLICATIONS FOR RESEARCH

This section begins with a general discussion, followed by discussions of research implications for the different, specific learning disorders treated in the previous chapters.

General Discussion

I have proposed a neuropsychological model of different domains of cognitive and social development; the proposed clinical nosology depends on the validity of that model. So one very basic research implication is the need to test this and related models of normal neuropsychological development. What is the normal developmental trajectory of these different domains and how are the domains related to each other? Is there discriminant validity for the different domains?

Some of the best evidence on this latter question comes from the studies of these learning disorders, in the form of double dissociations between disorders, such as those demonstrated between ADHD and dyslexia or between autism and dyslexia (see Table 9.1 for a list of documented and potential double dissociations). As can be seen, the best evidence so far is for the dissociability of phonological coding from several other neuropsychological domains. In the future, studies directly examining the other predicted double dissociations will obviously be important tests of the validity of this neuropsychological model. Although double dissociations appear compelling, they represent a confirmatory strategy and the hypotheses they support need to be tested in other ways.

Developmental and experimental studies are needed to help determine whether some of the domains are internally heterogeneous, as is very likely true for the domains of executive functions and social cognition. Another important research issue concerns how the neuropsychological parsing of cognition proposed here relates to other ways of dividing up cognition, such as that found in psychometric or Piagetian accounts. For instance, what is the overlap between executive functions, fluid intelligence, and formal operations; are they all different names for essentially the same thing?

Another important issue concerns the specificity of different neuropsychological deficits to different disorders. Executive functions and/or attention deficits appear to be common to several developmental disorders (e.g., autism, ADHD, some forms of conduct disorder, Tourette's syndrome, and possibly obsessive–compulsive disorder and some right hemisphere learning disorders). We need to better under-

TABLE 9.1 Double Dissociations Between Developmental Learning Disorder:
Demonstrated and Predicted

Pairs of disorders	Dissociated functions (measures)
Demonstrated	
Dyslexia vs. ADHD (Pennington, Groisser, & Welsh, in preparation)	Phonological coding (nonword reading) vs. executive functions: Planning (Tower of Hanoi) Vigilance (CPT, MFFT)
Dyslexia vs. autism (Rumsey et al., 1990)	Phonological coding (nonword reading) vs. social drive (clinical observations)
Dyslexia vs. nonverbal LD (Rourke, 1989)	Reading and spelling vs. spatial cognition (PIQ, Tactual Performance Test)
Predicted	
Dyslexia vs. amnesia	Phonological coding vs. verbal and nonverbal LTM
Dyslexia vs. Asperger's	Phonological coding vs. emotion perception
Amnesia vs. autism	Verbal and nonverbal LTM vs. theory of other minds
Amnesia vs. ADHD	Verbal and nonverbal LTM vs. executive functions
Amnesia vs. Asperger's	Verbal and nonverbal LTM vs. emotion perception
Amnesia vs. nonverbal LD	Verbal and nonverbal LTM vs. spatial cognition
Autism vs. nonverbal LD	Theory of other minds vs. spatial cognition
Autism vs. Asperger's	Theory of other minds vs. spatial cognition

stand what role such shared deficits play in each disorder and what other factors make each disorder distinctive. Disorders like autism (or schizophrenia with negative symptoms) may involve two distinct primary neuropsychological deficits, one in executive functions (the nonspecific deficit) and another in a distinct and specific neuropsychological domain. As can be seen in Table 9.1, double dissociations are *not* predicted between ADHD and either autism, Asperger's or nonverbal LD, because all of these disorders involve deficits in executive functions. Instead, we predict there will only be single dissociations in these comparisons.

Once we have some degree of confidence in this or some other neuropsychological model, a more practical task is to develop a well-standardized, battery of measures of the different domains, first for schoolage children. (Obviously, preschool and even infant batteries are desirable as well, but are more technically difficult to develop.)

This battery could then be used in an epidemiologic survey of the rates and comorbidities of these different learning disorders. Such a survey should overlap with an epidemiologic survey of childhood psychiatric disorders, since several of these disorders are DSM-III-R diagnoses. Moreover, several learning disorders have other childhood psychiatric disorders (e.g., dysthymia, depression) as correlated or secondary symptoms. Such an epidemiologic survey will provide much needed information about the prevalence, sex ratio, and comorbidities of these disorders.

If the survey includes appropriately selected twin samples, then behavior genetic methods can be applied to the problem of analyzing the basis of the comorbidities that will undoubtedly be found. Such analyses can help decide whether the comorbidity is due either to a common genetic etiology for both disorders or to one disorder producing the other as a secondary symptom.

Such a survey would also help address some of the subtype issues discussed in the previous chapters. Is Asperger's syndrome a neuropsychologically distinct syndrome? How common are right hemisphere LDs without social cognitive deficits? And what is the relative prevalence of these two subtypes of right hemisphere LD, one with and the other without social cognitive deficits? More generally, this epidemiological survey will also help identify purer subgroups appropriate for more intensive neuroscientific analysis, including genetic and neuroimaging studies.

Finally, all these learning disorders need to be understood from the perspective of developmental psychopathology. What are the developmental continuities and discontinuities in each disorder? What risk and protective factors are important in altering the course of each disorder?

We turn now to a discussion of research implications specific to each of the five learning disorders we have considered in this book.

Dyslexia

At this point, dyslexia is fairly well-characterized neuropsychologically in school-age samples. We need to know more about life-span development in dyslexia and to understand developmental continuities and discontinuities, including the mechanisms of compensation and even prevention. Longitudinal studies of infants and preschoolers at high familial risk for later dyslexia are needed, as are better studies of adult outcome. We also need more research on the basis of dyslexia's comorbidity with ADHD and other psychiatric conditions.

In terms of etiology, a lot is known about the genetics of this disorder, although further research is needed. Better information on the modes of genetic transmission is required. We need to clearly establish if there are major gene subtypes of dyslexia, and if so, we need to know how common they are. Much less is known about environmental influences that are specific to dyslexia and virtually nothing about environmental influences that are clearly independent of genetic influence. Research indicates that the preschool experience of being read to and playing language games that emphasize syllabic and subsyllabic segments within words are important for later reading development (Adams, 1990), but we do not know how these early experiences act apart from or in relation to genetic influences. Adoption or twin studies could help answer this question.

An indirect, but clinically important, way to address this question would be to conduct a rigorous preventive intervention study of children at high family risk for dyslexia. With careful definition of family risk and random assignment of children to different treatment conditions, such a study could both evaluate the environmental malleability of the genetic risk and potentially validate a method for early identification and treatment, a result of immense practical significance.

We do not understand the mechanisms underlying the sex differences in rates of occurance and compensation in dyslexia, if there truly is a sex difference in incidence. Twin studies that include opposite sex, dizygotic pairs can evalutate whether etiologic factors differ by sex.

Finally, better information about brain mechanisms in dyslexia will come from neuroimaging studies of dyslexics who are well-characterized in terms of both their genetic and neuropsychological characteristics.

Attention Deficit Hyperactivity Disorder and Other Executive Function Disorders

Because both heterogeneity and imprecision of clinical definition pose important threats to the construct validity of ADHD, one basic (and radical) recommendation is to redefine the syndrome, using criteria that are not just based on the symptom level of analysis. Too many distinct disorders produce a phenocopy of ADHD at the symptom level. This vagueness and imprecision certainly fuels the controversies about both the utility of the diagnosis and its treatment with stimulant medication—even though there is a subgroup of children for whom both the diagnostic label and stimulant treatment seem well justified. Perhaps we should require both positive symptoms *and* positive neuropsychological test results to make this diagnosis, as we do in the diagnosis of dyslexia. This two-tiered approach would eliminate many false positives and encourage a more systematic approach to differential diagnosis.

The next question, of course, is *which* tests should be used in a two-tiered approach. This question immediately takes us back to the familiar bootstraps problem. However, I think we are now much closer to useful neuropsychological models of both executive functions and attention, on which candidate tests could be based. A battery of such tests could then be studied to see how well it discriminates children with ADHD-only from diagnostic groups with comorbid ADHD. Because there appear to be genetic influences on ADHD, studying familial samples of both probands and nonreferred siblings might reduce the heterogeneity in the ADHD sample.

Obviously, more basic research is needed on the development and neuropsychology of executive functions and attention (and their relation to each other). Our current rough, working taxonomy of executive function includes four categories: (1) vigilance or sustained attention, (2) set maintenance, (3) planning, and (4) inhibitory motor control, but much more research is needed on the validity of this taxonomy and the development of various executive functions. Posner has proposed an exciting neuropsychological model of the components of the attentional system, but more research is needed on their development and the contribution of deficits in different components to different psychopathologies.

Although genetic and neuroimaging studies of ADHD are badly needed, their payoff will certainly be greater once we have a clearer handle on issues of diagnostic definition and neuropsychological phenotype.

Right Hemisphere Learning Disorders

This category potentially overlaps with ADHD and executive function disorders on the one hand, and social cognitive disorders, such as Asperger's syndrome, on the other. We need to know how many children with spatial cognitive deficits also have deficits in one or both of these other two domains.

Because very little research on right hemisphere learning disorders has been conducted, there is a lot that needs to be done. Two of the most basic research needs are for an epidemiologic study to examine the prevalence and discriminant validity of this learning disorder and for basic research on the development of spatial cognition.

Autism Spectrum Disorder and Social Cognitive Disorders

As we began to see in Chapters 6 and 7, it appears there may be several subtypes of social cognitive disorders, including autism, Asperger's syndrome, and possibly a right hemisphere social cognitive disorder that is not autism or Asperger's syndrome. So one pressing need is for a clearer taxonomy of social cognitive disorders. Development of such a taxonomy will proceed hand-in-hand with basic research on both the development and neuropsychology of social cognition. We need to know the subdomains of social cognition, and how they are related in development. Some potential subdomains include imitation, emotion perception, emotion expression, theory of other minds, empathy, pragmatics, and prosody. However, these skills have usually been studied separately; some may be different names for the same thing. We also need to know more about the genetic, bioenvironmental and social–environmental influences on the development of these skills. Finally, we need to have a clearer understanding of what role the prefrontal areas play in social cognition and how prefrontal social cognition is related to prefrontal executive function. For instance, an intriguing question is which social cognitive and/or executive functions are impaired in schizophrenia, and how do these deficits relate to those found in autism?

Long-Term Memory Disorders

Here there is certainly the largest knowledge gap between adult and child neuropsychology. Unlike the domains of social cognition or executive function, there already exists a sophisticated experimental psychology of memory and its adult disorders, but this knowledge has barely been applied to the study of memory disorders in children.

One fundamental question raised earlier is whether there are developmental LTM disorders. Are some forms of retardation mainly developmental amnesia? For instance, we know that there is a cholinergic deficit in Down syndrome and that cholinergic inputs are essential to the functioning of the limbic memory structures. Thus, is Down syndrome a developmental amnesia? Are there nonretarded developmental amnesias? The answer to these questions await future research, including the epidemiologic study discussed earlier.

Another fundamental question is how often relatively pure, acquired amnesic disorders occur in childhood. Case 10 in Chapter 8 is a potential example; some post-encephalitis cases are another (J. Fletcher, personal communication, April, 1990). This is really a question about the relative vulnerability of the limbic memory structures during development. Nelson (in review) has suggested that a closer examination of children who have suffered perinatal anoxic-ischemic episodes will likely reveal LTM impairment; this is clearly an important research question.

More generally, good measures of LTM function need to be included in studies of other developmental learning disorders. For instance, one theory of autism holds that it is a developmental amnesia, and proponents of this theory have provided some evidence of LTM impairment in autism (Boucher, 1981; Boucher & Lewis, 1989; Boucher & Warrington, 1976).

IMPLICATIONS FOR PRACTICE

The research presented in this book has important implications for both clinical training and practice in the various disciplines that deal with learning disordered children, including child and educational psychologists, child psychiatrists, pediatricians, pediatric neurologists, speech and language therapists, learning disability specialists, and occupational and physical therapists. The diagnosis and treatment of learning disorders is an interdisciplinary enterprise, but many practitioners are not trained in a broad, interdisciplinary perspective on the causes and treatments of learning disorders. Neuropsychology, and more generally neuroscience, offer a broadly integrative framework for understanding these disorders, but few of the practitioners involved get much training in neuropsychology or neuroscience.

For practitioners interested in using a neuropsychological framework, there are other obstacles beyond the training gap. In several of the neuropsychological domains discussed in this book, we lack good, well-standardized measures, even though promising experimental measures exist. There has been recent progress in this area, since well-standardized measures of skills like emotion perception, vigilance, and LTM have recently appeared or are in preparation.

I have been deliberately vague about which disciplines should do what in the evaluation of learning-disordered children. Partly because I am a psychologist, I feel psychologists have an important role to play. I think it would be very useful for some nonpsychologists to know enough about psychological testing to use some tests to screen for a disorder like dyslexia, because more affected children would be identified. For instance, it might be very useful in a public health sense to have pediatricians screen for ADHD and dyslexia, because a large proportion of children regularly see a pediatrician, whereas a much smaller proportion will ever encounter a child psychologist or child psychiatrist. I have already made clear that I feel psychological testing needs to be part of the full evaluation a child suspected of ADHD or dyslexia, and I think this testing can be done by an appropriately trained child psychologist. In contrast, the full evaluation of some learning disorders (i.e., acquired memory disorder and right hemisphere learning disorder) require a referral to a neuropsychologist, in my opinion.

A second obstacle concerns the relation between diagnosis and treatment. Practitioners, especially in the schools, are sometimes wary of complex diagnostic evaluations, especially when it is not clear how the diagnostic detail translates into treatment. Some complex and expensive diagnostic procedures do not lead to any specific treatment. Although we reviewed specific treatment suggestions for each of the five learning disorders discussed in this volume, much of that information is informal and based on clinical experience. There is certainly a pressing need for rigorous evaluation of treatments of learning disorders. Most of the treatments already in place in the nation's schools, for which billions of dollars are being spent, have not been adequately evaluated! This points to another training need for many educational practitioners, namely training in research evaluation of educational programs and treatments. Educational practice in the treatment of learning disorders has been and continues to be swept by fads. Unsubstantiated treatments easily claim a large following because of a lack of critical scrutiny.

Another practice issue that needs to be discussed is the relation between etiology and treatment. Many clinicians resist biological theories of etiology because they feel such theories inevitably imply that only biological treatments are efficacious. Instead, the nature of the etiology does not necessarily imply anything about the most effective treatment. Although there is a strong emphasis in this book on genetic and other biologic causes of learning disorders, nearly all the treatments described were environmental and experiential. When medications are indicated, they are most helpful in the context of an altered environment.

There is clearly much that needs to be done to advance research and practice in the area of learning disorders. However, unlike the mood of confusion and skepticism that has often characterized this field in the past, I think there is now reason for cautious optimism, based on the recent research progress reviewed here.

References

Aarkrog, D. (1968). Organic factors in infantile psychosis and borderline psychosis. *Danish Medical Bulletin,* 283–287.

Accordo, P.J. (1980). *A neurodevelopmental perspective on specific learning disabilities.* Baltimore: University Park Press.

Achenbach, T.M. (1982). *Developmental psychopathology.* New York: Wiley.

Achenbach, T.M., & Edelbrock, C.S. (1981). Behavioral problems and competencies reported by parents of normal and disturbed children aged 4 through 16. *Monographs of the Society for Research in Child Development, 46,* Serial No. 188.

Acredolo, L. (1988). Infant mobility and spatial development. In J. Stiles-Davis, M. Kritchevsky, & U. Bellugi (Eds.), *Spatial cognition: Brain bases and development* (pp. 157–166). Hillsdale, NJ: Lawrence Earlbaum.

Adams, M.J. (1990). *Learning to read.* Cambridge, MA: MIT Press.

Alberts-Corush, J., Firestone, P., & Goodman, P.T. (1986). Attention and impulsivity characteristics of the biological and adoptive parents of hyperactive and normal control children. *American Journal of Orthopsychiatry, 56,* 413–423.

Alexander, D., & Money, J. (1966). Turner's syndrome and Gerstmann's syndrome: Neuropsychologic comparisons. *Neuropsychologia, 4,* 265–273.

Allport, A. (1989). Visual attention. In M.I. Posner (Ed.), *Foundations of cognitive science.* Cambridge, MA: MIT Press.

American Psychiatric Association. (1987). *Diagnostic and statistical manual of mental disorders* (3rd. ed., rev.). Washington, DC: Author.

Andreason, N.C. (1988). Brain Imaging: Applications in psychiatry. *Science, 239,* 1381–1388.

Aram, D.M., & Nation, J.E. (1975). Patterns of language behavior in children with developmental language disorders. *Journal of Speech and Hearing Research, 18,* 229–241.

Bachevalier, J. (in press-a). Memory loss and socio-emotional disturbances following neonatal damage of the limbic system in monkeys: An animal model for childhood autism. *Advances in Psychiatry, 1, Schizophrenia.* New York: Raven Press

Bachevalier, J. (in press-b). Ontogenetic development of habit and memory formation in primates. In C.A. Nelson & M. Gunner (Eds.), *Development and neural bases of higher cognitive functions*. New York: Academy Press.

Baddeley, A.D. (1986). *Working memory*. Oxford: Clarendon Press.

Badian, N.A. (1984). Reading disability in an epidemiological context: Incidence and environmental correlates. *Journal of Learning Disabilities*, *17*, 129–136.

Baird, T.D., & August, G.J. (1985). Familial heterogeneity in infantile autism. *Journal of Autism and Developmental Disorders*, *15*, 315–321.

Ball, E.W., & Blachman, B.A. (1988). Phoneme segmentation training: Effect on reading readiness. *Annals of Dyslexia*, *38*, 208–225.

Barkley, R.A. (1977). The effects of methylphenidate on various types of activity level and attention in hyperkinetic children. *Journal of Abnormal Child Psychology*, *5*, 351–369.

Barkley, R.A. (1981). *Hyperactive children: A handbook for diagnosis and treatment*. New York: Guilford.

Baron-Cohen, S., Leslie, A.M., & Frith, U. (1985). Does the autistic child have a "theory of mind"? *Cognition*, *21*, 37–46.

Baron-Cohen, S., Leslie, A.M., & Frith, U. (1986). Mechanical, behavioral and intentional understanding of picture stories in autisic children. *British Journal of Developmental Psychology*, *4*, 113–125.

Baron-Cohen, S. (1988). Social and pragmatic deficits in autism: Cognitive or affective? *Journal of Autism and Developmental Disorder*, *18*, 379–402.

Baron-Cohen, S. (1989). Are autistic children behaviorists? An examination of their mental–physical and appearance–reality distinctions. *Journal of Autism and Developmental Disorders*, *19*, 579–600.

Bartak, L., Rutter, M., & Cox, A.A. (1975). A comparative study of infantile autism and specific developmental receptive disorder. *British Journal of Psychiatry*, *126*, 127–145.

Bartsch, K., & Wellman, H. (1989). Young children's attribution of action to beliefs and desires. *Child Development*, *60*, 946–964.

Battistia, M. (1980). Interrelationships between problem solving ability, right hemisphere processing facility and mathematics learning. *Focus on Learning Problems in Mathematics*, *2*, 53–60.

Bauman, M., & Kemper, T.L. (1985). Histoanatomic observations of the brain in early infantile autism. *Neurology*, *35*, 866–874.

Bellugi, U., Marks, S., Bihrle, A., & Sabo, H. (1988). Dissociation between language and cognitive functions in Williams syndrome. In D. Bishop & K. Mogford (Eds.), *Language development in exceptional circumstances* (pp. 177–189). London: Churchill Livingstone.

Bender, B.H., Lerner, J.A., & Kollasch, E. (1988). Mood and memory changes in asthmatic children receiving corticoasteroids. *Journal of the American Academy of Child and Adolescent Psychiatry*, *27*, 720–725.

Bender, B.H., Puck, M., Salenblatt, J., & Robinson, A. (1987). Cognitive development of children with sex chromosome abnormalities. In S. Smith (Ed.), *Genetics and learning disabilities* (pp. 175–201). San Diego: College Hill Press.

Beitchman, J.H., Nair, R., Clegg, M., Ferguson, B., & Patel, P.G. (1986). Prevalence of psychiatric disorders in children with speech and language disorders. *Journal of the American Academy of Child Psychiatry, 25,* 528–535.

Benson, D.F., & Geschwind, N. (1970). Developmental Gerstmann syndrome. *Neurology, 20,* 293–298.

Benson, J.B. (1990). The significance and development of crawling in human infancy. In J.E. Clark & J.H. Humphrey (Eds.), *Advances in motor development research* (pp. 91–142). New York: AMS Press.

Benson, J.B., & Uzgiris, I.C. (1985). Effect of self-initiated locomotion on infant search activity. *Developmental Psychology, 21,* 923–931.

Benton, A.L. (1977). Reflections on the Gerstmann syndrome. *Brain and Language, 4,* 45–62.

Benton, A.L., & Pearl, D. (1978). *Dyslexia.* New York: Oxford University Press.

Berch, D.V., & Bender, B.G. (1990). *Sex chromosome abnormalites and human behavior: Psychological studies.* Boulder CO: Westview Press.

Berger, M., Yule, W., & Rutter, M. (1975). Attainment and adjustment in two geographical areas. I: The prevalence of specific reading retardation. *British Journal of Psychiatry, 126,* 510–519.

Berkson, J. (1946). Limitations of the application of fourfold table analysis to hospital data. *Biometrics, 2,* 47–51.

Bisgaard, M.L., Eiberg, H., Moller, N., Niebuhr, E., & Mohr, J. (1987). Dyslexia and chromosome 15 heteromorphism: Negative lod score in a Danish material. *Clinical Genetics, 32,* 118–119.

Bishop, D.V. (1986). Unfixed reference, monocular occlusion and developmental dyslexia: A critique. *British Journal of Opthalmology, 73,* 209–215.

Boucher, L. (1981). Memory for recent events in autistic children. *Journal of Childhood Schizophrenia, 11,* 293–302.

Boucher, L., & Lewis, J. (1989). Memory impairment in relatively high functioning autism. *Journal of Child Psychology and Psychiatry, 30,* 99–122.

Boucher, L., & Warrington, E.K. (1976). Memory deficits in infantile autism: Some similarities to the amnesic syndrome. *Journal of Psychology, 67,* 73–87.

Breen, M.J. (1989). Cognitive and behavioral differences in ADHD boys and girls. *Journal of Child Psychology and Psychiatry, 30,* 711–716.

Brickson, M., & Bachevalier, J. (1984). Visual recognition in infant monkeys: Evidence for a primitive memory process. *Society for Neuroscience Abstracts, 10,* 137.

Brown, A.L., & Campione, J.C. (1986). Psychological theory and the study of learning disabilities. *American Psychologist, 41,* 1059–1068.

Bruck, M. (1984). The adult functioning of children with specific learning disabilities: A follow-up study. In I. Sigel (Ed.), *Advances in applied developmental psychology* (pp. 91–129). Norwood, NJ: Ablex.

Bruner, J.S. (1975). The ontogenesis of speech acts. *Journal of Child Language, 2,* 1–19.

Bryant, P., & Bradley, L. (1985). *Children's reading problems.* Oxford: Basil Blackwell.

Bryden, M.P., & Ley, R.G. (1983). Right-hemispheric involvement in the perception and expression of emotion in normal humans. In K.M. Heilman & P. Satz (Eds.), *The neuropsychology of human emotion* (pp. 6–44). New York: Guilford Press.

Burg, C., Rappaport, J., Bartley, L., Quinn, P., & Timmins, P. (1980). Newborn minor physical anomalies and problem behavior at age 3. *American Journal of Psychiatry, 137,* 791–796.

Campbell, M., Rosenbloom, S., Perry, R., George, A.E., Kircheff, I.I., Anderson, L., Small, A.M., & Jennings, S.L. (1982). Computerized axial tomography in young autistic children. *American Journal of Psychiatry, 139,* 570–512.

Campos, J.J., & Bertenthal, B.I. (1989). Locomotion and psychological development in infancy. In F.J. Morrison, C. Lord, & D.P. Keating (Eds.), *Applied developmental psychology.* New York: Academic Press.

Cantwell, D.P. (1972). Psychiatric illness in the families of hyperactive children. *Archives of General Psychiatry, 27,* 414–417.

Cantwell, D.P. (1975). Genetics of hyperactivity. *Journal of Child Psychology and Psychiatry, 16,* 261–264.

Cantwell, D.P., & Satterfield, J.H. (1978). The prevalence of academic underachievement in hyperactive children. *Journal of Pediatric Psychology, 3,* 168–171.

Case, R., Kurland, M., & Goldberg, J. (1982). Operational efficiency and the growth of short-term memory span. *Journal of Experimental Child Psychology, 33,* 386–404.

Catts, H.W. (1989). Phonological processing deficits and reading disabilities. In A.G. Kamhi & H.W. Catts (Eds.) *Reading disabilities, a developmental language perspective* (pp. 101–132). Boston: College-Hill Publication.

Chelune, G.J., & Baer, R.L. (1986). Developmental norms for the Wisconsin Card Sorting Test. *Journal of Clinical and Experimental Neuropsychology, 8,* 219–228.

Christensen, L.L., & Nielsen, J. (1981). A neuropsychological investigation of 17 women with Turner's syndrome. In W. Schmid & J. Nielsen (Eds.), *Human behavior and genetics* (pp. 151–166). Amsterdam: Elsevier/North-Holland.

Chugani, H.T., & Phelps, M.E. (1986). Maturational changes in cerebral function in infants determined by FDG positron emission tomography. *Science, 231,* 840–843.

Churchland, P.M. (1988). *Matter and consciousness.* Cambridge, MA: MIT Press.

Clark D.B. (1988). *Dyslexia: Theory and Practice of Remedial Instruction.* Parkton, MD: York Press.

Cohen, H. (1962). Psychological test findings in adolescents having ovarian dysgenesis. *Psychological Medicine, 24,* 249–256.

Conners, C.K. (1970). Symptom patterns in hyperkinetic, neurotic, and normal children. *Child Development, 41,* 667–682.

Conners, C.K., & Wells, K.C. (1986). *Hyperkinetic children: A neuropsychosocial approach.* Beverly Hills: Sage.

Conners, C.K., & Werry, J.S. (1979). Pharmacotherapy. In H.C. Quay & J.S. Werry (Eds.), *Psychopathological disorders of childhood* (pp. 336–386). New York: Wiley.

Courchesne, E., Yeung-Courchense, R., Press, G.A., Hesselink, J.R., & Jernigan, T.L. (1988). Hypoplasia of cerebellar vermal lobules VI and VII in autism. *New England Journal of Medicine, 318,* 1349–1354.

Creasey, H., Rumsey, T.M., & Schwartz, M. (1986). Brain morphometry in autistic men as measured by volumetric computed tomography. *Archives of Neurology, 43,* 669–672.

Cromwell, R., Baumister, A., & Hawkins, W. (1963). Research in activity level. In N. Ellis (Ed.) *Handbook of mental deficiency* (pp.632–663). New York: McGraw-Hill.

Cronbach, L.J., & Meehl, P.E. (1955). Construct validity in psychological tests. *Psychological Bulletin, 52,* 281–302.

Cunningham, C.E., & Barkley, R.A. (1978). The role of academic failure in hyperactive behavior. *Journal of Learning Disabilites, 11,* 15–21.

Cunningham, L., Cadoret, R., Loftus, R., & Edwards, J.E. (1975). Studies of adoptees from psychiatrically disturbed biological parents. *British Journal of Psychiatry, 126,* 534–539.

Dalby J.T. (1985). Taxonomic separation of attention deficit disorders and developmental reading disorders. *Contemporary Educational Psychology, 10,* 228–234.

Damasio, A.R., & Maurer, R.G. (1978). A neurological model for childhood autism. *Archives of Neurology, 35,* 777–786.

Damasio, A.R., Maurer, R.G., Damasio, A.R., & Chui, H.C. (1980). Computerized tomography scan findings in patients with autistic behavior. *Archives of Neurology, 37,* 504–510.

David, O.J., Hoffman, S.P., Svrid, J., & Clark, J. (1977). Lead and hyperactivity: Lead levels among hyperactive children. *Journal of Abnormal Child Psychology, 5,* 405–416.

Dawson, G., & Lewy, A. (1989a). Arousal, attention, and the socioemotional impairments of individuals with autism. In G. Dawson (Ed.), *Autism: Nature, diagnosis, and treatment* (pp. 49–74). New York: Guilford Press.

Dawson, G. & Lewy, A. (1989b). Reciprocal subcoritical—cortical influences in autism. In G. Dawson (Ed.), *Autism: Nature, diagnosis, and treatment.* New York: Guilford Press.

DeFries, J.C. (1989). Gender ratios in reading-disabled children and their affected relatives: A commentary. *Journal of Learning Disabilities, 22,* 544–555.

DeFries, J.C., Fulker, D.W., & LaBuda, M.C. (1987). Reading disability in twins: evidence for a genetic etiology. *Nature, 329,* 537–539.

Delong, G.R., & Dwyer, J.T. (1988). Correlations of familiy history with specific autistic subgroups. Asperger's syndrome and bipolar affective disease. *Journal of Autism and Developmental Disorders, 18,* 593–600.

Denckla, M.B. (1979). Childhood learning disabilities. In K.M. Heilman & E. Valenstein (Eds.), *Clinical neuropsychology* (pp. 535–573). New York: Oxford University Press.

Denckla, M.B. (1983). The neuropsychology of social-emotional learning disabilities. *Archives of Neurology, 40,* 461–462.

Diamond, A., & Goldman-Rakic, P.S. (1985a). Evidence for involvement of prefrontal cortex in cognitive changes during the first year of life: Comparison of human infants and rhesus monkeys on a detour task with transparent barrier. *Neurosciences Abstracts, 11,* 832.

Diamond, A., & Goldman-Rakic, P.S. (1985b). Evidence that maturation of frontal cortex of the brain underlies behavioral changes during the first year of life: I. The AB task, II. Object retrieval. Paper presented at the biennial meeting of the Society for Research in Children Development, Toronto.

Dodrill, C.B. (1981). Neuropsychology of epilepsy. In S.B. Filskov & T.J. Boll (Eds.), *Handbook of Clinical Neuropsychology* (pp. 366–395). New York: Wiley Interscience.

Douglas, V.I. (1988). Cognitive deficits in children with attention deficit disorder with hyperactivity. In L.M. Bloomindale & J. Sergeant (Eds.), *Attention deficit disorder: Criteria, cognition, intervention.* A book supplement of the Journal of Child Psychology and Psychiatry (No. 5). New York: Pergamon Press.

Douglas, V.I., Barr, R.G., O'Neill, M.E., Britton, B.G. (1986). Short term effects of methylphenidate on the cognitive, learning and academic performance of children with attention deficit disorder in the laboratory and the classroom. *Journal of Child Psychiatry and Psychology, 27,* 191–211.

Douglas, V.I., & Peters, K.G. (1979). Toward a clearer definition of the attentional deficit of hyperactive children. In G.A. Hale & M. Lewis (Eds.), *Attention and cognitive development.* New York: Plenum.

Dunleavy, R.A., & Boade, C.E. (1980). Neuropsychological correlates of severe asthma in children 9–14 years old. *Journal of Consulting and Clinical Psychology, 48,* 214–219.

Eiben, C.F., Anderson, T.P., Lockman, L., Matthews, D.J., Dryja, R., Martin, J., Burrill, C., Gottesman, N., O'Brien, P., & White, L. (1984). Functional outcome of closed had injury in children and young adults. *Archives of Physical Medicine Rehabilitation, 65,* 168–170.

Eimas, P. (1974). Linguistic processing of speech by young infants. In R. Schiefelbusch & L. Lloyd (Eds.), *Language perspectives: Acquisition, retardation and intervention* (pp. 55–74). Baltimore: University Park Press.

Eisenberg, L. (1978). Definitions of dyslexia: Their consequences for research and policy. In A.L. Benton & D. Pearl (Eds.), *Dyslexia* (pp. 29–42). New York: Oxford University Press.

Eliason, M.J. (1986). Neurofibromatosis: Implications for learning and behavior. *Developmental and Behavioral Pediatrics, 7,* 175–179.

Etcoff, N. (1984). Selective attention to facial identity and facial emotion. *Neuropsychologia, 22,* 281–295.

Fagan, J.F. III., & Singer, L.T. (1983). Infant recognition memory as a measure of intelligence. In L.P. Lipsitt (Ed.), *Advances in infancy research.* Norwood, NJ: Ablex.

Farah, M.J. (1988). The neuropsychology of mental imagery. In J. Stiles-Davis, M. Kritchevsky, & U. Bellugi (Eds.) *Spatial cognition: Brain bases and development* (pp. 33–56). Hillsdale, NJ: Lawrence Earlbaum.

Fein, D., Pennington, B.F., Markowitz, P., Braverman, M., & Waterhouse, L. (1986). Towards a neuropsychological model of infantile autism: Are the social deficits primary? *Journal of the American Academy of Child Psychiatry, 25,* 198–212.

Fein, D., Pennington, B.F., & Waterhouse, L. (1987). Implications of social deficits in autism for neurological dysfunction. In E. Schopler & G. Mesibov (Eds.), *Neurobiological issues in autism* (pp. 127–144). New York: Plenum.

Ferguson, H.B., & Rapoport, J.L. (1983). Nosological issues and biological validation. In M. Rutter (Ed.), *Developmental neuropsychiatry* (pp. 369–384). New York: Guilford Press.

Finucci, J.M. (1986). Follow-up studies of developmental dyslexia and other learning disabilites. In S. Smith (Ed.), *Genetics and learning disabilites* (pp. 97–121). San Diego: College-Hill Press.

Finucci, J.M., Guthrie, J.T., Childs, A.L. Abbey, H., & Childs, B. (1976). The genetics of specific reading disability. *Annual Review of Human Genetics, 40,* 1–23.

Fisher, J.H. (1905). Case of congenital word-blindness (inability to learn to read). *Ophthalmological Review, 24,* 315.

Fleischner, J., & Frank, B. (1979). Visual-spatial ability and mathematics achievement in learning disabled and normal boys. *Focus on Learning Problems in Mathematics, 1,* 7–22.

Fletcher, J.M. (1990). Personal communication.

Fletcher, J.M., & Satz, P. (1985). Cluster analysis and the search for learning disability subtypes. In B.P. Rourke (Ed.), *Neuropsychology of learning disabilities* (pp. 40–64). New York: Guilford Press.

Fletcher, J.M. (1985). External validation of learning disability typologies. In B.P. Rourke (Ed.), *Neuropsychology of learning disabilities* (pp. 187–211). New York: Guilford Press.

Foder, J.A. (1983). *The modularity of mind.* Cambridge, MA: MIT Press.

Folstein, S., & Rutter, M. (1977). Infantile autism: A genetic study of 21 twin pairs. *Journal of Child Psychology and Psychiatry, 18,* 297–321.

Folstein, S., & Rutter, M.L. (1988). Autism: Familial aggregation and genetic implications. *Journal of Autism and Developmental Disorders, 18,* 3–30.

Freeman, B.J., Ritvo, E.R., Mason-Brothers, A., Pingree, C., Yokota, A., Jenson, W.R., McMahon, W.M., Petersen, P.G., Mo, A., & Schroth, P. (1989). Psychometric assessment of first degree relatives of 62 autistic probands in Utah. *American Journal of Psychiatry, 146,* 361–364.

Fuster, J.M. (1985). The prefrontal cortex, mediator of cross-temporal contingencies. *Human Neurobiology, 4,* 169–179.

Gaffney, G.R., Kuperman, S., Tsai, L.Y., & Minchin, S. (1989). Forebrain structure in autism. *Journal of the American Academy of Child and Adolescent Psychiatry, 28,* 534–537.

Galaburda, A.M., & Kemper, T.L. (1979). Cytoarchitectonic abnormalities in developmental dyslexia: A case study. *Annals of Neurology, 6,* 94–100.

Galaburda, A.M., Sherman, G.F., Rosen, G.D., Aboitiz, F., & Geschwind, N. (1985). Developmental dyslexia: Four consecutive patients with cortical anomalies. *Annals of Neurology, 18,* 222–232.

Gardner, H. (1983). *Frames of mind: The theory of multiple intelligences.* New York: Basic Books.

Garron, D. (1977). Intelligence among persons with Turner's syndrome. *Behavior Genetics, 7,* 105–127.

Geschwind, N., & Behan, P.O. (1982). Left-handedness: Association with immune disease, migraine, and developmental learning disorder. *Proceedings from the National Academy of Science, USA, 79,* 5097–5100.

Gilger, J.W., Pennington, B.F., & DeFries, J.C. (in press). Risk for Reading Disabilities as a function of parental history of learning problems: Data from three samples of families demonstrating genetic transmission. *Reading and Writing.*

Gillberg, C. (1985). Asperger's syndrome and recurrent psychosis: A case study. *Journal of Autism and Developmental Disorders, 15,* 389–397.

Gillberg, C, & Gillberg, C. (1989). Asperger syndrome—Some epidemiological considerations: A research note. *Journal of Child Psychology and Psychiatry, 30,* 631–638.

Gillberg, C., Steffenbury, S., & Jakobson, G. (1987). Neurobiological findings in 20 relatively gifted children with Kannia type autism or Asperger's syndrome. *Developmental Medicine and Child Neurology, 29,* 641–649.

Gittelman, R., Mannuzza, S., Shenker, R., & Bonagura, N. (1985). Hyperactive boys almost grown up: I. Psychiatric status. *Archives of General Psychiatry, 42,* 937–947.

Golden, C.J. (1981). The Luria-Nebraska Children's Battery: Theory and formulation. In G.W. Hynd & J.E. Obrzut (Eds.), *Neuropsychological assessment and the school-age child* (pp. 277–302). New York: Grune & Stratton.

Goldman-Rakic, P.S. (1987). Circuitry of primate prefrontal cortex and regulation of behavior by representational knowledge. In F. Plum

(Ed.), *Handbook of physiology: Sec. 1. The Nervous System: Vol. 5. Higher Functions of the Brain* (pp. 373–417). New York: Oxford University Press.

Goldstein, F.C., & Levin, H.S. (1985). Intellectual and academic outcome following closed head injury in children and adolescents: Research strategies and empirical findings. *Developmental Neuropsychology, 3,* 195–214.

Goodman, K. (1967). Reading: A psycholinguistic guessing game. *Journal of the Reading Specialist, 6,* 126–135.

Goodman, R., & Stevenson, J. (1989). A twin study of hyperactivity-II. The etiological role of genes, family relationships and perinatal adversity. *Journal of Child Psychology and Psychiatry, 5,* 691–709.

Gualtieri, T., Evans, R.W., & Patterson, D.R. (1987). The medical treatment of autistic people: Problems an side effects. In E. Schopler & G.B. Mesibov (Eds.), *Neurobiological Issues in Autism* (pp. 373–388). New York: Plenum.

Hagerman, R.J. (1987). Fragile X syndrome. *Current Problems in Pediatrics, 17,* 627–674.

Hagerman, R.J., & Smith, A.C.M. (1983). The heterozygous female. In R.J. Hagerman, & P.M. McBogg (Eds.), *The fragile X syndrome: diagnosis, biochemistry and intervention.* Dillon, CO: Spectra.

Hallgren, B. (1950). Specific dyslexia (congenital word-blindness): A clinical and genetic study. *Acta Psychiatrica et Neurologica Supplement, 65,* 1–287.

Halperin, J.M., Gittelman, R., Klein, D.F., & Rudel, R.G. (1984). Reading-disabled hyperactive children: A distinct subgroup of attention deficit disorder with hyperactivity? *Journal of Abnormal Child Psychology, 12,* 1–14.

Harcherick, D.F., Cohen, D.J., Ort, S., Paul, R., Shaywitz, B.A., Volkman, F.R., Rothman, S.L.G., & Leckman, T.F. (1985). Computed tomographic brain scanning in four neuropsychiatric disorders of childhood. *American Journal of Psychiatry, 142,* 731–737.

Haslam, R.H., Dalby, J.T., Johns, R.D., & Rademaker, A.W. (1981). Cerebral asymmetry in developmental dyslexia. *Archives of Neurology, 38,* 679–304.

Hauser, S., Delong, R., & Rosman, P. (1975). Pneumographic findings in the infantile autism syndrome. *Brain, 98,* 667–688.

Heath, S.B. (1983). *Ways with words.* Cambridge: Cambridge University Press.

Heaton, R., Grant, I., & Charles, G.M. (in press). *Demographic corrections for an expanded Halstad Reitan Battery: Comprehensive norms, research findings and illustratived clinical applications.* Odyssa, FL: Psychological Assessment Resources.

Hecaen, H., & Albert, M.L. (1978). *Human neuropsychology.* New York: Wiley Interscience.

Held, R., & Hein, A. (1963). Movement-produced stimulation in the development of visually guided behavior. *Journal of Comparative and Physiological Psychology, 81,* 394–398.

Henry, S.A., & Witman, R.D. (1981). Diagnostic implications of Bannatyne's recategorized WISC-R scores for identifying learning disabled children. *Journal of Learning Disabilities, 14,* 517–520.

Herjanic, B., Campbell, J., & Reich, W. (1982). Development of a structured psychiatric interview for children: Agreement between child and parent on individual symptoms. *Journal of Abnormal Child Psychology, 10,* 307–324.

Hesselbrock, V.M., Stabenan, J.R., & Hesselbrock, M.N. (1985). Minimal brain dysfunction and neuropsychologic test performance in offspring of alcoholics. *Recent Developments in Alcoholism, 3,* 65–82.

Hier, D.B. (1980). Learning disorders and sex chromosome aberrations. *Journal of Mental Deficiency Research, 24,* 17–26.

Hier D.B., LeMay, M., & Rosenberger, P.B. (1979). Autism and unfavorable left-right asymmetries of the brain. *Journal of Autism and Developmental Disorders, 9,* 153–159.

Hier, D.B., LeMay, M., Rosenberger, P.B., & Perlo, V.B. (1978). Developmental dyslexia: Evidence of a subgroup with reversal of cerebral asymmetry. *Archives of Neurology, 35,* 90–92.

Hinshelwood, J. (1907). Four cases of congenital word-blindness occurring in the same family. *British Medical Journal, 2,* 1229–1232.

Hinshelwood, J. (1911). Two cases of hereditary word-blindness. *British Medical Journal, 1,* 608–609.

Hobson, R.P. (1989). Beyond cognition: A theory of autism. In G. Dawson (Ed.), *Autism: Nature, diagnosis, and treatment* (pp. 22–48). New York: Guilford Press.

Holobrow, P.L., & Berry, P.S. (1986). Hyperactivity and learning difficulties. *Journal of Learning Disabilities, 19,* 426–431.

Horn, J. (1985). Remodeling old models of intelligences. In B. Wolman (Ed.), *Handbook of intelligence: Theories, measurement, and applications.* New York: Wiley.

Horn, W.F., Wagner, A.E., & LaLongo, N. (1989). Sex differences in school-aged children with pervasive attention deficit hyperactivity disorder. *Journal of Abnormal Child Psychology, 17,* 109–124.

Horwitz, B., Rumsey, J.M., Grady, C.L., & Rappaport, S.I. (1988). The cerbral metabolic landscape in autism: Intercorrelations of regional glucose utilization. *Archives of Neurology. 45,* 749–755.

Hughes, J.R. (1982). The electroencephalogram and reading disorders. In R.N. Malatesha & P.G. Aaron (Eds.), *Reading disorders: Varieties and treatments.* New York: Academic Press.

Huttenlocher, P.R. (1979). Synaptic density in human frontal cortex—Developmental change and effects of aging. *Brain Research, 163,* 195–205.

Hynd, G.W., Semrud-Clikeman, M., Lorys, A.R., Novey, E.S., Eliopulas, D. (1990). Brain morphology in developmental dyslexia and attention deficit disorder/hyperactivity. *Archives of Neurology, 47,* 919–926.

Ingram, T.T.S. (1959). Specific developmental disorders of speech in childhood. *Brain, 82,* 450–467.

Just, M.A., & Carpenter, P.A. (1987). *The psychology of reading and language comprehension.* Boston: Allyn & Bacon.

Kanner, L. (1943). Autistic disturbances of affective contact. *Nervous Child, 2,* 217–250.

Kaufman, A.S. (1979). *Intelligent testing with the WISC-R.* New York: Wiley Interscience.

Kemper, M.B., Hagerman, R.J., Ahmad, R.S., & Mariner, R. (1986). Cognitive profiles and the spectrum of clinical manifestations in heterozygous fra X females. *American Journal of Medical Genetics, 23,* 139–156.

Kermoian, R., & Campos, J.J. (1988). Locomotor experience: A facilitatior of spatial cognitive development. *Child Development, 59,* 908–917.

Kerr, J. (1897). School hygiene, in its mental, moral, and physical aspects. Howard Medical Prize Essay. *Journal of the Royal Statistical Society, 60,* 613–680.

Kidd, K.K., & Records, M.A. (1979). Genetic methodologies for the study of speech. In X.O. Breakfield (Ed.), *Neurogenetics: Genetic approaches to the nervous system.* New York: Elsevier-North Holland (pp. 311–344).

Kinsbourne, M., & Warrington, E.K. (1963). A study of finger agnosia. *Brain, 85,* 57–66.

Klasen, E.L. (1968). *Legasthenia.* Bern: Huber.

Klein, R., Berry, G., Briand, K., D'Entremont, B., & Farmer, M. (1990). Letter identification declines with increasing retinal eccentricity at the same rate for normal and dyslexic readers. *Perception and Psychophysics, 47,* 601–606.

Klove, H., & Hole, K. (1979). The hyperkinetic syndrome: Criteria for diagnosis. In R.L. Trites (Ed.), *Hyperactivity in children: Etiology, measurement and treatment implications.* Baltimore: University Park Press.

Konstantareas, M.M., Homatidis, S., & Busch, J. (1989). Cognitive, communication and social differences between autistic boys and girls. *Journal of Applied Developmental Psychology, 10,* 411–424.

Kritchevsky, M. (1988). The elementary spatial functions of the brain. In J. Stiles-Davis, M. Kitchevsky and U. Bellugi (Eds.), *Spatial cognition: Brain bases and development* (pp. 111–140). Hillsdale, NJ: Lawrence Earlbaum.

LaBuda, M.C., DeFries, J.C., & Fulker, D.W. (1986). Multiple regression analysis of twin data obtained from selected samples. *Genetic Epidemiology, 3,* 425–433.

Lambert, N.M., & Sandoval, J. (1980). The prevalence of learning disabilties in a sample of children considered hyperactive. *Journal of Abnormal Child Psychology, 8,* 33–50.

Landau, B. (1988). The construction and use of spatial knowledge in blind and sighted children. In J. Stiles-Davis, M. Kritchevsky and U. Bellugi

(Eds.), *Spatial cognition: Brain bases and development* (pp. 343–371). Hillsdale, NJ: Lawrence Earlbaum.

Larsen, J.P., Hoien, T., Lundberg, I., & Odegaard, H. (1990). MRI evaluation of the size and symmetry of the planum temporal in adolescents with developmental dyslexia. *Brain and Language, 39,* 289–301.

Laufer, M.W., & Denhoff, E. (1957). Hyperkinetic impulse disorder in children. *Journal of Pediatrics, 50,* 463–474.

Lefly, D.L., & Pennington, B.F. (in review). Compensated adults: Are their reading and spelling skills really normal?

Leslie, A.M. (1987). Pretense and representation: The origins of a "theory of mind." *Psychological Review, 94,* 412–426.

Levin, H.S. (1979). The acalculias. In K.M. Heilman & E. Valenstein (Eds.), *Clinical neuropsychology* (pp. 128–140). New York: Oxford University Press.

Levin, H.S., Benton, A.L., Grossman, R.G. (1982). *Neurobehavioral consequences of closed head injury.* New York: Oxford University Press.

Levine, M.D., Obkerlaid, F., & Meltzer, L. (1981). Developmental output failure. *Pediatrics, 67,* 18–25.

Lewis, B.A., Ekelman, B.L., & Aram, D.M. (1989). A familial study of severe phonological disorders. *Journal of Speech and Hearing Research, 32,* 713–724.

Lewitter, F.I., DeFries, J.C., & Elston, R.C. (1980). Genetic models of reading disability. *Behavior Genetics, 10,* 9–30.

Liberman, I.Y. (1973). Segmentation of the spoken word and reading acquisition. *Bulletin of the Orton Society, 23,* 65–77.

Liberman, I.Y., & Shankweiler, D. (1979). Speech, the alphabet, and teaching to read. In L.B. Resnick & P.A. Weaver (Eds.), *Theory and practice of early reading, vol 2,* (pp. 109–132). Hillsdale, NJ: Erlbaum Associates.

Liberman, I.Y., Shankweiler, D., Fischer, F.W., & Carter, B. (1974). Reading and the awareness of linguistic segments. *Journal of Experimental Child Psychology, 18,* 201–212.

Liberman, I.Y., Shankweiler, D., Orlando, C., Harris, K.S., & Berti, F.B. (1971). Letter confusions and reversals of sequence in the beginning reader: Implications for Orton's theory of developmental dyslexia. *Cortex, 7,* 127–142.

Lieberman, P. (1984). *Biology and evolution of language.* Cambridge, MA: Harvard University Press.

Lindamood, C., & Lindamood, P. (1969). *Auditory discrimination in depth.* Boston: Teaching Resources.

Loring, D.W., & Papanicolaou, A.C. (1987). Memory assessment in neuropsychology: Theoretical considerations and practical utility. *Journal of Clinical and Experimental Neuropsychology, 4,* 340–358.

Lou, H.C., Henriksen, L., & Bruhn, P. (1984). Focal cerebral hypoperfusion and/or attention deficit disorder. *Archives of Neurology, 41,* 825–829.

Lou, H.C., Henriksen, L., Bruhn, P., Borner, H., & Nielson, J.B. (1989).

Striatal dysfunction in attention deficit and hyperkinetic disorder. *Archives of Neurology, 46,* 48–52.

Lovaas, O.J. (1987). Behavioral treatment and normal educational and intellectual functioning in young autistic children. *Journal of Consulting and Clinical Psychology, 55,* 3–9.

Luria, A. (1966). *Higher cortical functions in man.* New York: Basic Books.

Lynch, G., McGaugh, J.L., & Weinberger, N.M. (1984). *Neurobiology of learning and memory.* New York: Guilford Press.

Madison, L.S., George, C., & Moeschler, J.B. (1986). Functioning in the fragile X syndrome: A study of intellectual memory and communication skills. *Journal of Mental Deficiency, 3,* 129–148.

Maclean, M., Bryant, P., & Bradley, L. (1987). Rhymes, nursery rhymes, and reading in early childhood. *Merrill-Palmer Quarterly, 33,* 255–282.

Mahler, M. (1952). On child psychosis and schizophrenia: Autistic and symbiotic infantile psychosis. *Psychoanalytic Study of the Child, 7,* 286–305.

Manuzza, S., & Gittelman, R. (1984). The adolescent outcome of hyperactive girls. *Psychiatry Research, 13,* 19–29.

Mattes, J.A., & Gittelman, R. (1979). *A pilot trial of amantadine in hyperactive children.* Paper presented at the NCDEU meeting, Key Biscayne, FL.

McCauley, E., Kay, T., Ito, J., & Treder, R. (1987). The Turner Syndrome: Cognitive deficits, affective discrimination, and behavior problems. *Child Development, 58,* 464–473.

McGee R., Williams, S., & Silva, P.A. (1985). The factor structure and correlates of ratings of inattention, hyperactivity and antisocial behavior in a large sample of nine year old children from the general population. *Journal of Consulting an Clinical Psychology, 53,* 480–490.

McGee, R., Williams, S., & Silva, P.A. (1987). A comparison of girls and boys with teacher-identified problems of attention, *Journal of the American Academy of Child and Adolescent Psychiatry, 26,* 711–714.

McGee, R., & Share, D.L. (1988). Attention deficit disorder-hyperactivity and academic failure: Which comes first and what should be treated? *Journal of the American Academy of Child and Adolescent Psychiatry, 27,* 318–325.

McGlone, J. (1985). Can spatial deficits in Turner's syndrome be explained by focal CNS dysfunction or atypical speech lateralization? *Journal of Clinical and Experimental Neuropsychology, 7,* 375–394.

Meehl, P.E. (1973). Schizotaxia, schizotypy, schizophrenia. *American Psychology, 17,* 827–838.

Meltzoff, A.N. (1987). The roots of social and cognitive development: Models of man's original nature. In T.M. Field & N. Fox (Eds.), *Social perception in infants.* New Jersey: Ablex.

Menyuk, P., & Menn, L. (1979). Early strategies for the perception and production of words and sounds. In P. Fletcher & M. Garman (Eds.), *Language acqustion* (pp. 49–70). Cambridge: Cambridge University Press.

Miezejeski, C.M., Jenkins, E.C., Hill, A.L., Wisniewski, K., French, J.H., & Brown, W.T. (1986). A profile of cognitive deficit in females from fragile X families. *Neuropsychology, 24*, 405–409.

Milich, R.S., & Loney, J. (1979). The role of hyperactive and aggressive symtomatology in predicting adolescent outcome among hyperactive children. *Journal of Pediatric Psychology, 4*, 93–112.

Money, J. (1973). Turner's syndrome and parietal lobe functions. *Cortex, 9*, 387–393.

Morgan, W.P. (1896). A case of congenital word-blindness. *British Medical Journal, 2*, 1543–1544.

Morely, M.E. (1965). *The development and disorders of speech in childhood.* London: Churchill Livingstone.

Morris, R. (1984). *Multivariate methods for neuropsychology—techniques for classification, identification, and prediction research.* Paper presented at International Neuropsychological Society Meeting, Houston, TX.

Morrison, J.R., & Stewart, M.A. (1973). The psychiatric status of the legal families of adoptive hyperactive children. *Archives of General Psychiatry, 28*, 888–891.

Morrow, L., & Ratcliff, G. (1988). Neuropsychology of spatial cognition: Evidence from cerbral lesions. In J. Stiles-Davis & M. Kritchevsky, (Eds.), *Spatial cognition brain bases and development.* Hillsdale, NJ: Lawrence Erlbaum.

Mundy, P., & Sigman, M. (1989). The theoretical implications of joint-attention deficits in autism. *Development and Psychopathology, 1*, 173–183.

Myklebust, H.R. (1975). Nonverbal learning disabilities: Assessment and intervention. In H.R. Myklebust (Ed.), *Progress in learning disabilities: Vol.3.* New York: Grune & Stratton.

Naeye, R.C., & Peters, E.C. (1987). Antenatal hypoxia and low IQ values. *American Journal of Diseases in Children, 141*, 50–54.

Naidoo, S. (1972). *Specific dyslexia.* London: Pitman.

Nelson, C.A. (1987). The recognition of facial expressions in the first two years of life: Mechanisms of development. *Child Development, 58*, 889–909.

Nelson, C.A. (in press). Neural correlates of recognition memory in the first post-natal year of life. In G. Dawson & K. Fisher (Eds.), *Human behavior and the developing brain.* New York: Guilford Press.

Nelson, C.A., Colins, P.F., & Torres F. (1991). Brain activity in seizure patients preceding temporal lobectomy. *Archives of Neurology, 48*, 141–147.

Nelson, C.A., Ellis, A.E., Collins, P., & Lang, S.F. (1990). Infant's neuroelectric responses to missing stimuli: Can missing stimuli be novel stimuli? *Developmental Neuropsychology, 6*, 339–349.

Nichols, P., & Chen, T.C. (1981). *Minimal brain dysfunction: A prospective study.* Hillsdale, NJ: Lawrence Erlbaum.

Nittrouer, S., & Studdart-Kennedy K. (1987). The role of coarticulatory effects in the perception of fricatives by children and adults. *Journal of Speech and Hearing Research, 30,* 319–329.

O'Dougherty, M., Wright, F.S., Loewenson, R.B., & Torres, F. (1985). Cerebral dysfunction after chronic hypoxia in children. *Neurology, 35,* 42–46.

Olson, R.K. (1985). Disabled reading processes and cognitive profiles. In D.B. Gray & J.K. Kavanaugh (Eds.), *Biobehavioral measures of dyslexia.* Parkton, MD: York Press.

Olson, R.K., Gillis, J.J., Rack, J.P., DeFries, J.C., & Fulker, D.W. (in press). Confirmatory factor analysis of word recognition and process measures in the Colorado Reading Project. *Reading and Writing.*

Olson, R.K., Wise, B., Conners, F., Rack, J., & Fulker, D. (1989). Specific deficits in component reading and language skills: Genetic and environmental influences. *Journal of Learning Disabilities, 22,* 339–348.

Orton, S.T. (1937). *Reading, writing, and speech problems in children.* New York: Norton.

Ott, J. (1985). Estimation of the recombination fraction in human pedigrees: Efficient computation of the likelihood for human studies. *American Journal of Human Genetics, 26,* 588–597.

Owen, F.W, Adams, P.A., Forrest, T., Stolz, L.M., & Fisher, S. (1971). Learning disorders in children sibling studies. *Monographs of the Society for Research for Child Development, 36,* serial #144.

Ozonoff, S., Pennington, B.F., & Rogers, S. (1990). Are there emotion perception deficits in young autistic children? *Journal of Child Psychology and Psychiatry.*

Ozonoff, S., Pennington, B.F., & Rogers, S.J. (in press). Executive function deficits in high functioning autistic children: Relationship to theory of mind. *Journal of Child Psychology and Psychiatry.*

Ozonoff, S., Rogers, S., & Pennington, B.F. (in press). Contrasting deficits in Asperger's syndrome vs. high functioning autism. *Journal of Child Psychology and Psychiatry.*

Parry, P. (1973). *The effect of reward on the performance of hyperactive children.* Unpublished doctoral dissertation, McGill University, Montreal.

Passler, M.A., Isaac, W., & Hynd, G.W. (1985). Neuropsychological development of behavior attributed to frontal lobe functioning in children. *Developmental Neuropsychology, 1,* 349–371.

Paterhite, C.E., & Loney, J. (1980). Childhood hyperkinesis: Relationships between symptomatology and home environment. In C.K. Whalen & B. Henker (Eds.), *Hyperactive children: The social ecology of identification and treatment.* New York: Academic Press.

Paul, R. (1987) Natural History. In D.J. Cohen, A.M. Donnellan, & R. Paul (Eds.), *Handbook of autism and pervasive developmental disorders* (pp. 121–130). New York: Wiley.

Pauls, D.L. (1987). The familiality of autism and related disorders: A review of the evidence. In D.J. Cohen, A.M. Donnellan, & R. Paul (Eds.),

Handbook of Autism and Pervasive Developmental Disorders (pp. 192–198). New York: Wiley.

Pauls, D.L., & Leckman, J.F. (1986). The inheritance of Giles de la Tourette syndrome and associated behaviors: Evidence for autosomal dominant transmission. *New England Journal of Medicine, 315,* 993–997.

Pelham, W.J. Jr. (1988). The effects of psychostimulant drugs on learning and academic achievement in children with attention deficit disorder and learning disabilites. In J.K. Torgensen & B. Wong (Eds.), *Psychological and educational perspectives on learning disabilites* (pp. 259–295). New York: Academic Press.

Pennington, B.F., Bender, B., Puck, M., Salbenblatt, J., & Robinson, A. (1982). Learning disabilities in children with sex chromosome anomalies. *Child Development, 53,* 1182–1192.

Pennington, B.F., Gilger, J.W., Pauls, D.L., Smith, S.D., Smith, S.A., & DeFries, J.C. (in review). Evidence for major gene transmission in dyslexia.

Pennington, B.F., Groisser, D.B., & Welsh, M.C. (in preparation). Contrasting neuropsychological profiles in ADHD vs. dyslexia.

Pennington, B.F., Heaton, R.K., Karzmark, P., Pendleton, M.G., Lehman, R., & Shucard, D.W. (1985). The neuropsychological phenotype in Turner syndrome. *Cortex, 21,* 391–404.

Pennington, B.F., Lefly, D.L., Van Orden, G.C., Bookman, M.O. & Smith, S.D. (1987). Is phonology bypassed in normal or dyslexic development? *Annals of Dyslexia, 37,* 62–89.

Pennington, B.F., McCabe, L.L., Smith, S.D., Lefly, D.L., Bookman, M.O., Kimberling, W.J., & Lubs, H.A. (1986). Spelling errors in adults with a form of familial dyslexia. *Child Development, 57,* 1001–1013.

Pennington, B.F., Schreiner, R.A., & Sudhalter, V. (in press-a). Towards a neuropsychology of fragile X syndrome. In R.J. Hagerman & A. Cronister (Eds.), *The fragile X syndrome,* Baltimore: Johns Hopkins University Press.

Pennington, B.F., Smith, S.R., Kimberling, W., Green, P.A., & Haith, M.M. (1987). Left-handedness and immune disorders in familial dyslexics. *Archives of Neurology, 44,* 634–639.

Pennington, B.F., Van Doorninck, W.J., McCabe, L.L., & McCabe, E.R.B. (1985). Neuropsychological deficits in early treated phenylketonurics. *American Journal of Mental Deficiency, 89,* 467–474.

Pennington, B.F., Van Orden, G., Kirson, D., & Haith, M.M. (in press-b). What is the causal relation between verbal STM problems and dyslexia? In S. Brady & D. Shankweiler (Eds.), *Phonological processes in literacy.* Hillsdale, NJ: Erlbaum.

Pennington, B.F., Van Orden, G., Smith, S.D., Green, P.A., & Haith, M.M. (1990). Phonological processing skills and deficits in adult dyslexics. *Child Development, 61,* 1753–1778.

Perecman, E. (1987). *The frontal lobes revisited.* New York: IRBN Press.

Perfetti, C.A. (1985). *Reading ability*. New York: Oxford University Press.

Perner, J., Frith, U., Leslie, A.M., & Leekam, S. R. (1989). Exploration of the autistic child's theory of mind: Knowledge, belief and communication. *Child Development, 60*, 689–700.

Plomin, R. (1986). *Development, genetics, and psychology*. Hillsdale, NJ: Erlbaum.

Plomin, R. (1990). The role of inheritance in behavior. *Science, 248*, 183–188.

Porrino, I.J., Rapoport, J.L., Behar, D., Sceery, W., Ismond, D.R., & Bunney, W.E., Jr. (1983). A naturalistic assessment of the motor activity of hyperactive boys. *Archives of General Psychiatry, 40*, 681–687.

Porges, S.W., Walter, G.F., Korb, R.J., & Sprague, R.L. (1975). The influence of methylphenidate on heart rate and behavioral measures of attention in hyperactive children. *Child Development, 46*, 727–733.

Posner, M.I. & Petersen, S.E. (in press). The attention system of the human brain. *Annual Review of Neuroscience*.

Posner, M.I., Petersen, S.E., Fox, P.T., & Raichle, M.E. (1988). Localization of cognitive operations in the human brain. *Science, 240*, 1627–1631.

Price, B.H., Daffner, K.R., Stowe, R.M., & Mesulam, M.M. (1990). The comportmental learning disabilities of early frontal lobe damage. *Brain, 113*, 1383–1393.

Quart, E.J., Buchtel, H.A., & Sarnaik, A.P. (1987). Long-lasting memory deficits in children recovered from Reye's Syndrome. *Journal of Clinical and Experimental Neuropsychology, 10*, 409–420.

Rakic, P., Bourgeois, J.P., Zecevic, N., Eckenhoff, M.F., & Goldman-Rakic, P.S. (1986). Concurrent overproduction of synapses in diverse regions of the primate cerebral cortex. *Science, 232*, 232–235.

Rapin, I. (1987). Searching for the cause of autism: A neurologic perspective. In D.J. Cohen & A.M. Donnellan (Eds.), *Handbook of autism and pervasive developmental disorders* (pp. 710–717). New York: Wiley.

Rapin, I. & Allen, D. (1982). Developmental language disorders: Nosologic considerations. In U. Kirk (Ed.), *Neuropsychology of language, reading and spelling* (pp. 155–184). New York: Academic Press.

Rapoport, J.L., & Quinn, P.O. (1975). Minor physical anomalies (stigmata) and early developmental deviation: A major biological subgroup of "hyperactive children." *International Journal of Mental Health, 4*, 29–44.

Raynor, K. (1986). Do faulty eye movements cause dyslexia? *Developmental Neuopsychology, 1*, 3–15.

Realmuto, G.M., Garfinkel, B.D., Tuchman, M., Tsai, M.Y., Chang, P.N., Fisch, R.O., & Shapiro, S. (1986). Psychiatric diagnosis and behavioral characteristics of phenylketonuric children. *Journal of Nervous and Mental Disease, 174*, 144–148.

Reiss, A.L., Hagerman, R.J., Vinogradov, S., Abrams, M., & King, R. (1988). Psychiatric disability in female carriers of the fragile X chromosome. *Archives of General Psychiatry, 45*, 25–30.

Rimland, B. (1971). The differentiation of childhood psychosis: An analysis of checklists for 2,218 psychotic children. *Journal of Autism and Childhood Schizophrenia, 1,* 161–174.

Ritvo, E.R., Freeman, B.J., Scheibel, A.B., Doung, P.T., Robinson, H., & Guthrie, D. (1986). Decreased Purkinje cell density in four autistic patients: Initial findings of the UCLA-NSAC Autopsy Research Project. *American Journal of Psychiatry, 43,* 862–866.

Robinson, A., Lubs, H.A., & Bergson, D. (1979). *Sex chromosome aneuploidy: Prospective studies on children.* New York: Alan R. Liss.

Roberts R.J., Varney N.R., Reinarz S.J., & Parkens R.A. (1988). CT asymmetries in developmentally dyslexic adults. *Developmental Neuropsychology, 43,* 231–237.

Robertson, C.M.T., Finer, N.N., & Grace, M.G.A. (1989). School performance of survivors of neonatal encephalopathy associated with birth asphyxia at term. *Journal of Pediatrics, 114,* 753–760.

Rodgers, B. (1983). The identification and prevalence of specific reading retardation. *British Journal of Educational Psychology, 53,* 369–373.

Rogers, S.J. & Lewis, H. (1989). An effective day treatment model for young children with pervasive developmental disorders. *Journal of the American Academy of Child and Adolescent Psychiatry, 28,* 207–214.

Rogers, S.J., & Pennington, B.F. (in press). A theoretical approach to the deficits in infantile autism. *Development and Psychopathology.*

Rosenberger, P.B., & Hier, D.B. (1979). Cerebral asymmetry and verbal intellectual deficits. *Annals of Neurology, 8,* 300–304.

Ross, D.M., & Ross, S.A. (1982). *Hyperactivity: Current issues, research and theory* (2nd ed). New York: Wiley.

Rourke, B.P. (1989). *Nonverbal learning disabilities: The syndrome and the model.* New York: Guilford Press.

Rourke, B.P., & Finlaysen, M.A.J. (1978). Neuropsychological significance of variations in patterns of academic performance: Verbal and visual disabilities. *Journal of Abnormal Child Psychology, 6,* 121–133.

Rourke, B.P., & Strang, J.D. (1978). Neuropsychological significance of variations in patterns of academic performance: Motor, psychomotor, and tactile-perceptual abilities. *Journal of Pediatric Psychology, 2,* 62–66.

Rourke, B.P., Young, G.C., Strang, J.D., & Russell, D.L. (1986). Adult outcomes of central processing deficiencies in childhood. In I. Grant & K.M. Adams (Eds.), *Neuropsychological assessment in neuropsychiatric disorders: Clinical methods and empirical findings* (pp. 245–267). New York: Oxford University Press.

Rumelhart, D.E., McClelland, J.L. (1986). *Parallel distributed processing: Explorations in the microstructure of cognition. Volume 1.* Cambridge, MA: MIT Press.

Rumsey, J. (1985). Conceptual problem-solving in highly verbal, nonretarded autistic men. *Journal of Autism and Developmental Disorders, 15,* 23–36.

Rumsey, J.M., Dorwort, R., Vermess, M., Denckla, M.B., Kruesi, M., & Rapoport, J.L. (1986). Magnetic resonance imaging of brain anatomy in severe developmental dyslexia. *Archives of Neurology, 43,* 1045–1046.

Rumsey, J.M., Rapoport, J.L, & Sceery, W.R. (1985). Autistic children as adults: Psychiatric, social and behavioral outcomes. *Journal of the American Academy of Child Psychiatry, 24,* 465–473.

Rumsey, J., & Hamberger, S.D. (1988). Neuropsychological findings in high-functioning men with infanitle autism, residual state. *Journal of Clinical and Experimental Neuropsychology, 10,* 201–221.

Rumsey, J.M., & Hamburger, S.D. (1990). Neuropsychological divergence of high-level autism and severe dyslexia. *Journal of Autism and Developmental Disorders, 20,* 155–168.

Rutter, M. (1983). Cognitive deficits in the pathogenesis of autism. *Journal of Child Psychology and Psychiatry, 24,* 513–531.

Rutter, M., Graham, P., & Yule, W. (1970). A neuropsychiatric study in childhood. *Clinics in Developmental Medicine,* Philadelphia: Lippincott.

Rutter, M., Macdonald, H., Le Couteur, A., Harrington, R., Bolton, P., & Bailey, A. (1990). Genetic factors in child psychiatric disorders—empirical findings. *Journal of Child Psychology and Psychiatry, 31,* 39–83.

Rutter, M., Tizard, J., & Whitmore, K. (1970). *Education, health and behavior.* London: Longman.

Rutter, M., & Yule W. (1975). The concept of specific reading retardation. *Journal of Child Psychology and Psychiatry, 16,* 11–197.

Sacks, O. (1972). *Awakenings.* New York: Vintage.

Safer, D.J., & Allen, R.P. (1976). *Hyperactive children: Diagnosis and management.* Baltimore: University Park Press.

Satz, P., & Zaide, J. (1983). Sex differences: Clues or myths on genetic aspects of speech and language disorders. In C.L. Ludlow, & J.A. Cooper (Eds.). *Genetic Aspects of Speech and Language Disorders* (pp. 85–105). New York: Academic Press.

Scarborough, H. (1989). Prediction of reading disability from familial and individual differences. *Journal of Educational Psychology, 81,* 101–108.

Scarborough, H. (1990). Very early language deficits in dyslexic children. *Child Development, 61,* 1728–1743.

Schacter, D.L., & Moscovitch, M. (1984). *Infant memory.* New York: Plenum Press.

Schopler, E. (1985). Convergence of learning disability, higher-level autism and Asperger's syndrome. *Journal of Autism and Developmental Disorders, 15,* 359–360.

Schopler, E., Reichler, R.J, DeVillis, R.F., & Daly, K. (1980). Toward objective classification of childhood autism: Childhood Autism Rating Scale (CARS). *Journal of Autism and Developmental Disorders, 10,* 91–103.

Schulman, J., & Leviton, A. (1978). Reading disabilites: An epidemiologic approach. In H.R. Myklebust (Ed.), *Progress in learning disabilites:* Vol. 4. New York: Grune & Stratton.

Semrud-Clikeman, M., & Hynd G.W. (1990). Right hemispheric dysfunction in nonverbal learning disabilities: Social, academic, and adaptive functioning in adults and children. *Psychological Bulletin, 107,* 196–209.

Shaffer, J.W. (1962). A specific cognitive deficit observed in gonadal aplasia (Turner's Syndrome). *Journal of Clinical Psychiatry, 18,* 403–406.

Shallice, T. (1982). Specific impairments in planning. In D.E. Broadbent & L. Weiskrantz (Eds.), *The neuropsychology of cognitive function* (pp. 199–209). London: The Royal Society.

Shallice, T. (1988). *From neuropsychology to mental structure.* New York: Cambridge University Press.

Shankweiler, D., & Crain, S. (1987). Language mechanisms and reading disorder: A modular approach. In P. Bertelson (Ed.) *The onset of literacy.* Cambridge: MIT Press.

Shaywitz, B.A., Cohen, D.J., & Bowers, M.B. (1977). CSF monoamine metabolites in children with minimal brain dysfunction: Evidence for alteration of brain dopamine. *Journal of Pediatrics, 90,* 67–71.

Shaywitz, B.A., Cohen, D.J., & Shaywitz, B.A. (1980). Behavior and learning difficulties in children of normal intelligence born to alcoholic mothers. *Journal of Pediatrics, 96,* 978–982.

Shaywitz, S.E., & Shaywitz, B.E. (1988). Attention deficit disorder: Current perspectives. In J.F. Kavanaugh & T.J. Truss (Eds.), *Learning disabilities: Proceedings of the national conference* (pp. 369–523). Parkton, MD: York Press.

Shaywitz, S.E., Shaywitz, B.A., Cohen, D.J., & Young, J.G. (1983). Monoaminergic mechanisms in hyperactivity. In M. Rutter (Ed.), *Developmental neuropsychiatry* (pp. 330–347). New York: Guilford Press.

Shaywitz, S.E., Shaywitz, B.A., Fletcher, J.M., & Escobar, M.D. (1990). Prevalence of reading disabilities in boys and girls: Results of the Connecticut Longitudinal Study. *Journal of American Medical Association, 264,* 998–1002.

Shepard, R. (1988). The role of transformation in spatial cognition. In J. Stiles-Davis, M. Kritchevsky, & U. Bellugi (Eds.), *Spatial cognition brain bases and development.* Hillsdale, New Jersey: Lawrence Erlbaum.

Shepard, R.N., & Metzler, J. (1971). Mental rotation of three-dimensional objects. *Science, 171,* 701–703.

Shute, G.E., & Huertas, V. (1990). Developmental variability in frontal lobe function. *Developmental Neuropsychology, 6,* 1–11.

Siegel, C., Waldo, M., Mizner, G., Adler, L.E., & Freedman, R. (1984). Deficits in sensory gating in schizophrenic patients and their relatives. *Archives of General Psychiatry, 41,* 607–612.

Siegel, L.S., & Ryan, E.B. (1989). The development of working memory in normally achieving and subtypes of learning disabled children. *Child Development, 60,* 973–980.

Sigman, M., Ungerer, J.A., Mundy, P., & Sherman, T. (1987). Cognition in autistic children. In D.J. Cohen, A.M. Donnellan, & R. Paul (Eds.), *Handbook of autism and pervasive developmental disorders* (pp. 103–120). New York: Wiley.

Silbert, A., Wolff, P.H., & Lillienthal, J. (1977). Spatial and temporal processing in patients with Turner's syndrome. *Behavior Genetics*, 7, 11–21.

Singer, S., Stewart, M., & Pulaski, L. (1981). Minimal brain dysfunction: Differences in two groups of index cases and their relatives. *Journal of Learning Disabilities*, 14, 470–473.

Slater, H., Morrison, V., & Rose, D. (1982). *British Journal of Developmental Psychology*, 13, 519–525.

Smalley, S.L., & Asarnow, R.F. (1990). Cognitive subclinical markers of autism. *Journal of Autism and Developmental Disorders*, 20, 271–278.

Smalley, S.L., Asarnow, R.F., & Spence, M.A. (1988). Autism and genetics: A decade of research. *Archives of General Psychiatry*, 45, 953–961.

Smith, F. (1978). *Understanding reading: A psycholinguistic analysis of reading and learning to read*. New York: Holt, Rinehart, & Winston.

Smith, S.D., Kimberling, W.J., Pennington, B.F., & Lubs, H.A. (1983). Specific reading disability: Identification of an inherited form through linkage and analysis. *Science*, 219, 1345–1347.

Smith, S.D., Pennington, B.F., Kimberling, W.J., & Ing, P.S. (1990). Familial dyslexia: Use of genetic linkage data to define subtypes. *Journal of the American Academy of Child and Adolescent Psychiatry*, 29, 204–213.

Spence, M.A., Ritvo, E.R., Marazita, M.L., Funderbunk, S.J., Sparkes, R.S., & Freemena, B.J. (1985). Gene mapping studies with the syndrome of autism. *Behavior Genetics*, 15, 1–18.

Spreen, O. (1982). Adult outcomes of reading disorders. In R.N. Malatesha & P.G. Aaron (Eds.), *Reading disorders: Varieites and treatments* (pp. 473–498). New York: Academic Press.

Spreen, O., Tupper, D., Risser, A., Tuckko, H., & Edgell, D. (1984). *Human developmental neuropsychology*. New York: Oxford University Press.

Squire, L. (1987). *Memory and brain*. New York: Oxford University Press.

Stanovich, K.E. (1986). Matthew effects in reading. Some consequences of individual differences in the acquistion of literacy. *Reading Research Quarterly*, 21, 360–406.

Stanovich, K.E., Nathan, R.G., & Vala-Rossi, M. (1986). Developmental changes in the cognitive correlates of reading ability and the developmental lag hypothesis. *Reading Research Quarterly*, 21, 267–283.

Stanovich, K.E., Nathan, R.G., & Zolman, J.E. (1988). The developmental lag hypothesis in reading: Longitudinal and matched reading-level comparisons. *Child Development*, 59, 71–86.

Stanovich, K.E., & West, R.F. (1983). The generalizability of context effects on word recognition: A reconsideration of the roles of parafoveal priming and sentence context. *Memory & Cognition*, 11, 49–58.

Stephenson, S. (1907). Six cases of congenital word-blindness affecting three generations of one family. *Ophthalmoscope*, 5, 482–484.

Stern, D.N. (1985). *The interpersonal world of the infant: A view from psychoanalysis and developmental psychology*. New York: Basic Books.

Stevenson, J. (1988). Which aspects of reading ability show a "hump" in their distribution? *Applied Cognitive Psychology*, 2, 77–85.

Stevenson, J. (in press). Which aspects of processing text mediate genetic effects? *Reading and Writing*.

Stevenson, J., & Fredman, G. (1990). The social environmental correlates of reading ability. *Journal of Child Psychology and Psychiatry*, 31, 681–698.

Stevenson, J., Graham, P., Fredman, G., & McLoughlin, V. (1986). A twin study of genetic influences on reading and spelling ability and disability. *Journal of Child Psychology and Psychiatry*, 28, 231–247.

Stevenson, J., Hawcraft, J., Lobascher, M., Smith, I., Wolff, O.H., & Graham, P.J. (1979). Behavioral deviance in children with early-treated phenylketonuria. *Archives of Disease in Childhood*, 54, 14.

Stiles-Davis, J. (1988). Spatial dysfunctions in young children with right hemisphere injury. In J. Stiles-Davis, & M. Kritchevsky (Eds.), *Spatial cognition brain bases and development* (pp. 251–272). Hillsdale, NJ: Lawrence Erlbaum.

Stiles-Davis, J., Kritchevsky, M., & Bellugi, U. (1988). *Spatial cognition and brain bases and development*. Hillsdale, NJ: Lawrence Erlbaum.

Strang, J.D., & Rourke, B.P. (1985). Arithmetic disability subtypes: The neuropsychological significance of specific arithmentic impairment in childhood. In B.P. Rourke (Ed.), *Neuropsychology of learning disabilities: Essentials of subtype analysis* (pp. 167–183). New York: Guilford Press.

Strauss, A., & Lehtinen, L. (1947). *Psychopathology and education in the brain injured child*. New York: Grune & Stratton.

Stuart, M., & Coltheart, M. (1988). Does reading develop in a sequence of stages: *Cognition*, 30, 139–181.

Stuss, D.T., & Benson, D.F. (1986). *The frontal lobes*. New York: Raven Press.

Sykes, D.H., Douglas, V.I., & Morgenstern, G. (1973). Sustained attention in hyperactive children. *Journal of Child Psychology and Psychiatry*, 14, 213–220.

Sykes, D.H., Douglas, V.I., Weiss, G., & Minde, K.K. (1971). Attention in hyperactive children and the effect of methylphenidate (Ritalin). *Journal of Child Psychology and Psychiatry*, 12, 129–139.

Szatmari, P., Bartolucci, G., & Bremner, R. (in press). Asperger's syndrome and autism: Comparisons on early history and outcome. *Developmental Medicine and Child Neurology*.

Szatmari, P., Bartolucci, G., Bremner, R., Bond, S., & Rich, S. (1989). A follow-up study of high-functioning autistic children. *Journal of Autism and Developmental Disorders*, 19, 213–225.

Taylor, E.A. (1986). *The overactive child*. Philadelphia: Lippincott.

Taylor, H.G. (1988). Learning disabilities. In E.J. Mash & L.G. Terdal (Eds.), *Behavioral assessment of childhood disorders* (pp. 402–450). New York: Guilford.

Templin, M. (1957). *Certain language skills in children*. Minneapolis: University of Minnesota Press.

Thomas, C.J. (1990). Congenital "word-blindness" and its treatment. *Ophthalmoscope, 3,* 380–385.

Tranel, D., Hall, L.E., Olson, S., & Tranel, N.N. (1987). Evidence for a right-hemisphere developmental learning disability. *Developmental Neuropsychology, 3,* 113–127.

Trevarthen, C. (1977). Descriptive analyses of infant communicative behavior. In H.R. Schaffer (Ed.), *Studies in mother-infant interaction.* New York: Academic Press.

Tsai, L., Stewart, M.A., & August, G. (1981). Implication of sex differences in the familial transmission of infantile autism. *Journal of Autism and Developmental Disorders, 11,* 165–174.

Tulving, E. (1983). *Elements of episodic memory.* New York: Oxford University Press.

Van Orden, G.C. (1987). A ROWS is a ROSE: Spelling sound and reading. *Memory & Cognition, 15,* 181–198.

Van Orden, G.C. (1991). Phonologic mediation is fundamental to reading. In D. Besner & G.W. Humphreys (Eds.), *Basic processes in reading: Visual and word recognition* (pp. 77–103). Hillsdale, NJ: Erlbaum.

Van Orden, G.C., Johnston, J.C., & Hale, B.L. (1988). Word identification in reading proceeds from spelling to sound to meaning. *Journal of Experimental Psychology: Learning, Memory, and Cognition, 14,* 371–385.

Van Orden, G.C., Pennington, B.F., & Stone, G.O. (1990). Word identification in reading and the promise of subsymbolic psycholinguistics. *Psychological Review, 97,* 488–522.

Veenema, H., Veenema, T., & Geraedts, J.P. (1987). The fragile X syndrome in a large family. II. Psychological investigations. *Journal of Medical Genetics, 24,* 32–38.

Vellutino, F.R. (1979). *Dyslexia: Theory and research.* Cambridge, MA: MIT Press.

Voeller, K.K.S. (1986). Right-hemisphere deficit syndrome in children. *American Journal of Psychiatry, 143,* 1004–1009.

Vogler, G.P., DeFries, J.C., & Decker, S.N, (1985). Family history as an indicator of risk for reading disability. *Journal of Learning Disabilities, 18,* 419–421.

Volkmar, F.R., Paul, R., & Cohen, D.J. (1985). The use of "Asperger's Syndrome." *Journal of Autism and Developmental Disorders, 15,* 437–439.

Waber, D.P. (1979). Neuropsychological aspects of Turner syndrome. *Developmental Medicine and Child Neurology, 2,* 58–70.

Wagner, R.K. & Torgesen, J.K. (1987). The nature of phonological processing and its causal role in the acquisition of reading skills, *Psychological Bulletin, 101,* 192–212.

Wallach, M.A., & Wallach, L. (1976). *Teaching all children to read.* Chicago: University of Chicago Press.

Wallach, L., Wallach, M.A., Dozier, M.G., & Kaplan, N.E. (1977). Poor children learning to read do not have trouble with auditory discrimination but do have trouble with phoneme recogntion. *Journal of Educational Psychology, 69,* 36–39.

Weintraub, S., & Mesulam, M.M. (1983). Developmental learning disabilities of the right hemisphere: Emotional, interpersonal, and cognitive components. *Archives of Neurology, 40,* 463–468.

Welsh, M.C., & Pennington, B.F. (1988). Assessing frontal lobe functioning in children: Views from developmental psychology. *Developmental Neuropsychology, 4,* 199–230.

Welsh, M.C., Pennington, B.F., & Grossier, D.B. (in press). A normative-developmental study of executive function: A window on prefrontal function in children? *Developmental Neuropsychology.*

Welsh, M., Pennington, B.F., Ozonoff, S., Rouse, & McCabe (1990). Neuropsychology of early-treated phenylketonuria: Specific executive function deficts. *Child Development, 61,* 1697–1713.

Werry, J.S., Minde, K., Guzman, D., Weiss, G., Dogan, K., & Hoy, R. (1972). Studies of the hyperactive child. VIII: Neurological status compared with neurotic and normal children. *American Journal of Orthopsychiatry, 42,* 441–450.

Whalen, C.K. (1983). Hyperactivity, learning problems, and the attention deficit disorders. In T.H. Ollendick & M. Hersen (Eds.), *Handbook of child psychopathology* (pp. 151–199). New York: Plenum.

Wilkins, A.J., Shallice, T., & McCarthy, R. (1987). Frontal lesions and sustained attention. *Neuropsychologia, 25,* 359–365.

Willerman, L. (1973). Activity level and hyperactivity in twins. *Child Development, 44,* 288–293.

Wilson, B.A. (1987). *Rehabilitation of memory.* New York: Guilford.

Wing, L. (1981). Asperger's syndrome: A clinical account. *Psychological Medicine, 11,* 115–129.

Wing, L. (1986). Clarification of Asperger's syndrome. *Journal of Autism and Developmental Disorders, 16,* 513–515.

Wise, B., & Olson, R.K. (1991). Remediating reading disabilites. In J.E. Obrzut & G.W. Hynd (Eds.), *Advances in the neuropsychology of learning disabilities: Issues, methods, and practice.* NY: Academic Press.

Witelson, S.F. (1987). Neurobiological aspects of language in children. *Child Development, 58,* Number 3.

Witelson, S.F. & Swallow, J.A. (1988). Neuropsychological study of the development of spatial cognition. In J. Stiles-Davis, M. Kritchevsky, & U. Bellugi (Eds.), *Spatial cognition: Brain bases and development* (pp. 373–409). Hillsdale, NJ: Lawrence Earlbaum.

Wolff, S., Narayan, S., & Moyes, B. (1988). Personality characteristics of parents of autistic children: A controlled study. *Journal of Child Psychology and Psychiatry, 29,* 143–153.

Wolff, P.A., Michel, G.F., Ovrat, N.L., & Drake, C. (1990). Rate and timing precision of motor coordination in developmental dyslexia. *Developmental Psychology, 26,* 349–359.

Woodcock, R.W., & Johnson, M.B. (1989). Woodcock-Johnson Psychological-educational battery–revised. Allen, TX: DLM Teaching Resources.

Wright, J.D. (1989). Irlen lenses: Their claims have not been substantiated, Position paper of the Massachusetts Society of Eye Physicians and Surgeons. The Learning Disabilities Network Exchange, 7, 1–4.

Yakovlev, P.I., & Lecours, A.R. (1967). The myelogenetic cycles of regional maturation of the brain. In A. Minkowski (Ed.), Regional development of the brain in early life. Oxford: Blackwell Scientific.

Zahalkova, M., Vrzal, V., & Kloboukova, E. (1972). Genetical investigations in dyslexia. Journal of Medical Genetics, 9, 48–52.

Zametkin, A.J., Nordahl, T.E., Gross, M., King, A.C., Semple, W.E., Rumsey, J., Hamburger, S., & Cohen, R. (1990). Cerebral glucose metabolism in adults with hyperactivity of childhood onset. The New England Journal of Medicine, 323, 1361–1415.

Zametkin, A.J., & Rapoport, J.L. (1986). The pathophysiology of attention deficit disorder with hyperactivity. In B.B. Lahey & A.E. Kazdin (Eds.), Advances in clinical child psychology. (Vol. 9). New York: Plenum Press.

Zametkin, A.J., & Rapoport, J.L. (1987). Neurobiology of attention deficit disorder with hyperactivity: Where have we come in 50 years? Journal of the American Academy of Child and Adolescent Psychiatry, 26, 676–686.

Index

AB̄ task, 21
Achenbach, T. M., 34, 193n
Acquired memory disorders, 166–180
  behavioral observations, 170
  brain mechanisms, 169
  case descriptions, 172–179
  closed head injury (CHI), 167
  definition, 166, 167
  developmental course, 169
  diagnosis, 170–172
  etiologies, 167, 168
  future research, 189, 190
  history, 170
  prevalence, 167
  research review, 166–169
  risk factors, 166–168
  seizure disorders, 167
  sex ratio, 167
  symptoms, 169, 170
  test results, 170–172
  treatment, 179, 180
Adams, M. J., 55, 73, 187, 193n, 207n
ADHD, see Attention deficit hyperactivity
    disorder
Amnesic syndrome, 21
Amygdala, 6
Anoxic insults, 21
Aram, D. M., 8, 64, 66, 193n, 204n
Articulation disorders, 8, 64, 65
Artifactual symptoms, 29, 30
Asperger's syndrome, 12, 135–137, 146
  etiologies, 136, 137
  prevalence, 136
  sex ratio, 136
Attention deficit hyperactivity disorder
    (ADHD), 13, 82–110
  behavioral observations, 99

brain mechanisms, 90–92
case descriptions, 102–110
comorbidity with dyslexia, 87–90
definition, 83–84
developmental course, 97, 98
diagnosis, 98–100
environmental influences, 87
etiologies, 84–87
familiality, 85, 86
future research, 187, 188
genetics of, 84–87
heritability, 85
history, 98, 99
hyperactivity, 85, 86
neuropsychological phenotype, 93–97
prevalence, 83–84
research review, 82–98
sex ratio, 84
symptoms, 98
test results, 100
threats to syndrome validity, 82, 83
treatment, 100–102
Autism, 16, 17
Autism spectrum disorder, 135–165
  behavioral observations, 150
  brain mechanisms, 140, 141
  case descriptions, 153–165
  definition, 135, 136
  developmental course, 147, 148
  diagnosis, 149–151
  environmental influences, 138, 139
  etiologies, 136–139
  familiality, 138, 139
  future research, 189
  genetics of, 136–139
  heritability, 138, 139
  history, 149

Autism spectrum disorder (*continued*)
  neuropsychological phenotype, 141–147
  prevalence, 136
  research review, 135–146
  segregation analysis, 137
  sex ratio, 136
  symptoms, 149–151
  test results, 150, 151
  theory of mind, 144, 145, 158, 159, 164
  treatment, 152–153

Bachevalier, J., 20, 21, 142, 169, 193n–195n
Baddeley, A. D., 8, 194n
Barkley, R. A., 82, 101, 194n, 197n
Baron-Cohen, S., 143–145, 194n
Behavioral observations
  acquired memory disorders, 170
  attention deficit hyperactivity disorder,
    99
  autism spectrum disorder, 150
  dyslexia, 70, 71
  right hemisphere learning disorders, 122,
    123
Bender, B. H., 48, 84, 168, 194n, 195n, 207n,
    208n
Benson, J. B., 10, 12, 13, 112, 195n
Benton, A. L., 46, 112, 167, 195n, 204n
Boucher, L., 142, 190, 195n
Brain mechanisms
  acquired memory disorders, 169
  attention deficit hyperactivity disorder,
    90–92
  autism spectrum disorder, 140, 141
  dyslexia, 56–58
  right hemisphere learning disorders, 116
Broca's area, 7
Bryant, P., 11, 62, 75, 196n, 205n

Campos, J. J., 10, 196n, 203n
Cantwell, D. P., 85, 88, 99, 196n
Case descriptions
  acquired memory disorders, 172–179
  attention deficit hyperactivity disorder,
    102–110
  autism spectrum disorder, 153–165
  dyslexia, 77–81
  right hemisphere learning disorders, 125–
    134
Cingulate gyrus, 6
Clinical implications of speech and language
  disorders, 67, 68

Clinical training and practice, dyslexia, 190,
    191
Closed head injuries (CHI), 167
Comorbidity of attention deficit
    hyperactivity disorder with dyslexia,
    87–90
Conners, C. K., 83, 94–96, 101, 197n
Construct validity, 24
Convergent validity, 25
Correlated symptoms, 28

Damasio, A. R., 17, 140, 197n
Dawson, G., 142, 197n
Declarative memory, 18, 19
DeFries, J. C., 46, 49–51, 89, 197n, 198n,
    200n, 203n, 204n, 215n
Delayed nonmatching to sample (DNMS)
    task, 20, 21
Denckla, M. B., 11, 100, 111, 113, 198n
Developmental course
  acquired memory disorders, 169
  attention deficit hyperactivity disorder,
    97, 98
  autism spectrum disorder, 147, 148
  dyslexia, 61–64
  right hemisphere learning disorders, 120,
    121
Developmental Gerstmann syndrome, 112
Developmental language disorders (DLD),
    64–67
Developmental phonology disorders, 64,
    65
Diagnosis, 32–38
  acquired memory disorders, 170–172
  advantages, 33
  attention deficit hyperactivity disorder,
    98–100
  autism spectrum disorder, 149–151
  dyslexia, 67–73
  hypothesis, 32, 33
  "medical model" approach, 33, 34
  right hemisphere learning disorders, 121–
    125
"Diagnostic space," 35
Diamond, A., 16, 198n
Differential diagnosis model, 34–38
Differential vulnerability of brain systems, 4
Discriminant validity, 25
Domains of brain function, 5–22
Double dissociation, dyslexia, 184, 185
Douglas, V. I., 93–95, 101, 198n, 214n

Dyslexia, 8, 45–81
  behavioral observations, 70, 71
  brain mechanisms, 56–58
  case descriptions, 77–81
  clinical training and practice, 190, 191
  comorbidity of attention deficit
    hyperactivity disorder, 87–90
  definition, 45–47
  developmental course, 61–64
  diagnosis, 67–73
  double dissociation, 184, 185
  environmental causes, 55
  ethnographic research, 55, 56
  etiologies, 47–56
  familiality, 48–50
  future research, 186, 187
  gene locations, 53–55
  genetics of, 47–55
  heritability, 50–52
  history, 69, 70
  neuroanatomical differences, 57, 58
  neuropsychological phenotype, 58–61
  phoneme awareness, 62, 63
  phoneme segmentation, 61
  prevalence, 46
  reading errors, 70
  research review, 45–64
  sex ratio, 46, 47
  Specific Dyslexia Algorithm (SDA), 72,
    73
  spelling errors, 71
  symptoms, 45, 46, 68, 69
  test results, 71–73
  treatment, 73–77

Early treated phenylketonuria (PKU), 16–18
Eimas, P., 8, 199n
Emotional expression, 12
Emotional recognition, 12
Environmental influences
  attention deficit hyperactivity disorder, 87
  autism spectrum disorder, 138, 139
  dyslexia, 55
  right hemisphere learning disorders, 115
Etcoff, N., 111, 199n
Ethnographic research, dyslexia, 55, 56
Etiologies
  acquired memory disorders, 167, 168
  Asperger's syndrome, 136, 137
  attention deficit hyperactivity disorder,
    84–87

autism spectrum disorder, 136–139
dyslexia, 47–56
right hemisphere learning disorders, 113–
  115
Executive function developmental
  pathologies, 16–18
Executive functions, 4, 12–18
  and social cognition in autistics, 146
External validity, 23–25

Familiality
  attention deficit hyperactivity disorder,
    85, 86
  autism spectrum disorder, 138, 139
  dyslexia, 48–50
Feedback
  providing, 38–42
  to child patient, 41, 42
  parents, 38–40
  schools, 40–41
Fein, D., 12, 143, 199n
Finucci, J. M., 49, 52, 63, 199n
Fletcher, J. M., 23, 24, 46, 189, 199n, 200n,
  212n
Fodor, J. A., 3, 200n
Folstein, S., 26, 137–139, 200n
Frith, U., 144, 194n, 208n
Frontal functions model, 14
Fuster, J. M., 12–14, 200n
Future research
  acquired memory disorders, 189, 190
  attention deficit hyperactivity disorder,
    187, 188
  autism spectrum disorder, 189
  dyslexia, 186, 187
  long-term memory disorders, 189, 190
  right hemisphere learning disorders, 188,
    189
  social cognitive disorders, 189

Galaburda, A. M., 57, 200n
Gardner, H., 5, 6, 11, 200n
Gene locations, dyslexia, 53–55
Genetics
  attention deficit hyperactivity disorder,
    84–87
  autism spectrum disorder, 136–139
  dyslexia, 47–55
  right hemisphere learning disorders, 113–
    115
Geschwind, N., 53, 57, 112, 195n, 200n

Gillberg, C., 12, 113, 136, 200n
Goldman-Rakic, P. S., 12–16, 198n, 201n, 209n
Guessing in reading, 74

Habit memory, 18, 19
Hagerman, R. J., 84, 115, 201n, 203n
Handwriting disorders, 112
Heritability
  attention deficit hyperactivity disorder, 85
  autism spectrum disorder, 138, 139
  dyslexia, 50–52
Hier, D. B., 56, 84, 202n, 210n
Hippocampus, 6
History
  acquired memory disorders, 170
  attention deficit hyperactivity disorder, 98, 99
  autism spectrum disorder, 149
  dyslexia, 69, 70
  right hemisphere learning disorders, 120, 121
Hynd, G. W., 15, 57, 91, 111, 202n, 207n, 211n
Hyperactivity, attention deficit hyperactivity disorder, 85, 86
Hypothesis, diagnosis, 32, 33

Imitation, 12
Immediate memory, 19
Implications
  for practice, 190, 191
  for research, 184–190
Infantile amnesia, 19, 20
Internal validity, 23, 24

Learning disorders, 4
Leslie, A. M., 144, 194n, 204n, 208n
Liberman, I. Y., 59, 71, 204n
Lieberman, P., 4, 204n
Limbic system, 12, 16
Loney, J., 87, 206n, 207n
Long-term memory disorders
  future research, 189, 190
Long-term memory (LTM), 18–21
Lou, H. C., 91, 204n

Math disorders, 112
McGee, R., 88, 89, 205n
Memory
  declarative, 18, 19

habit, 18, 19
  immediate, 19
  long-term (LTM), 18–21
  procedural, 18
  short-term (STM), 19
Mesulam, M. M., 11, 111, 113, 115–118, 120, 147, 209n, 215n
Modular brain systems, 3, 4

Nelson, C. A., 12, 19, 20, 169, 190, 206n
Neuroanatomical differences
  dyslexia, 57, 58
Neuropsychological model, 3–22
Neuropsychological phenotype
  attention deficit hyperactivity disorder, 93–97
  autism spectrum disorder, 141–147
  dyslexia, 58–61
  right hemisphere learning disorders, 116–119
Normal development of prefrontal function, 15–16
Normal eye movements in reading, 74

Obsessive-compulsive disorder, 17
Olson, R. K., 51, 52, 55, 75, 207n, 214n
Orbital frontal area, 6
Ozonoff, S., 17, 207n, 215n

Parents' role
  in dyslexia, 76
  in providing feedback, 38–40
Pauls, D. L., 17, 138, 207n
Pennington, B. F., 15, 17, 47–49, 51, 53, 54, 59–62, 71, 89, 90, 113–115, 141, 143, 145, 146, 199n, 200n, 204n, 207n, 208n, 210n, 212n, 215n
Perisylvian region, 6
Phoneme awareness, dyslexia, 62, 63
Phoneme awareness skills, 75
Phoneme segmentation, dyslexia, 61
Phonological coding, 51, 52, 59–61
Phonological processing, 4, 7, 8
Plomin, R., 54, 85, 138, 208n
Posner, M. I., 92, 96, 208n, 209n
Pragmatics, 12
Prefrontal function, 13–16
Prevalence
  acquired memory disorders, 167
  Asperger's syndrome, 136
  attention deficit hyperactivity disorder, 83, 84

autism spectrum disorder, 136
 dyslexia, 46
 right hemisphere learning disorders, 113
Primary symptoms, 27, 28
Procedural memory, 18
Prosody, 12

Rapin, I., 23, 27, 66, 209n
Rapoport, J. L., 141, 148, 209n, 210n, 216n
Reading, guessing in, 74
Research review
 acquired memory disorders, 166–169
 attention deficit hyperactivity disorder,
  82–98
 autism spectrum disorder, 135–146
 dyslexia, 45–64
 right hemisphere learning disorders, 113–
  121
Right hemisphere learning disorders, 11,
  111–134
 behavioral observations, 122, 123
 brain mechanisms, 116
 case descriptions, 125–134
 definition, 111–112
 developmental course, 120, 121
 diagnosis, 121–125
 environmental influences, 115
 etiologies, 113–115
 future research, 188, 189
 genetics, 113–115
 history, 120, 121
 neuropsychological phenotype, 116–119
 prevalence, 113
 research review, 113–121
 sex ratio, 113
 symptoms, 121
 test results, 123, 124
 treatment, 124, 125
 Turner syndrome, 113–115
Risk factors for acquired memory disorders,
  166–168
Ritvo, E. R., 140, 141, 209n
Rogers, S. J., 143–146, 152, 207n, 210n
Rourke, B. P., 11, 111–113, 115, 117–120,
  122, 125, 136, 210n, 213n
Rumsey, J. M., 17, 57, 141, 148, 202n, 210n
Rutter, M., 26, 30, 46, 82, 83, 86, 91, 137–
  139, 151, 195n, 200n, 210n, 211n

Satz, P., 46, 47, 199n, 211n
Scarborough, H., 49, 62

Schizophrenia, 16
Schopler, E., 135, 150, 211n
Secondary symptoms, 28
Segregation analysis, 137
Seizure disorders, 167
Sex ratio
 acquired memory disorders, 167
 Asperger's syndrome, 136
 attention deficit hyperactivity disorder, 84
 autism spectrum disorder, 136
 dyslexia, 46, 47
 right hemisphere learning disorders, 113
Shallice, T., 3, 13, 14, 19, 93, 211n, 216n
Shankweiler, D., 59, 60, 71, 204n, 211n
Shaywitz, B. A., 26, 46, 47, 87–89, 91, 92,
  97, 100, 101, 211n, 212n
Shaywitz, S. E., 26, 46, 47, 87–89, 92, 97,
  100, 101, 212n
Shepard, R. N., 10, 212n
Short-term memory (STM), 19, 60
Sigman, M., 151, 212n
Smalley, S. L., 136–139, 212n
Smith, S. D., 53, 54, 71, 208n, 212n
Social cognition, 11, 12
 and executive functions in autistics, 146
Social cognitive disorders
 future research, 189
Spatial cognition, 8–11
Specific Dyslexia Algorithm (SDA), 72, 73
Specific reading disability (SRD), 46
Spelling errors, dyslexia, 71
Stanovich, K. E., 46, 63, 74, 89, 213n
Stevenson, J., 18, 30, 50, 84, 86, 201n, 213n
Stiles-Davis, J., 8–10, 213n
Stuttering, 8, 65, 66
Subtype validity, 24, 26–30
Symptoms, 26–30
 acquired memory disorders, 169, 170
 artifactual, 29, 30
 attention deficit hyperactivity disorder,
  98, 99
 autism spectrum disorder, 149–151
 correlated, 28
 dyslexia, 45–46, 68, 69
 primary, 27, 28
 right hemisphere learning disorders,
  121
 secondary, 28
Syndromes, criticism, 30
Syndrome validation, 23–31
Synthetic phonics approaches, 75

Test results
  acquired memory disorders, 170–172
  attention deficit hyperactivity disorder, 100
  autism spectrum disorder, 150, 151
  dyslexia, 71–73
  right hemisphere learning disorders, 123, 124
Theory of mind
  autism spectrum disorder, 144, 145, 158, 159, 164
Theory of multiple intelligences, 5, 6
Tourette's syndrome, 16, 17
Treatment
  acquired memory disorders, 179, 180
  attention deficit hyperactivity disorder, 100–102
  autism spectrum disorder, 152–153
  dyslexia, 73–77
  right hemisphere learning disorders, 124, 125
Turner syndrome, 113–115

Validity
  construct, 24
  convergent, 25
  discriminant, 25
  external, 23–25
  internal, 23, 24
  of subtypes, 24, 26–30
Van Orden, G. C., 59–61, 71, 208n, 214n, 215n
Voice disorders, 65

Wallach, L., 55, 56, 215n
Wallach, M. A., 55, 56, 215n
Welsh, M. C., 15, 17, 85, 90, 208n, 215n
Wernicke's area, 7
Witelson, S. F., 7, 10, 216n

Zametkin, A. J., 91, 92, 216n